long
time
gone

VIEWPOINTS ON AMERICAN CULTURE

Edited by Catherine Clinton

Viewpoints on American Culture offers timely reflections for twenty-first century readers. A sensible guide to knowledge in a scholarly field, something one can pick up—literally and figuratively—seems to be facing extinction. Volumes in our series will provide intellectual relief and practical solution.

The series targets topics where debates have flourished and brings together the voices of established and emerging writers to share their own points of view in a compact and compelling format. Our books offer sophisticated, yet accessible, introductions into an array of issues under our broad and expanding banner.

Sifters: Native American Women's Lives
Edited by Theda Perdue

Long Time Gone: Sixties America Then and Now
Edited by Alexander Bloom

long time gone

SIXTIES AMERICA
THEN AND NOW

Edited by Alexander Bloom

OXFORD
UNIVERSITY PRESS

2001

OXFORD
UNIVERSITY PRESS

Oxford   New York
Athens   Auckland   Bangkok   Bogotá   Buenos Aires   Calcutta
Cape Town   Chennai   Dar es Salaam   Delhi   Florence   Hong Kong   Istanbul
Karachi   Kuala Lumpur   Madrid   Melbourne   Mexico City   Mumbai
Nairobi   Paris   São Paulo   Shanghai   Singapore   Taipei   Tokyo   Toronto   Warsaw

and associated companies in
Berlin   Ibadan

Copyright © 2001 by Oxford University Press, Inc. Intro © Alexander Bloom

Published by Oxford University Press, Inc.
198 Madison Avenue, New York, New York 10016

Oxford is a registered trademark of Oxford University Press.

Library of Congress Cataloging-in-Publication Data
Long time gone : sixties America then and now / edited by Alexander Bloom.
p.   cm.—(Viewpoints on American culture)
ISBN 0-19-512514-2, ISBN 0-19-512515-0 (pbk.)
1. United States—History—1961–1969.   2. United States—Social conditions—1960–1980.
3. Nineteen sixties.   I. Bloom, Alexander.   II. Series.
E841 .F67 2001
973.923—dc21   00-061122

9 8 7 6 5 4

Printed in the United States of America
on acid-free paper

For
Peggy

Acknowledgments

Editing this volume has been a unique and special experience for me. I was initially approached to undertake it by Catherine Clinton, the general series editor, and Thomas LeBien, then an editor at Oxford. Their notion was to compile a volume around a single topic with a mixture of established and younger scholars. My idea was to add public figures to the mix, along with traditional academics. Both Catherine and Thomas have been enthusiastic and thoughtful partners in this project, offering advice and encouragement. Thomas has even continued to provide quiet counsel since joining another press. I appreciate deeply both their initial confidence in me and their ready assistance at every step.

My first task after agreeing to do this book was to draw up a list of potential contributors, what became a kind of "dream team" of sixties writers, scholars, and activists. My assumption was that a number of them would turn me down and younger scholars would then fill in the gaps. But with one exception, all my first choices readily agreed. It is with profound gratitude that I acknowledge the willing and eager participation of these exceptional scholars, respected journalists, and well-known political and social activists. The work of the younger scholars—Karen Miller and Bradford Martin—not only keeps pace with that of their more established cocontributors, but offers a fine balance between those from the era and those looking back.

Along the way, a number of friends have been extraordinarily helpful in suggesting contributors, listening to ideas, thinking of titles, and responding to my queries. These include Patricia Sullivan, Kathryn Tomasek, Anni Baker, Peter Warner, and, especially, Judith Smith. I want to specifically acknowledge Christian Appy. Chris, in addition to knowing more about the Vietnam War than anyone I know, has been an ideal coauthor and a good friend. Our working relationship has been a pleasure and model of collegiality. My research assistants have helped with everything—running down the smallest facts and sources, handling the various drafts, and helping assemble the final manuscript. I could not have finished this without them and they have my gratitude—Jessica Vickerson, Jessica Benjamin, Amy Lowe, Zachary Bloom, and, especially, Kathryn Kyricos.

Susan Ferber inherited this project at Oxford. She has brought to it a wonderful sense of enthusiasm as well as the finest copy pencil I have ever experienced in an editor. She is able to hold the big picture and the smallest punctuation mark simultaneously in her mind. She has made nearly every line in this book better.

My sons, Stefan and Zachary Bloom, have grown up with my books. Years ago, their main role in these books was to serve as objects of dedication. Now they are young men with whom I can talk about ideas and share my enthusiasms, and they can both appreciate and contribute to my work. I am prouder of them than anything I have ever written.

Peggy Stockman listened to my ideas, helped me think of contributors and titles, read drafts and chapters, provided moral support when frustrations developed, and kept my perspective wide. Academics can often become insular, looking inward and at each other, and frequently miss the real-world truths. Peggy has always kept it, and me, real.

Brighton, Massachusetts   A. B.
May 2000

Contents

Sixties Timeline   xi

Introduction: Why Read about the 1960s at the
Turn of the Twenty-first Century?   3

The Movement We Helped to Make   11
    Julian Bond

"Of This Generation": The New Left and the
Student Movement   23
    Wini Breines

Vietnam War Mythology and the Rise of
Public Cynicism   47
    Christian Appy
    Alexander Bloom

Running Battle: Washington's War at Home   75
    Tom Wells

Lyndon Johnson and the Roots of Contemporary
Conservatism   99
    Tom Wicker

Negroes No More: The Emergence of
Black Student Activism   123
    Karen K. Miller

Everything Seemed Beautiful: A Life in the
Counterculture   145
    Barry Melton

Politics as Art, Art as Politics: The Freedom Singers,
the Living Theatre, and Public Performance   159
    Bradford Martin

Sources of the Second Wave: The Rebirth of
Feminism   189
    Sara M. Evans

Placing Gay in the Sixties   209
    John D'Emilio

Sixties Timeline

1960   First lunch counter sit-ins, Greensboro, North Carolina
Woolworth's
Student Nonviolent Coordinating Committee (SNCC)
founded
Students for a Democratic Society (SDS) founded
John Kennedy elected president

1961   Freedom rides to desegregate interstate travel
Kennedy establishes President's Commission on the
Status of Women

1962   Port Huron Statement
Integration of the University of Mississippi by federal
marshals
Cuban Missile Crisis

1963   SDS attempts to organize the urban poor with ERAP
Project
Publication of Betty Friedan's *The Feminine Mystique*
Murder of Medgar Evers, Mississippi NAACP leader
Ritual suicide of a Buddhist monk protesting the
American-backed Diem regime
Civil Rights March on Washington
Military coup overthrows Diem
Assassination of John Kennedy

1964   Beatles first American tour
Economic Opportunity Act (begins War on Poverty)
Freedom Summer
Three civil rights workers killed in Mississippi

Civil Rights Act passed

Gulf of Tonkin Resolution

Berkeley Free Speech Movement (FSM)

Lyndon Johnson elected president

1965   Malcolm X assassinated

United States introduces American ground troops
in Vietnam

Selma March

First campus teach-ins and demonstrations against the
Vietnam War

Voting Rights Act

Watts Riots

United Farm Workers' Cesar Chavez announces national
boycott of grapes to support striking farmworkers

Congress begins enacting Great Society legislation

1966   Martin Luther King moves campaign north to Chicago

Bill Graham begins rock shows at San Francisco's
Fillmore Auditorium

Nationally televised Congressional hearings on Vietnam

Black Panther Party founded in Oakland, California

Founding of National Organization for Women (NOW)

Ronald Reagan elected governor of California

1967   Human Be-In, San Francisco

Muhammed Ali stripped of heavyweight championship
for refusing military induction

"Summer of Love"

Urban riots in Detroit and Newark, New Jersey

Monterey Pop Festival

March on the Pentagon

1968   Tet Offensive

Senators Eugene McCarthy and Robert Kennedy
challenge Lyndon Johnson for the Democratic
Party nomination

George Wallace runs as third-party candidate for president

My Lai massacre

Lyndon Johnson suddenly withdraws from the race
Martin Luther King, Jr., assassinated
Columbia University Student Strike
French Student Strike
Robert Kennedy shot and killed
Poor Peoples' March on Washington
Demonstrations at and boycott of Mexico City Olympics
   by African-American athletes
Miss America Demonstrations
Riotous Democratic Party National Convention
   in Chicago
Richard Nixon elected president

1969   Student strike at San Francisco State
Trial of the "Chicago Eight," accused of disrupting 1968
   Democratic Convention
People's Park, Berkeley
Stonewall Riots, New York
Woodstock Festival
Weather Underground's "Days of Rage"
Altamont rock concert

1970   First Earth Day
Creation of Environmental Protection Agency (EPA)
Nixon orders incursion into Cambodia
National guardsmen shoot and kill student demonstrators
   at Kent State
Police open fire and kill students at Jackson State
   University in Mississippi
First Gay Pride March
Women's Equality Day demonstrations celebrating fiftieth
   anniversary of suffrage
Jimi Hendrix dies
Janis Joplin dies
The Beatles break up

1971   William Calley convicted for My Lai murders
Pentagon Papers published
Jim Morrison dies

1972   Nixon announces mining of North Vietnamese harbors
Ms. magazine founded
Antiwar presidential campaign of George McGovern
Richard Nixon re-elected
"Christmas bombing" of North Vietnam

1973   *Roe v. Wade* decision legalizing abortion
Paris Peace Accords
American Indian occupation of Wounded Knee
Watergate scandal

1974   Richard Nixon resigns

1975   American withdrawal from Vietnam and the defeat of
South Vietnamese government

**long
time
gone**

Introduction

Why Read about the 1960s at the Turn of the Twenty-first Century?

The 1960s remain alive for Americans thirty years after the decade ended. When the United States fought the Gulf War in 1991, the aim was not only to drive the Iraqis out of Kuwait, but, as was explicitly stated by President George Bush, to finally expiate the "Vietnam syndrome" from our culture. When the reaction to the verdict in the Rodney King case sparked urban upheaval in Los Angeles in 1992, the Bush administration blamed the riots on the "failed politics of the '60s." During the 1992 presidential campaign, Bill Clinton's draft record emerged and reemerged throughout the campaign, as well as whether or not he inhaled marijuana.

Once elected, Bill Clinton, and first lady Hillary Clinton, became targets of their political opponents not merely because of their politics or even their financial dealings or personal behavior but, as Newt Gingrich put it, because they were "counterculture McGoverniks." In fact, the so-called Republican Revolution of 1994 was often phrased as a reaction against the 1960s. "Sixties values," Gingrich declared, "cripple human beings, weaken cities, make it difficult for us to, in fact, survive as a country." They are "to blame for most of the current major diseases which have struck this society." During Clinton's impeachment struggle, Christian Coalition head Pat Robertson lamented that the office once occupied "by Washington and Jefferson and Lincoln" had become "the playpen for the sexual freedom of the poster child of the 1960s."

Casting the contemporary world in a 1960s framework is not only the province of politicians. In a recent academic forum titled "The Columbine Incident and the Radical Tradition in America," one participant argued that "kids killing kids may be the radical protest of our age." The young killers "may be the Mark Rudd and Abbie Hoffman [two radical leaders in the 1960s] figures of today. . . . heirs of the youth rebellion of the '60s. . . . They may have upped the ante on their radical forebears. . . . These boys have truly embraced 'revolution for the hell of it,' maybe better than Abbie ever did."

At the same time, the Rolling Stones continue to pack stadiums across the country and, even more significantly, young people journeyed across the country in mock 1960s garb to follow the Grateful Dead. These fans imitated their idea of a '60s lifestyle, and hoped to recapture some lost sense of community and idealism epitomized by the band and its following. The public reaction to the death of Jerry Garcia in 1995 and the void in the culture left by the band's decision to call it quits suggest a very different kind of grip this past era has on our own.

The 1960s seem to hold on to us—or, at least, our mythologized vision of the era. The decade maintains a unique place in contemporary life, unlike that of any previous era. Decades or periods usually take on a cohesive popular meaning once they have passed into history. A consensus about the shape and identity of the decade settles into popular imagination. The public conjures images of the *roaring* 1920s, the *hard times* of the 1930s, the *happy days* of the 1950s. These impressions are selective, overgeneralized, and frequently unaware or dismissive of individuals or situations that defy the generalizations. Scholars set about pointing out these omissions and attempt to set the record straight.

What is unique about the 1960s is that we are living with a number of competing (and, sometimes, contradictory) popular meanings—not one consensus but several. We have a divided—perhaps schizophrenic—legacy from this era. Like the other generalized views of past eras, each of these contains errors and simplifications. But what is most striking is the way these visions of the 1960s can contradict one another and still coexist in the popular imagination.

The 1960s remain alive in the culture in a manner different from any previous decade. We are still debating issues that emerged during that decade, still living in the conscious aftermath of its events and transformations. It is a decade that seems to hold our imaginations long after its time has passed.

We tend to think of historical periods as a single entity, as though the "sixties" exploded full blown on the American scene, with all its elements fully realized. In fact, it is hard even to date the era. Some have suggested that the sixties began with the first lunch counter sit-ins at the Greensboro, North Carolina, Woolworth's in early 1960. Others mark the era's birth with the organization of Students for a Democratic Society at Port Huron, Michigan, in 1962; or with the assassination of John Kennedy in 1963; or with the first major student demonstration, the Berkeley free speech movement, in 1964.

There is no clear moment when the "sixties" began. In fact, what this listing of events suggests is the emergence of a new political sensibility in the first years of the decade. Over these years and across the country, groups began to challenge basic assumptions and institutions, from segregation to campus restrictions to presumptions about personal development and national goals. Individuals drew inspiration from other events and actions—the tactics, vocabulary, and idealism from one situation feeding the next.

One common denominator of the first moments of this new activism was the participation of young people, epitomized by the names of their organizations—the *Student* Nonviolent Coordinating Committee (SNCC) or *Students* for a Democratic Society (SDS). Young people played central roles in the important events of the early 1960s. They sat in at lunch counters and in department stores throughout the segregated South in 1960, rode as Freedom Riders to desegregate interstate travel in 1961, mounted the SDS attempt to organize the urban poor in 1963, challenged restrictive rules and impersonal educations with the free speech movement in 1964, and organized the first campus teach-ins and demonstrations against the Vietnam War in 1965.

By mid-decade it was evident to all Americans that something powerful was shaking the fundamental structures of American life. This only intensified as the decade progressed. The southern civil rights movement gave way to a national struggle for black power, cultural identity, and race consciousness. The Black Panther Party was founded in Oakland, California, in 1966, to protect urban citizens from police brutality, articulating its messages in a new, more militant tone. Martin Luther King, Jr., struggled for integration in the South, then took his message to the North with a campaign against housing discrimination in Chicago in 1966, as well as publicly criticizing the Vietnam War in 1967. He planned to organize all those living in poverty with the Poor People's March on Washington in 1968. King's assassination in April of that year not only sparked riots throughout the country, but is often seen as one of the events that dissipated the idealism that marked much of the decade.

King's opposition to the Vietnam War suggests the interrelation of the movements. In the first years of the 1960s, Vietnam remained an issue off center stage, gaining attention only with a headline-grabbing event, such as the 1963 ritual suicide of a Buddhist monk who was protesting the U.S.-backed Diem regime, or the military coup that overthrew Diem later that year. In 1965, however, when SDS called for a march on Washington to protest the war, organizers were amazed when twenty-five thousand turned out. From that point on, regular protests occurred throughout the country, the number of demonstrators escalating along with the number of soldiers in Southeast Asia. In 1968, five hundred thousand people turned out in the nation's capital for an anti-Vietnam War protest, with millions of others gathered in locales across the country.

Vietnam moved to center stage, with nationally televised congressional hearings, antidraft protests, draft-card burnings, public counseling about draft resistance for young men, opposition on campuses to the presence of military recruiters, and, finally, a direct antiwar challenge in 1968 within the Democratic Party to President Johnson's desire for renomination. First, Minnesota Senator Eugene McCarthy and, then, New York Senator Robert Kennedy announced their intention to seek the nomination on antiwar platforms. Two days before the Wisconsin primary, when it appeared LBJ was going down in defeat to McCarthy, the president suddenly withdrew from the race. Later that primary season, after winning in California, Robert Kennedy was shot and killed as he walked from the ballroom where he had just given his victory speech.

The war had brought down a president and set in motion the forces that would come together at the calamitous Democratic Convention in Chicago later that summer. There, before national television cameras, Chicago police tear-gassed and beat antiwar demonstrators in what an investigatory commission later termed a "police riot." Inside the convention hall, as the delegates smelled tear gas and heard the chanting of demonstrators, speakers from the platform berated the administration and the convention host, Chicago Mayor Richard Daley, accusing him of employing "Gestapo tactics."

The new president, Richard Nixon, seemed to promise an end to the war in his winning campaign, but instead shifted tactics, slowly withdrawing American troops but massively increasing American air strikes. Demonstrations against the war continued, and after Nixon ordered an incursion into Cambodia in the spring of 1970, protests erupted across the nation. One confrontation, between students and national guardsmen at Kent State University in Ohio, turned horribly tragic, as the guard opened fire on the demonstrators, killing four and wounding nine. Ten days later, state police opened fire on students at Jackson State University in Mississippi, killing two more. Like the King and Kennedy assassinations, these shootings further shattered people's idealism, leaving them frustrated, disillusioned, and hostile.

Yet amid the tumult and confrontation, other elements that define the 1960s emerged, focusing on personal introspection, human interaction, and individual improvement in the quality of life. Challenges to "the system" not only focused on the war, the economy, or racial discrimination. The system was also seen as offering people less meaningful lives, binding men and women to prescribed and unfulfilling roles, and limiting human potential. Interconnected with critiques of foreign or domestic policy were visions offering new ways of constructing lives. Personal and sexual exploration, redefined social arrangements, and artistic endeavors that strived to provide deeper understandings all emerged from the same wellsprings as the political movements.

Perhaps only a small minority could actually journey to San Francisco in the "summer of love" of 1967, but the meaning and example of alternative lifestyles permeated society. From clothing styles to sexual freedom, the ideas of the counterculture filtered through the nation. *Life* magazine might have focused on San Francisco and Haight-Ashbury as the capital of "hippiedom," but these were only its most prominent outcropping. The impact was felt on college campuses, at high schools, in big cities, in small towns, at the movies, and on records—especially on records. Music seemed central to the entire '60s experience, not the narrowly defined cultural role it plays today. Rock bands and folk singers participated in civil rights marches and antiwar rallies. But that is only the surface relationship. The music embodied the same underlying themes, the same sense of creating something new and something better, as did the political and social movements. These all seemed part of the same large endeavor.

Each new challenge inspired others. The vocabulary of civil rights—about equal access, breaking down barriers, ending discrimination—was easily transferred to others who lived under unfair constraints. Many racial and ethnic groups began to explore their own histories, cultures, and backgrounds. Women made the logical jump from racial prejudice to discrimination based on sexist views. And by decade's end, gays and lesbians began to exert their own resistance to the prejudicial treatment they had long suffered. Many of these endeavors, especially for women and gays, only began in the 1960s; the major efforts and achievements came in later eras.

It is as difficult to mark the end of the 1960s as it is the beginning. The deaths at Kent State in 1970 are often cited as one ending point. Others see the failed antiwar presidential campaign of George McGovern in 1972 or the Watergate scandals of 1973 and 1974 as the end. Still others cite the American withdrawal from Vietnam and the defeat of South Vietnam in 1975 as bringing down the final curtain on the era. As with dating the beginning of the "sixties," locating its conclusion is speculative and ultimately unnecessary. Americans know the era has ended and yet feel as though we are living in its aftermath, still debating its issues, and still trying to decide whether it had a positive or negative impact on contemporary American life.

It is the intention of this collection to look back at the 1960s and to understand the issues of the day on their own terms, as well as to think about their meanings for today. The aim is to dispel the myths and to try to construct both an accurate vision of the past and an understanding of its contemporary influences.

Lost in the modern imagery of "sixties" life is the interconnection of the political, the cultural, and the social. Individuals' lives, ideas, and actions wound together—the personal became political, and the cultural and political seemed to be two parts of a whole. A second intention of this collection is to reestablish *this* sense of the "sixties" experience. Thus, a number of the essayists have introduced personal stories—either their own or those of their subjects—to try to recapture the inner resonance of life in the 1960s, that intimate interconnection among elements that seem so disparate today.

Some of the contributors—Julian Bond, Barry Melton, Tom Wicker, Sara Evans, Wini Breines, John D'Emilio, and I—were active participants in the worlds we describe. Others came of age after the decade had passed, but understand the relationship between their subjects' lives and the political or cultural activities in which they were engaged—that at any one moment, a political or social event might move to the fore, but at every moment all the elements remained in play, each influencing the other.

Each essay was written specifically for this volume. They move through the decade, from the first civil rights sit-ins of 1960 to the emergence of a gay rights movement at the end of the decade. Each is built around a single topic from the period yet the impact of each can only be understood fully when explored in relation to the others. Barry Melton's notion that his rock group, "Country Joe and the Fish," became a "house band for the antiwar movement" captures this intimate interconnection between the spheres.

Topics from one essay pop up in others. Julian Bond sketches the rise of SNCC in his essay on the civil rights movement. Bradford Martin uses SNCC's Freedom Singers as an example of the merging worlds of art and politics in his essay on the counterculture. The developments late in the decade within the New Left, in Wini Breines's essay, point directly to the topics discussed in Karen Miller's essay on black student activism, in Sara Evans's on the women's movement, and in John D'Emilio's on the emergence of gay rights. There are also obvious connections between the essays on Vietnam, on Lyndon Johnson, and on the antiwar movement.

Some of the essays offer sweeping overviews, while others choose a moment or smaller example to epitomize their topic. Always, the intent is to describe the central issues and attitudes at the time. The second intent is to assess, sometimes implicitly but often explicitly, the meaning of these years and these issues for our contemporary world. We still live with the 1960s insofar as it holds our imaginations and continues to shape the rhetoric of our political dialog. Debates about policy or social concerns represent a playing out of political and social momentum generated in that period. We need to understand what those forces actually were and what they mean today.

The 1960s are both the province of history and a powerful memory shaping contemporary discussion. Both our history and our political dialog should always be as accurate as possible. These essays are intended to provide some of that accuracy—to help set the historical record and the modern discourse straight.

The Movement We Helped to Make

Julian Bond

On a February day in 1960, I was sitting in a cafe near my college campus in Atlanta. It was a place where students went between or instead of classes. A student named Lonnie King approached me. I knew Lonnie only as a football player on Morehouse's losing team and, as a Navy veteran, some years older than our schoolmates. He was holding a copy of that day's *Atlanta Daily World*, the city's black newspaper. He pointed to the headline: Greensboro Students Sit-in for Third Day!

The story told, in precise detail, how black college students from North Carolina Agricultural and Technical College in Greensboro had, for the third consecutive day, entered a Woolworth's Five-and dime store and asked for service at the whites-only lunch counter. It described their demeanor, their dress, and their determination to return the following day and for as many successive days as it took if they were not served.

"Have you seen this?" he demanded.

"Yes, I have," I replied.

"What do you think about it?" he inquired.

"I think it's great!"

"Don't you think it ought to happen here?" he asked.

"Oh, I'm sure it will happen here," I responded. "Surely someone here will do it." Then came a query, an invitation, a command:

"Why don't *we* make it happen here?"

He took one side of the cafe and I took the other, talking to students, inviting them to discuss the Greensboro news and to duplicate it in Atlanta. The Atlanta student movement had begun.

In a few days we had gathered students from Clark, Morehouse, Spelman, Morris Brown, Atlanta University, and the Interdenominational Theological Center— the heart of the black college community in Georgia. It did not take long for word of what we were planning to reach the ear of Atlanta University president Rufus Clement. He called us in and told us that much was expected of Atlanta students. But he urged us to present a statement of purpose to the Atlanta community before we committed any action. So another student and I wrote "An Appeal for Human Rights," borrowing liberally from a pamphlet titled *A Second Look at Atlanta*, published by a group of young black businessmen and intellectuals. Dr. Clement arranged to have our version printed in Atlanta's three daily newspapers. It created a sensation. With our recruited schoolmates we formed an organization, reconnoitered at downtown lunch counters, and within a few weeks, seventy-seven of us had been arrested.

Like many southern black youths of my generation, my path to the civil rights movement extended from my college experience. I grew up on black college campuses. My father, the late Dr. Horace Mann Bond, was president of Fort Valley State College for Negroes in Georgia and Lincoln University in Lincoln, Pennsylvania. From 1957 on I lived in university housing owned by Atlanta University, where my father ended his career as dean of the School of Education. Local and state racial politics often froze the black college, its faculty and administrators and students, into political inactivity and grudging acceptance of the status quo. The best of schools did, however, keep alive the rich tradition of protest and rebellion that had existed throughout black communities since slavery.

This was my experience at Fort Valley and Lincoln, and in Atlanta. At the age of 3, I posed with my sister Jane, my father, and noted black scholars E. Franklin Frazier and W. E. B. DuBois while the elders pledged us to a life of scholarship. At seven, I sat at the knee of the great black singer and political activist Paul Robeson as he sang of the Four Insurgent Generals. I watched as NAACP Executive Secretary Walter White visited the Lincoln campus, escorted by an impressive phalanx of black-booted Pennsylvania state troopers whose shiny motorcycles were surely designed to attract the attention of small boys and impress them with the importance of the white-looking black man whom they protected. When my father came to Atlanta University, I entered Morehouse College, the alma mater of Martin Luther King, Jr., and Sr. Both Kings and a long list of race men and women, dedicated to the uplift of their people, were paraded before us in daily, required sessions of morning chapel.

But school alone did not fuel my civil rights fires; my father's house and my mother's table served daily helpings of current events, involving the world and the race. The race's problems and achievement were part of everyday discussion. When a fourteen–year-old named Emmett Till was kidnapped, beaten,

JULIAN BOND has been active in the movement for civil rights and social justice for four decades. He is currently the chair of the board of directors of the National Association for the Advancement of Colored People (NAACP) as well as distinguished scholar in residence at American University and professor of history at the University of Virginia. A veteran of the civil rights struggle, he served as communications director for the Student Nonviolent Coordinating Committee (SNCC) from 1960 to 1965. He won election to the Georgia House of Representatives in 1965, as an antiwar and civil rights candidate, and served in that body until 1974, when he was elected to the Georgia state senate, where he served until 1987. In the summer of 1968——at the Democratic National Convention in Chicago—his name was placed in nomination for vice president, making him the first African American ever so nominated by a major political party. Only twenty-eight, he had to withdraw his name, as he was seven years under the constitutional age requirement for the vice presidency.

castrated, and murdered in Mississippi, it terrified the fifteen-year-old me. I asked myself, "If they will do that to him, what won't they do to me?"

When I was in college in 1960, the dominant organization fighting for civil rights was the National Association for the Advancement of Colored People (NAACP). The NAACP's history stretched back to the beginning of the century. In 1905, DuBois wrote a call for the all-black Niagara Movement, an organization later incorporated into the new interracial NAACP, born in 1909:

> We must complain, yes plain, blunt complaint, ceaseless agitation, unfailing exposure of dishonesty and wrong—this is the unerring way to liberty, and we must follow it. . . .
>
> Next, we propose to work. These are the things that we as Black men must try to do. To press the matter of stopping the curtailment of our political rights; to urge Negroes to vote honestly and effectively; to push the matter of civil rights; to organize business cooperation; to build schoolhouses and increase the interest in education; to bring Negroes and labor unions into mutual understanding; to study Negro history: to attack crime among us. . . . to do all in our power, by word and by deed, to increase the efficiency of our race, the enjoyment of its manhood rights, and the performance of its just duties.

The NAACP's founding gave the movement an organized base. It soon developed an aggressive strategy of litigation aimed at striking down racial restrictions enshrined in law, triumphing in 1954 with *Brown v. Board of Education*, the Supreme Court case that ended segregation in public schools. That decision effectively ended segregation's legality; it also gave a nonviolent army the license to challenge segregation's morality.

From *Brown* forward, the movement expanded its targets, tactics, and techniques. Organizations and leadership expanded as well. The 1955–56 Montgomery bus boycott introduced a new leader, Martin Luther King, Jr., who articulated a new method of nonviolent resistance for fighting segregation. The new method required mass participation. Reliance on slow appeals to courts began to subside.

The NAACP had long lobbied Congress and presidents to adopt antisegregation measures. While the civil rights movement expanded, most politicians, including Dwight Eisenhower, John Kennedy, and Lyndon Johnson, approached race relations gingerly, if at all. Eisenhower was a benign racist who lobbied Supreme Court Chief Justice Earl Warren, whom he had appointed, against integrating schools. Eisenhower's vacillation served only to encourage the resistant white South. Although he courted black votes in 1960, Kennedy did not endorse equal rights and civil right legislation until the year before his term and life were cut short. In Lyndon Johnson, however, the movement found a match: a politician who wanted to be remade from Southerner to Westerner to American; a figure conscious that history would be his judge; a bighearted man more sensitive to appeals for racial justice than any president before or after him.

Whoever was in power, the NAACP and other groups and many individuals fought against a system of racial domination that whites had regularized over time. This system protected the privileges of white society and generated tremendous human suffering for blacks. In both urban and rural areas of the South, blacks were controlled economically, politically, and personally—relegated to the worst jobs; prevented, often by force and terror, from free participation in the political process; and denied due process of law and personal freedoms all whites routinely enjoyed. A consequence of the segregation system was the development of institutions in close-knit communities, such as churches, schools, and organizations, that nurtured and encouraged the fight against white supremacy.

The young people who began the 1960 student sit-in movement lived and learned amid such institutions. Eager to push beyond the legalistic approach of the NAACP, they envisioned a new kind of civil rights organization. In an early 1960 freedom song, the young students who joined together to create the southern student movement described themselves this way:

> The time was 1960, the place the USA,
> That February 1st became a history-making day.
> From Greensboro across the land, the news spread far and wide,
> As quietly and bravely, youth took a giant stride.
>
> (*Chorus*) Heed the call Americans all, side by equal side.
> Sisters, sit in dignity, brothers sit in pride.
>
> From Mobile, Alabama, to Nashville, Tennessee,
> From Denver, Colorado, to Washington, D.C.,
> There rose a cry for freedom, for human liberty. (Chorus)
>
> The time has come to prove our faith in all men's dignity.
> We serve the cause of justice, of all humanity.
> We're soldiers in the army, with Martin Luther King,
> Peace and love our weapons, nonviolence is our creed. (Chorus)

In early spring 1960 we received a letter from Martin Luther King, Jr., and Ella Baker, the acting executive director of the Southern Christian Leadership Conference (SCLC), inviting us to a student-centered meeting over Easter weekend in Raleigh, North Carolina. In Raleigh we found three hundred like-minded young black people and joined together to found the Student Nonviolent Co-ordinating Committee (SNCC). SNCC's goals were described to the Democratic Convention's Platform Committee in 1960 by its first chair, Marion Barry, who much later became mayor of Washington, D.C. We sought "a community in which a man can realize the full meaning of self, which demands an open relationship with others." In a nine-page statement, Barry said that southern students wanted an end to racial discrimination in housing, education, employment, and voting. SNCC's goals were similarly described by its executive secretary, James Forman, in 1961, as working full-time against the whole value system of the United States and by working toward revolution; in a 1963 organization brochure it defined itself as a program of developing, building, and strengthening indigenous leadership; and at the 1963 March on Washington the third SNCC chair, John Lewis, called for the building of a serious social revolution against American politics dominated by politicians who built their careers on immoral compromises and allied themselves with open forms of political, economic, and social exploitation.

At its founding conference, in April 1960, SNCC Executive Committee member Charles Jones declared that this organization would affect areas beyond lunch counters and move into areas such as politics and economics. Another recommendation noted that students had a natural claim to leadership in this project. We had pioneered in nonviolent direct action. Now we could show we understood the political implications of our movement. We were convinced of the necessity of all local areas joining in the campaign to secure the right to vote. No right was more basic to the American citizen, none more basic to a democracy.

Within four months of SNCC's founding, volunteer worker Robert Moses planned a student-staffed voter registration project in all-black Mound Bayou in the Mississippi Delta for the summer of 1961. The state of Mississippi became a laboratory for SNCC's unique methods of organizing. The students' work began in southwestern Mississippi, but when SNCC workers were driven from the area by local violence, state suppression, and federal indifference, the organization regrouped in Jackson and in Mississippi's Delta counties in early 1962.

Within a year, SNCC evolved from a coordinating agency into an activist organization helping local leadership in rural communities and small towns across the South participate in a variety of protests and political and economic organizing campaigns. Its members' youth and independence enabled the organization to remain close to grass-roots currents that rapidly escalated the southern movement from sit-ins to freedom rides to voter drives to political organizing.

By 1965, SNCC fielded the largest staff of any civil rights organization operating in the South. It had organized nonviolent direct action against segregated facilities and voter registration projects in Alabama, Arkansas, Maryland, Missouri, Louisiana, Virginia, Kentucky, Tennessee, North and South Carolina, Georgia, and Mississippi. It had built two independent political parties and organized labor unions and agricultural cooperatives. It had helped to expand the limits of debate within black America and refocused the civil rights movement. Unlike mainstream civil rights groups, which sought integration of blacks into the existing order, SNCC sought integration accompanied by structural changes in American society.

The rural South that SNCC entered in 1961 had a long history of civil rights activism. In many instances, however, SNCC staffers were often the first *paid* civil rights workers to base themselves in isolated rural communities, daring to take the message of freedom into areas where the bigger civil rights organizations feared to tread. The SNCC workers differed from those of other civil rights organizations, and their method of operation was different as well.

SNCC's unofficial slogan was "Do what the people say to do." Rather than impose our civil rights plan on a community, we believed the people of a community could best determine what their goals and methods would be. We were also convinced that leadership could be found anywhere—among sharecroppers and unlettered folks as well as in the more privileged classes who frequently believed middle-class status entitled them to be decision makers.

In addition, SNCC ventured into areas where few, if any, civil rights workers had been in recent years. The NAACP had been outlawed in Alabama in 1956 and did not begin operating there again until 1964, although many NAACP activists continued their work under other sponsorship. In 1962, the NAACP had only one field secretary in South Carolina, Florida, Alabama, and Mississippi and a regional staff based in Atlanta. Another civil rights organization, the Congress of Racial Equality (CORE) had a southern staff that fluctuated between five and ten in 1962 and 1963; in 1964, CORE had eighteen field secretaries in Mississippi; there were four CORE staff in Alabama in 1965. The Southern Christian Leadership Conference hired its first field secretary in 1960; in 1964 the staff numbered sixty-two. By the summer of 1965, SCLC had field secretaries in every southern state except Florida and Tennessee, and much of the organization's work, like the NAACP's, was conducted through affiliates. One historian has written that SCLC had to adopt a strategy of hit and run, striking one target at a time.

By contrast, in the spring of 1963, SNCC had eleven staff members in south-west Georgia alone, and twenty in six different offices spread throughout Mississippi. By August, SNCC had projects and permanent staff in a dozen Mississippi communities, as well as in Selma, Alabama; Danville, Virginia; and Pine Bluff, Arkansas. There were 12 staffers in the Atlanta headquarters, 60 field secretaries, and 121 full-time volunteers.

When SNCC chose a community in which to begin civil rights activities we researched the economic and political history of the area. Field workers were supplied with detailed information on a community's economic and financial power structure, tracing connections of local bankers and business leaders in the local White Citizens Council to the largest American banks and corporations. Other research provided the economic and political status of the community's black population. A SNCC organizer spent his or her first weeks in a new community meeting local leaders, working with them to create an action plan for more aggressive registration efforts, and recruiting new activists through informal conversation, painstaking house-to-house canvassing, and regular mass meetings.

Registering rural southern blacks, a SNCC worker wrote, would greatly liberate U.S. politics as a whole. At the very least, these new voters would defeat the powerful, hidebound southern Democrats who were holding the reins of Congress on the basis of being elected year after year from districts where black citizens were denied the franchise. The SNCC workers and those of other organizations fought white terror and helped create a willingness to risk danger to register to vote. At every turn they and the people they hoped to register confronted verbal and physical abuse from the white power structure. Organizers from SNCC built or strengthened aggressive, locally led movements in the communities where it worked.

To demonstrate that disenfranchised Mississippi blacks wanted to vote, SNCC mounted a Freedom Vote campaign in November 1963. More than eighty thousand blacks cast votes in a mock election for governor and lieutenant governor. With dozens of northern white students working in this campaign, it attracted the attention of the Department of Justice and national media as black registration workers had never before done, paving the way for the Freedom Summer campaign in 1964.

The Freedom Summer campaign brought one thousand young white volunteers to Mississippi for the summer of 1964. The volunteers tried to register voters and continued to build the new political party SNCC had helped to organize, the Mississippi Freedom Democratic Party (MFDP). They also staffed twenty-eight freedom schools intended by their designer, SNCC's Charlie Cobb, to provide an education that would make it possible to challenge the myths of our society about black intellectual inferiority, to perceive more clearly contemporary realities, and to find alternatives and, ultimately, new directions for action.

Unencumbered by allegiances to the national Democratic Party that frequently constrained other, older organizations, SNCC staffers encouraged the Rev. R. L. T. Smith of Jackson to run for Congress from the state's 2nd Congressional District. With Robert Moses as his unofficial campaign manager, Smith ran to shake loose the fear among Mississippi blacks and to show them what meaning politics might have in their lives. Smith lost, as expected, but his campaign opened new political possibilities for Mississippi blacks. Over the next several years, SNCC-backed candidates ran for Congress in Albany, Georgia; Selma, Alabama; Danville, Virginia; and Enfield, North Carolina. The organization also assisted first time black candidates for Agricultural Stabilization and Conservation Service (ASCS) boards in Alabama, Arkansas, Georgia, North Carolina, and Mississippi and aided school board candidates in a number of states.

The capstone of the electoral efforts was the plan by the MFDP to challenge the seating for the regular, all-white delegation from Mississippi at the 1964 National Democratic Convention in Atlantic City, which would nominate the party's presidential and vice presidential candidates, and, in 1965, challenge the seating of Mississippi's congressional delegation. The MFDP held its own state convention, selected an integrated delegation and sent it to Atlantic City. Televised hearings before the party's credentials committee offered compelling testimony from MFDP delegates, including delegation vice chair Fannie Lou Hamer and Rita Schwerner, widow of one of the three civil rights workers murdered that summer in Mississippi.

Given the Democrats' support of the Civil Rights Bill and Lyndon Johnson's own commitment to civil rights, the MFDP delegates were optimistic about their challenge. Nevertheless their efforts ended in failure. Lyndon Johnson, desiring a smooth renomination, wanted no controversy at the convention. Pressure from Johnson erased the support from party liberals that had once been promised to Freedom Democrats. A compromise offer was made—the all-white Mississippi regulars would be seated as well as two at-large convention seats for the MFDP, but chosen by the national party and not the Freedom Democrats. Despite pressure from liberals and moderates to accept the compromise, Fannie Lou Hamer summed up her compatriots' feelings when she said: "We didn't come for no two seats when all of us is tired!" The offer was rejected, and the Freedom Democrats left for home.

Each electoral challenge—from local races to the **MFDP challenge**—served as an object lesson for strengthening black political **independence**. The organizing and lobbying efforts laid the groundwork for the next steps. Despite Johnson's resistance to the MFDP in Atlantic City, in 1965 he proposed the Voting Rights Act passed by Congress that year. In his televised speech announcing the bill, Johnson echoed the ultimate call of the civil rights movement, declaring that in this effort "we shall overcome."

The voting effort continued throughout the decade. The MFDP's legal efforts against white resistance to political equality proved important to black political efforts across the South. An MFDP-directed court suit resulted in the Supreme Court's landmark 1969 decision in *Allen v. State Board of Elections*, which was critical to continuing black political progress throughout the South. For the first time the Supreme Court recognized and applied the principle of minority vote dilution—that the black vote could be affected as much by dilution as by an absolute prohibition on casting a ballot. This became the basis for numerous redistricting cases that led to the election of black or minority representatives to Congress and to state legislatures.

The mid-1960s were a turning point in the southern human rights struggle. Federal legislation passed in 1964 and 1965 accomplished the immediate goals of many in the civil rights movement. When the federal government passed bills that supposedly supported black voting and outlawed public segregation, SNCC lost the initiative in these areas. Northern urban riots in 1964, 1965, 1966, and 1967 made the nation and southern civil rights workers aware that victories at lunch counters and ballot boxes meant little to blacks locked in northern ghettoes. At the same moment that Lyndon Johnson moved closer to the civil rights organizations, they began to move away from him on another issue. In 1965, the McComb MFDP branch became the first black political organization to express opposition to the war in Vietnam. State MFDP officials not only refused to repudiate the McComb statement, but reprinted it in the MFDP state newsletter, giving it wider circulation and breaking ground for future black opponents of the war.

My own campaign for the Georgia House of Representatives in 1965 was an attempt to take the techniques SNCC had learned in the rural South into an urban setting, and to carry forward SNCC's belief that grass-roots politics could provide answers to the problems faced by American blacks. But it also pointed to the new combination of issues that would mark politics in the second half of the decade.

Federal lawsuits had reapportioned the Georgia General Assembly, overturning a legislature where grossly disproportional districts meant that some cows and horses were better represented than some human beings. The court ordered new, equal districts created in urban Fulton County and ordered elections in them for one-year terms. I decided to run in one of them when a movement friend, Ben Brown, qualified in an adjacent district.

In keeping with SNCC's style, a platform was developed in consultation with the voters. The Bond campaign supported a $2 minimum wage law in Georgia, repeal of the right-to-work law, and abolition of the death penalty. We won overwhelmingly, and I was to take the oath of office on January 10, 1966. But on January 6, SNCC became the first civil rights organization to link the prosecution of the Vietnam War with the persecution of blacks at home. It issued a statement that accused the United States of deception in its claims of concern for the freedom of colored peoples in such countries as the Dominican Republic, the former Congo, South Africa, the former Rhodesia, and in the United States itself. The United States is no respecter of persons or laws, the statement said, when such persons or laws run counter to the nation's needs and desires.

The statement created a sensation. In the civil rights community, it marked a break in the relationship between the more militant civil rights organizations and the administration of President Johnson and further widened the gap between SNCC and the moderate civil rights mainstream.

At the time, I was SNCC's communications director, and, when I appeared to take the oath of office on January 10, hostility from white legislators was nearly absolute. They prevented me from taking the oath, declared my seat vacant, and ordered another election to fill the vacancy. I won that election and was expelled again. By the time I approached a third election, this time for a two-year term, I had filed suit in federal court. Judge Griffin Bell (later attorney general under Jimmy Carter) wrote the majority decision for the three-judge court that refused to overturn the Georgia legislature's decision to deny me the seat I had already won twice. I appealed to the U.S. Supreme Court.

I had never been to the Court before. There I sat and listened as Georgia Attorney General Arthur Bolton argued that Georgia had a right to refuse to seat me. I found myself hypnotically nodding in agreement. Victor Rabinowitz, one of my lawyers, elbowed me and whispered, "Stop that!" Following Bolton's argument, the justices asked a few questions. When Justice Byron White asked, "Is that all you have? You've come all this way, and that's all you have?" I knew we had won. Chief Justice Earl Warren's unanimous decision in *Bond v. Floyd* was more than a victory for the First Amendment; it was a reaffirmation of my constituents' right to free choice in casting their votes. A year after my first attempt, I became a member of the Georgia House of Representatives.

Speaking in 1901, my slave-born grandfather viewed the century before him with hope.

The false partitions set up to separate classes and races are falling down. Illogical and un-Christian distinctions, though still disgracing the age and hampering the spirit of progress must soon yield to justice and right. . . . Then forward in the struggle for advancement.

Wrong for a time may seem to prevail and the good already accomplished seem to be overthrown. But forward in the struggle, inspired by the achievements of the past, sustained by a faith that knows no faltering, forward in the struggle.

As we recall the struggles of the recent past, many of us are confused about what the movement's aims and goals were, what it accomplished and where it failed, and what our responsibilities are to complete its unfinished business today.

Looking back at that movement from today, we now have a very different view of the events and personalities of the period.

Instead of the towering figures of Kings and Kennedys standing alone, we now also see an army of anonymous women and men.

Instead of famous orations made to multitudes, we now also see the planning and work that preceded the triumphant speeches.

Instead of a series of well-publicized marches and protests, we now also see long organizing campaigns and brave and lonely soldiers often working in near solitude.

Instead of prayerful petitions for government's deliverance, we now see aggressive demands and an ethic of self-help.

History's view of the movement's goals has been too narrow. African Americans did not want to be integrated into a burning house; rather, they wanted to build a better house for everyone. They marched on Washington for freedom and jobs, not for abstract freedom alone.

Instead of a sudden upsurge in black activism in Montgomery in 1955, we now see a long and unceasing history of aggressive challenges to white supremacy that began as long ago as slavery time.

And instead of a movement that ended in 1968 with the death of Martin Luther King, Jr., we now see a continuous movement stretching from the ancient past until this moment, with different forms and personalities, in many places and locales, with differing methods and techniques, whose central goal has always been the elimination of strictures based on race.

We tend today to look back on the King years with nostalgia, as if those were the only years in which we were truly able to overcome. Our inability to do so today is caused, at least in part, by the way we recall Dr. King. For most of us he is little more than an image of a gifted preacher who had a dream seen in grainy black-and-white television film taken in Washington almost four decades ago.

But King, of course, was much more than that, and the movement was much more than Martin Luther King, Jr. He didn't march from Selma to Montgomery by himself; he didn't speak to an empty field at the March on Washington. There were thousands marching with him and before him, and thousands more who did the dirty work that preceded the triumphant march.

Black Americans really didn't just march to freedom. We worked our way to civil rights through the difficult business of organizing: knocking on doors, one by one. Registering voters, one by one. Creating a community organization, block by block. Financing the cause of social justice, dollar by dollar. Building a state-wide movement, town by town. Creating an interracial coalition, nationwide.

Yesterday's movement succeeded because the victims became their own best champions. When Rosa Parks refused to stand up on a Montgomery bus or when Martin Luther King, Jr., stood up to speak, mass participation came to the movement for civil rights.

For too many people today, the fight for equal justice has become a spectator sport, a kind of National Basketball Association in which all the players are black, and all the spectators are white. But in this true-to-life competition between good and evil, the players are of every color and condition, the fate of all the fans tied to the points scored on the floor. When good prevails, all the spectators win, too.

Because young black people faced arrest at southern lunch counters forty years ago, the laws that resulted from their actions now protect older Americans from age discrimination, protect Jews and Moslems and Christians from religious discrimination, and protect the disabled from exclusion because of their condition. It took but one woman's courage to start a movement in Montgomery, the bravery of four young men in Greensboro to set the South on fire.

The current racial scene in the United States is dismal but not without hope. My grandfather's words—from the beginning of the twentieth century—might well be remembered as we begin the twenty-first.

> The pessimist from his corner looks out upon the world of wickedness and sin, and blinded by all that is good or hopeful in the condition and progress of the human race, bewails the present state of affairs and predicts woeful things for the future.
>
> In every cloud he beholds a destructive storm, in every flash of lightning an omen of evil and in every shadow that falls across his path a lurking foe.
>
> But he forgets that the clouds also bring life and hope, that the lightning purifies the atmosphere, that shadow and darkness prepare for sunshine and growth, and that hardships and adversity nerve the race, as the individual, for greater efforts and grander victories.

"Of This Generation"

The New Left and the Student Movement

Wini Breines

We are people of this generation, bred in at
least modest comfort, housed now in
universities, looking uncomfortably to the
world we inherit.

Port Huron Statement, 1962

College and university attendance exploded in the postwar period. There were two million college students in 1950, three million in 1960, five million by 1965 (the first baby boomers were college age in 1964), seven million by 1968 and, by 1973, ten million. In 1970, 50 percent of all people in the United States from eighteen to twenty-two years old were attending college, primarily large public universities. Educational democratization was under way, thanks in part, ironically, to the increasingly tight partnership between the federal government and the universities. Federal money poured into the universities, much of which was tied to military-sponsored research. For the first time in American history, masses of young people, female and male, lived together away from their families.[1] I was one of them. In the midst of a growing student population, early white student movement activists often do not stand out from the rest of the conservatively dressed and buttoned-down students in campus photographs. The young men had short hair and wore white shirts, dark trousers, and sometimes even ties. Young women wore skirts. As a girl in the 1950s, I remember having to wear white gloves for dress occasions.

The 1950s were a conservative time in America, and campuses reflected it. The policy of *in loco parentis* meant that college administrators were considered parents away from home—and students were treated like children. At coed and women's institutions this translated into keeping close tabs on undergraduate women through curfews, rules, and strict dormitory life. Young women were not permitted in men's dormitory rooms, and men were not permitted in women's rooms; they socialized in dormitory lobbies and lounges. At my university, if you were in the dormitory lounge with a young man, three out of four of your feet had to be on the ground at all times! Students were expelled if they broke social rules devised to contain and control—and protect—them. Once over Thanksgiving vacation, when the dorms were closed and I had nowhere to stay, I "illegally" stayed in my boyfriend's room in an off-campus men's rooming house. We were reported and both almost expelled. Instead, the dean of men— yes, there was a dean for males and one for females—warned my boyfriend that "a stiff prick knows no conscience," and we were both put on probation. Vir-

---

WINI BREINES teaches sociology and women's studies at Northeastern University in Boston. She is the author of several books including *The Great Refusal: Community and Organization in the New Left* (1989) and *Young, White and Miserable: Growing Up Female in the Fifties* (1992), and she co-edited, with Alexander Bloom, *"Takin' It to the Streets": A Sixties Reader* (1995). She was active in the New Left, antiwar, and women's liberation movements in Madison, Wisconsin, and Boston, and continues to work and ruminate on them. She is currently working on a project concerning gender issues and the troubled relationships of black and white women in the civil rights and black power movements that led to the development of separate feminisms.

ginity until marriage was expected of young women, and colleges did their best to enforce it. Ironically, although education has been the path to upward mobility, middle-class white girls' means to security was by earning their "MRS. degree"—finding a husband in college, and, implicitly, the institutions facilitated the project.

Campuses in the 1950s were not political places; college administrators discouraged students from exploring serious politics, and most students were apolitical. Administrators and university trustees often had World War II–related experience and federal government connections, and were politically conservative. They were committed to the dominant Cold War perspective that embraced a notion of the world in which the United States represented the best and most democratic society possible and had a moral and political responsibility to expunge communism.[2] The basic premise was that there was little to be concerned about since everything was good in the United States. The country was strong and prosperous. White families were buying consumer goods, moving to the suburbs, and sending their children to college. From this perspective, what would students have to criticize?

It is difficult to believe that out of this comfortable but conformist and apparently innocent world, a New Left and student movement would develop. Most Americans, including many parents, were shocked when it did.[3] In the years before World War II, especially during the Depression, an old Left centered on the American Communist Party had played an important role in American politics, particularly in organizing unions. But by the 1950s, discredited by vituperative anticommunism and its own internal weaknesses, the old Left was virtually powerless. White youth inaugurated a *New* Left to distinguish their ideas from those of the old Left and to pursue fresh critiques of American society. The most dramatic difference between the old and new Lefts lay in the lack of interest that young people had in the Soviet Union, the site of the first communist revolution and society, and in defending international communism. They were also repelled by postwar–Cold War anti-communism, which they considered irrelevant to solving American social and political problems. Without championing the Soviet Union, they criticized the culture, economy, and politics of the United States.

Some early new leftists did come from old Left families—they were raised by parents who had been, or still were, affiliated with or sympathetic to the American communist movement. The children had grown up in an environment critical of capitalism and of class and racial discrimination in the United States and of the federal government's interventionist and undemocratic foreign policy. From the beginning, then, the New Left, which preceded the student movement, included young people from a variety of backgrounds. All were critical of American society, most were anticapitalist, and many eventually defined themselves as socialist. Over time they developed a position that American capitalism, based on private property and profit, was profoundly undemocratic, and they supported a political vision that ensured, as every individual's right, adequate income, housing, education, and medical care. They came together around local magazines and journals, peace and civil rights activity, the defense of the 1959 Cuban socialist revolution and Fidel Castro, and campus-focused political action groups. One of these was at the University of Michigan, at which students for a Democratic Society (SDS) the most important new Left student organization in the 1960s, was founded. New leftists were passionately engaged in politics and in developing both a strategic and theoretical understanding of capitalism and socialism, of racism and imperialism. Mainstream Americans considered them utopian, communist, socialist, deviant, or unpatriotic and were disturbed to see student rebels who "should" have been grateful and content. Their student activism sharply contrasted with the mainstream university life of the 1950s—football games, fraternity pranks, and panty raids.

While they had some mentors, the New Left and student movement were very much invented by young people themselves. They had little choice, for there were few elder leftist leaders or organizations to guide them.[4] At first, most knew little about the history of Left and radical opposition in the United States. Scattered in colleges and universities around the country, only a few professors prodded students to question their society. The Columbia University radical sociologist C. Wright Mills inspired many of the founders of SDS. In *The Power Elite* (1956) Mills argued that an interlocking, powerful elite of the government, corporations, and the military made a mockery of the United States as a democracy. His 1960 "Letter to the New Left" encouraged students to become agents of social change. But the early New Left's central inspiration was the civil rights movement. Throughout the 1950s the movement gathered steam in such struggles as the Montgomery bus boycott and the Little Rock school desegregation battle. Black people had moved young whites with their courage, determination, and dignity. The Student Nonviolent Coordinating Committee (SNCC), the most important youthful and radical civil rights organization of the early 1960s, became a model for the New Left. Although there were civil rights initiatives throughout the 1940s and 1950s, and they had important older mentors—especially SNCC executive director Ella Baker, local activists in southern communities, and Martin Luther King, Jr.—it was the young people who pushed in the direction of radical direct action. My first college political activity was picketing at a Madison, Wisconsin, Woolworth's store in support of the black southern student civil rights activists who in 1960 began sit-ins at segregated chain-store lunch counters to protest racial apartheid.

The values of the civil rights movement—equality, justice, freedom, and community—transformed the way that many young whites saw their country. They were horrified by racial segregation and discrimination and the recognition of the disparity between the articulated values of American political life and the reality. While official rhetoric spoke of democracy, student activists recognized hypocrisy all around them. Most African Americans were not treated equally, had little opportunity to succeed, and did not receive justice. They were excluded from middle-class prosperity and consumerism and the expectation of secure futures. This contradicted the values that young northern whites had been taught. Young student activists were idealistic. They believed in the values the United States was supposed to stand for, and they embraced John F. Kennedy's rhetoric of hope and civic commitment. Their relatively secure lives, the civil rights movement, and the Kennedy presidency contributed to students' deeply internalized hopes and ideals. That idealism fueled the movements.

Most early activists were middle class, usually from metropolitan areas, and attended elite eastern colleges and major state universities. Adults assumed that 1950s prosperity and optimism would generate satisfied and conformist young people, but for a significant minority it did not. Particularly moved by discrimination against African Americans, early activists were deeply concerned about values of truth and justice and about meaning in their own lives. They began to reject materialism and conformity and sought ways to live honestly, equally, and ethically in relation to others. Throughout the 1960s it became increasingly apparent to new leftists that the U.S. government was part of what came to be called a "military industrial complex" or a "power elite" with enormous control over the lives of ordinary Americans and people around the world, particularly poor people and people of color.[5] At the same time, early new leftists were discontented with their own middle-class lives and longed for a sense of community. Despite their material comfort, they felt relatively powerless and spoke often of wanting their lives to be more "real" and authentic. Many girls growing up in the 1950s experienced their suburban lives as inadequate. They felt separated from real life and meaningful experiences.[6] Dissatisfied youth were attracted to the Beat writers who rejected a materialistic, Puritan, future-oriented work ethic; to the young hero of *The Catcher in the Rye*; to James Dean in *Rebel Without a Cause*; and to existentialist philosophy.

One aspect of the New left that distinguished it from the old Left and traditional politics of all kinds was an effort to link political issues with personal life. Activists recognized that private life was deeply influenced by the organization of power, by economics and culture. Problems that were defined as personal often had social explanations. In addition, they believed that how they lived their lives, in the movement and out, had political implications. In SNCC, the nonviolent "beloved community" consisted of a committed and caring group in the midst of political action; it was this community that provided sustenance in the continuing struggle as well as a model for future relationships. Civil rights workers were building a new society at the same time that they fought to change the old. Influenced by their example, the New Left and student movement attempted to create a political movement that embodied democratic values, a prefigurative politics based on participatory democracy, equality, respect, and community. New leftists, then, were engaged in complicated political work: they were attempting to change society, to understand the influence of politics on personal life, and to create new, less hierarchical, relationships. It was not until the women's liberation movement that this project was fully explored.

Many of these ideas were expressed in the 1962 SDS Port Huron Statement, which has been called "one of the most pivotal documents in postwar American history."[7] It is a long manifesto, written at a retreat in Port Huron, Michigan, primarily by SDS leader Tom Hayden, with help from students from the University of Michigan and other midwestern and eastern SDS chapters. Participants wrote and argued and debated continually, feeling the need to understand and analyze, and to develop theories that informed action. More important than its specific proposals, the Port Huron Statement articulated a sensibility and way of considering the world. It begins: "We are people of this generation, bred in at least modest comfort, housed now in universities, looking uncomfortably to the world we inherit." It covers a range of issues, most of which are colored by hope and idealism and a fervent belief in democracy. One of the most quoted lines states, "We seek the establishment of a democracy of individual participation governed by two central aims: that the individual share in those social decisions determining the quality and direction of his life; that society be organized to encourage independence in men and provide the media for common participation." (Male pronouns and nouns were used throughout the manifesto, as they were in almost all New Left and radical documents until the women's liberation movement raised the issue of language and of male dominance.) These words articulate the notion of participatory democracy, an idea passionately embraced by the New Left and of great appeal to students everywhere. The simple idea was that everyone should be able to participate in the decisions that affect her or his life. It was radical because most people could not (and cannot), especially the poor. Participatory democracy led to critiques of U.S. race relations, class configurations, political and social hierarchy everywhere, even within SDS itself. The Port Huron Statement's formulations capture the early New Left's high regard for intellectual and political ideas and its serious moral commitment to a profoundly democratic society.

Community Organizing

By 1963, a number of SNCC activists and SDS leaders were suggesting that instead of young whites organizing black people in the civil rights movement, they should go to the source of the problem, white racists, and attempt to organize them against racism. SDSers understood that poor whites had more in common with poor blacks than they did with prosperous and powerful whites but that instead of directing their frustration toward those in power, poor whites expressed feelings of superiority to and hatred of black people. Heeding the suggestion and wanting to organize off the campus, SDS set up the Economic and Research Action Project (ERAP) in 1963. The idea was for SDS members to become involved in community organizing in white urban neighborhoods with the goal of organizing an "interracial movement of the poor" which would eventually link whites and blacks together in coalitions for social change. An important minority of SDS members, many of them in the leadership, participated in ERAP projects. They wanted to "live" their politics in the "real" world, not just on campus, and to convince poor people that they could change their situation through collective action, that poor people of different races faced similar economic problems. With dedication and idealism, these white new leftists, numbering no more than several hundred, became community organizers in impoverished urban neighborhoods in Chicago, Newark, Cleveland, and elsewhere.

ERAP was a topic of heated discussions within SDS. The young people who joined ERAP projects supported the idea that students had to give up their privileges and go to where the people were the most disadvantaged and voiceless to help them to organize themselves. Opponents argued that the student movement was where things were happening and where attention should be focused. They suggested that leaving the campus to live among the poor was based on guilt and a misguided notion of who was going to spearhead social change in America. Debates raged about how a more democratic and just society might come about, whether or not students were legitimate agents of revolution, how to mobilize poor and working-class groups, and what organizational forms made sense. There were also intense debates within ERAP about which issues to organize around—large economic themes, like jobs and livable incomes, or local and neighborhood concerns, like negligent landlords and inadequate services such as the absence of traffic lights and garbage removal.

The ERAP projects were experiments in group living and democratic process. All decisions and problems were discussed fully with equal participation, and everyone had house and community responsibilities. Organizers tried to live the idea that the personal is political by living and working together democratically and organizing with respect and mutuality, as a way to encourage local residents to become spokespeople and leaders of their communities. They voluntarily relinquished their privileges and tried to earn the trust of and learn from people with whom they ostensibly had little in common.

ERAP, however, was not a glowing success. The projects did not manage to organize viable community groups that recognized common interests with other poor people and went on to challenge the capitalist system. They did not organize an interracial movement of the poor. They did, though, have small local successes. Women organized women to become community leaders and to force cities to respond to the need for playgrounds, safe streets, housing, and welfare rights. Some ERAP organizers sowed the seeds of community organizations that became important in subsequent years. ERAPers learned that social change is slow and hard work, that people with few resources are frequently discouraged and hostile, and that poor whites are often overtly racist. They learned, too, that participatory democracy is time consuming and often inefficient.[8]

Campus Demonstrations

The 1964 free speech movement (FSM) at the Berkeley campus of the University of California is the episode that dramatically brought the student movement into American consciousness. Prior to 1964 the movement had been building around the country, primarily at large state universities in the Midwest and West and on private liberal arts campuses on the East Coast. Small, isolated groups had organized to oppose nuclear bomb testing and advocate peace in the world. The aggressive tactics of the House Un-American Activities Committee a congressional committee committed to exposing and destroying communism in America, galvanized student protest. The anticommunist, liberal National Student Association had also been active throughout the 1950s. Support groups for SNCC and chapters of northern civil rights organizations grew, and white students went South to participate in freedom rides and voter registration drives. SDS chapters spread throughout the country.

In 1964 Berkeley students became involved in an explosive struggle over their right to engage in politics on campus. That fall the university administration ruled that students could not use the campus to advocate for off-campus political causes, nor to publicize, solicit, raise money for or recruit for political organizations. Prohibitions against raising money for SNCC sparked the student response. A number of FSM leaders had been involved in the civil rights movement and linked the two. At a rally during the free speech movement, leader Mario Savio stated, "Last summer I went to Mississippi to join the struggle there for civil rights. This fall I am engaged in another phase of the same struggle, this time in Berkeley. . . . The same rights are at stake in both places—the right to participate as citizens in democratic society and the right to due process of law. . . . It is a struggle against the same enemy."[9] Students argued that it was a question of constitutional free speech, that they should be able to discuss anything on campus, and questioned who was making decisions and for what reasons. Besides the free speech issue, they rebelled against the top-down and bureaucratic decision making of the administrators who controlled their lives.

When the administration decided to arrest a number of students for violating the ban, the campus erupted. Even students who were not involved in politics supported free speech on campus and were shocked at the summary actions of the administration, which eventually suspended eight students. Several well-publicized demonstrations ensued. During one, students surrounded a police car that held an arrested activist and enthusiastically discussed politics, philosophy, and strategy for thirty-two hours. At another, they occupied the main administration building, Sproul Hall, until the police were called to eject them. Almost eight hundred students risked their academic careers by getting arrested. It was the largest mass arrest in California history.[10] Eventually a majority of the Faculty Senate supported the students against the administration. Through committed and persuasive nonviolent action, the students had succeeded. The ban was rescinded by the university regents. Students were permitted to advocate political causes on the Berkeley campus.

What is most significant about FSM is that it riveted and encouraged students around the country and raised critical issues of politics and strategy that preoccupied the student movement for the rest of the decade. I remember the elation I felt when I heard about FSM in the fall of 1964. I was impressed that students were on the move in California, contributing to what seemed to be becoming a national student movement. I was not alone in being moved by their principled activism: scores of East Coast students streamed into the Bay Area when they learned about Berkeley radical activism. Themes of participatory democracy, opposition to authoritarian and hierarchical organization, student alienation, student identification with the powerless and those deprived of their rights, disapproval of bureaucracy, and the role of the university as an institution of learning removed from corporate and government interests—all these appeared regularly in speeches and writing from this period and struck responsive chords in students on campuses everywhere.

Throughout the months of FSM a pattern emerged that characterized campus demonstrations throughout the country for years after. Radical students would ask for or demand changes or rights that did not appear to be particularly unreasonable. The university administration would overreact, apparently unable to respond in measured terms to what they considered a threat to their authority. This would mobilize greater numbers of students. The scenario would repeat itself. Eventually the authorities would respond in an extreme manner: suspensions, expulsions, stonewalling, police busts. Discontented students who might never have been mobilized were drawn into the movement. Often they were as outraged at the punitive responses of the university leadership as they were motivated by the issues under consideration. Overreaction on the part of the authorities politicized and radicalized young people, who were particularly sensitive to abuses of power.

The university attempted to discourage discontent—saying, in effect, that campus policy was not debatable. When students undertook nonviolent demonstrations, they were often met by police. Protesters' desire for change was transformed into confrontational struggles as those in power turned hostile to the demonstrators' desire for social change or even for negotiation. This dynamic unfolded in the antiwar movement as it had earlier in the civil rights movement. The civil rights movement began with black people peacefully asking for their rights and escalated into a bloody struggle because of resistance and fury on the part of the authorities attempting to maintain the status quo and their own power. In the case of the war, students began by requesting information about the war in Vietnam, questioning American intentions and attempting to speak to those in power; they received no reasonable response. Peace advocates recognized the same dynamic in the U.S. government's prosecution of the war in Vietnam itself; instead of negotiation, more force was applied. The efforts to "speak truth to power" were not successful in the 1960s.

The Student Movement Expands

Distinguishing the New Left from the student movement is difficult. One way to view the development is as an expansion from the New Left, those student intellectuals and activists in the late 1950s and early 1960s who self-consciously saw themselves developing a Left critique of American society, to the larger student movement of the late 1960s, which took on a variety of issues. By the mid-'60s, due in large part to its leadership of the movement against the war in Vietnam, the New Left expanded rapidly into a student movement with tens of thousands of adherents. It centered on SDS and other small pacifist and socialist organizations that wanted more than an end to the war in Vietnam or equality for African Americans. New leftists understood the war in Vietnam as American imperialism, part of a pattern of American intervention in the affairs of other, usually Third World, countries. Many became socialists. But most of those who "joined" or identified with the student movement in the second half of the 1960s were not new leftists. They were not generally engaged in thinking about socialism or revolution, community organizing, exposing corporate liberalism, or consciously fighting against capitalist institutions. The newer participants were more likely to be against the war in Vietnam and angry and frustrated with the narrowness of the norms and values of American society. They were antiauthoritarian, suspicious of leaders and experts, and discontented with the roles and rules set out for young people.

Another way of thinking about the distinction is in terms of movement generations. Those who were twenty years old in Ann Arbor in 1961, where SDS was founded, for example, were twenty-nine in 1970, while thousands of young people, a decade or more younger, had become active by the end of the decade. As increasing numbers of lower-middle-class and working-class students identified with the student and antiwar movements and younger people, including high school students, joined, the student movement became more heterogeneous.[11] The younger activists were usually galvanized by Vietnam, the Black Power movement, the counterculture, repressive high school or campus regulations, or an interest in drugs, sex, and rock 'n' roll. Unlike older new leftists, they were even less interested in and more suspicious of organized and institutionalized politics because they had come of age as the government was being discredited by its brutal policies at home and in Vietnam and by the social movements against it.

Another point is worth making. While confrontations at Berkeley in 1964, Columbia University in 1968, San Francisco State in 1969, and Kent State in 1970 were among the most significant student movement events of the 1960s, students throughout the country grew increasingly active, on campuses small and large, rural and urban, at community colleges and religious institutions, both private and public. They often did not receive the media attention beamed at the large major public universities and elite colleges, but upheaval was everywhere. It was a social movement precisely because so many students were in motion.

Finally, the relationship between the student movement and counterculture can not be ignored. The American youth movement was accompanied and
constituted by political popular music. Folk music, rhythm and blues, soul,
Motown, and rock drew in young people and contributed to their sense of sepa-
rateness from mainstream America and the adult world. The generational rupture is suggested by Bob Dylan's lyric from the "Ballad of a Thin Man": "Something is happening, and you don't know what it is, do you, Mr. Jones?" Dylan
and Joan Baez, to mention only the most famous young folk musicians, sang
songs of social significance, some of which, like "Blowin' in the Wind," became
radical anthems. Rock 'n' roll lyrics were increasingly political, articulating
antiwar and racial themes, and confrontational in their endorsement of youth
culture, particularly drugs. From folk music and blues in the late 1950s and early
1960s to the Beatles, Janis Joplin, Marvin Gaye, the Doors, the Grateful Dead,
Sly and the Family Stone, James Brown and numerous others, music spoke to
and for dissident young people.

It is inaccurate if not impossible to separate interwoven strands of rebellion and opposition. In the midst of growing concerns about Vietnam, the "summer of love" unfolded in 1967. Young people flocked to the Haight Ashbury
section of San Francisco and other counterculture enclaves in college towns
across America. Accompanied by the new rock music, they experimented with
sex and drugs. They created and identified with a youth culture that rejected
conformity, materialism, war, delayed gratification, and destruction of the earth.
Concerned with more than traditional party politics, young people questioned
social roles of all sorts. Asking who they were and who they wanted to be, they
embarked on a journey of deprogramming themselves from mainstream norms.
A youth revolt of vast proportions was under way. Political movements of the
late 1960s were infused with lifestyle explorations, and although there were clear
demarcations between hippies and political activists, elements of each were
adopted by the other. The separation between the political movements and the
counterculture was never neat. Student activists often identified with both
political and cultural rebellion. SDSers and new leftists kept their focus on politics, particularly the war, but many were engaged in cultural revolution too.
They changed their style of dress, grew their hair long, smoked marijuana, experimented with LSD, and explored sexual relationships. The well-groomed
young radicals of the early 1960s were nowhere to be seen by 1967. Photographs
from the time show my New Left husband a graduate student, who had pledged
a fraternity in his freshman year, with long hair and bell bottoms. The New
Left became the student movement and the student movement became the
antiwar movement—and the counterculture affected nearly everyone involved.

Ultimately ERAP and other political concerns of the New Left and civil rights movement were upstaged by the war in Vietnam. It is difficult not to wonder how the movements would have developed without the war. From 1965 on, Vietnam became the central issue of the decade. Just as it is difficult to separate the New Left and the student movement, it is impossible to distinguish the student movement from the antiwar movement. The war was the issue that created protesters, although not usually new leftists, out of white students and contributed to black students' growing conviction that the government was racist. The war provided a way for students to think critically about American foreign policy, racism, and the role of the military on campuses and in society—and about broader issues of power and democracy. And although most of those who turned out for demonstrations against the war in Vietnam just wanted the war to end, many did begin to question politics as usual.

Various levels of criticism, alienation, and rebellion operated simultaneously. The student movement swelled because of the war. Ending the fighting became the central goal. Early in the war, male college students were exempt from the draft during their four undergraduate years. They benefited from student deferments that were unavailable to other, usually working-class, men, and many felt guilty. They were threatened nonetheless, knowing they would be called up after graduation, and they could not help but recognize how vulnerable other young men were. By the end of the decade, as the war escalated, high school students multiplied the ranks of the student and antiwar movements. And while they all protested the war, they simultaneously set out to change their lives.

The Late Sixties

Nineteen sixty-eight was an amazing year. The sheer number of dramatic political events is staggering. Even at the time activists recognized the year as a turning point of some kind. By 1968, the New Left and student and antiwar movements were active throughout the country, and there was a feeling that major social change was under way. Because events unfolded so rapidly and dramatically, it was difficult to resist an apocalyptic sense of history changing before one's very eyes. Deep, passionate, and angry divisions developed in the country between those who wanted the war to end and American society to become more just and democratic, and those who supported the status quo. Many Americans were bewildered that so much seemed out of control and contested.

The year began with the Tet offensive in Vietnam. This military show of strength and determination by the National Liberation Front of South Vietnam (NLF) and the North Vietnamese demonstrated that optimistic statements about "victory just around the corner" were fraudulent. Exposing the weaknesses of the U.S. position in Vietnam, the Tet offensive turned millions of Americans against the war and expanded antiwar sentiment well beyond college campuses. Overnight, citizens became deeply suspicious of their leaders. In March, President Johnson announced he was withdrawing from the presidential race because of the unpopularity of the war. Eugene McCarthy and Robert Kennedy campaigned on an antiwar platform for the Democratic Party nomination, raising hopes that a peace candidate, a "dove," would be chosen as the party's presidential candidate. McCarthy and Kennedy seemed to promise that mainstream party politics might work; millions of young people and minorities campaigned for both candidates.

Four days after Lyndon Johnson's withdrawal, Martin Luther King, Jr., was murdered. In June, on the night of his last Democratic Party primary victory in California, Robert Kennedy was murdered. Both assassinations dashed the hopes and dreams of innumerable people. Ghetto rebellions broke out across the United States after King's assassination. Images of violence in the streets, on the campuses, and in Vietnam bombarded Americans. The strength and militance of the Black Panthers and Black Power movement transformed the nature of the racial debate. At the Olympics in Mexico City in October two black American athletes gave the black power salute as the national anthem played and their medals were awarded.

That spring the brave democratic Czechoslovakian experiment, Prague Spring, was under way ("socialism with a human face") and, in May, French students and workers revolted, nearly toppling the government. Internationally, students were in motion in opposition to the power elites and governments in their countries, to end the war in Vietnam and, fundamentally, in favor of more democratic societies. These were all utopian, imaginative, alive, engaged, outraged, and enraged. I spent that spring and summer demonstrating in Berlin against the U.S. government's war in Vietnam with German students, many of whom were members of the German New Left organization also called SDS. It was the year that Bill Clinton joined English antiwar demonstrations and wrote his draft board from Oxford University of his opposition to the war. An international student movement had developed, united by its opposition to U.S. intervention in Vietnam and belief in self-determination in their own countries and abroad. That same May the Columbia University student strike, occupation, and police bust became one of the most spectacular of all student movement events.

By the end of the summer the Soviet Union had invaded Czechoslovakia and crushed the Prague experiment. In Chicago thousands of demonstrators were beaten by Chicago police at the Democratic Party convention while millions watched the violence on television. Hubert Humphrey, who had entered no primaries, won the party nomination. For many progressives and liberals the Democratic Party was discredited. Richard Nixon won the election in November, in part by implying that he had a "secret" plan to end the war. The combined impact of all these events changed the tone of American life—and of the student and antiwar movements.

Like the rest of the society, campuses became increasingly polarized in the last years of the decade. Struggles erupted among new leftists, militant antiwar protesters, moderate antiwar students who opposed SDS and confrontational tactics, students who supported the war and despised all protesters, and the authorities. Militant student demonstrators targeted government officials, the police, ROTC (Reserve Officers Training Corps) programs, university military research projects, campus administrators, and racist university policies. Administrators were criticized for and discredited by their universities' ties to the military and for their handling of campus protests. The days of mannerly nonviolent protest were in the past. With the most respected liberal leaders gone, there was no one in government to appeal to. Politics as usual, working through legitimate channels, had not worked.

The student movement had been wildly successful. Only several years earlier, small isolated groups of radical students had raised questions about U.S. society. There were few expectations that the student movement might become a mass movement. Yet by 1968 hundreds of campus demonstrations had taken place over local campus rules, student involvement in university governance, campus racial policies, university complicity with the military, and the war in Vietnam. And in that year, major segments of the U.S. population had turned against the war, expanding the antiwar movement well beyond college campuses.

Race continued to be a central issue. The Black Power movement and the Black Panther Party defiantly celebrated their identity as black people. Their militancy, courage, confrontational style, community activism, and socialist analysis inspired white new leftists to support and imitate them, particularly in the face of the FBI's campaign against them. In 1970 I joined thousands of protesters in New Haven, Connecticut, to express support for jailed Panthers and outrage at the government's attack on them. (I was still a political activist, twenty-eight years old, pregnant, and worried about tear gas if the demonstration got violent. Determined to stay on the outskirts of the action, I went anyway because I felt so strongly that whites should support the Panthers.) By the end of 1968, the central campus issues were the war and race—not segregation in the South so much as racism at home, in the North, in the university, and the world. A powerful white nation, the United States, had invaded a poor Third World nation, Vietnam, with little regard for its culture and life, just as it had little regard for the people of color within its own borders, except to conscript them to fight against Asians in that war.

Yet SDS foundered. Just at the moment when millions of students identified with the student movement, when the student and antiwar movement became truly mass movements, the central New Left student organization splintered into factions that destroyed its political relevance. While national demonstrations in favor of a moratorium on the war were held in 1969 and 1970, with hundreds of thousands of people peacefully protesting and pleading with the government to negotiate and withdraw, SDS was engaged in sectarian and divisive politics. One major group identified with Marxism-Leninism and the other, called Weatherman, saw itself as a vanguard that could spark a revolution in America through violence and provocation and alliances with militant blacks. Most SDSers did not identify with either faction, but by 1969 the organization split under the weight of the factional infighting.

Activists' despair mounted as the war escalated and violence shook U.S. cities. From their perspective, the government persistently ignored the massive opposition to the war. By the end of the year, older New Left and student activists felt deeply disillusioned with U.S. society, and many began to consider themselves revolutionaries. New and younger activists shared their anger and disappointment. Young people, white and black, had become cynical about government and politics. One of the most devastating results of antiwar candidate Eugene McCarthy's campaign to become the Democratic Party presidential candidate was how much energy liberal students had devoted to it and how little they achieved. They had gone door-to-door for McCarthy and become deeply involved in electoral politics, as did those who rallied to Robert Kennedy, only to be cruelly disabused of their hopes by assassination, power politics, and police violence in Chicago. After eight years of political activity, hopes were shattered that society could be reformed through government response to appeals for justice and peace. One of the central experiences of young activists in the late 1960s, black and white, was disillusionment. In descriptions of their political development, they refer repeatedly to shock, disappointment, and disenchantment with their country and its leaders. A central dramatic story of the 1960s is of the transformation of hope in the early years of the decade to frustration and hopelessness by the end. With this rupture of optimism came a militance and realism about American power that generated movements and ideas markedly different from the hopeful and nonviolent groups of the early

1960s. Events required, or seemed to require, an escalation of tactics, new strategies, grim confrontational politics, a rejection of speaking truth to power, and the repudiation of protest in the name of resistance, even revolution. These years signified a kind of "growing up" for many whites. They recognized that morality alone was not enough to change American society.

Campus Wars

By the late 1960s the student movement had become a mass movement. There were hundreds of campus episodes. With the rise of black consciousness and the idea of Third World revolution spreading among young blacks, in the fall of 1969 the Black Student Union at San Francisco State College demanded the establishment of a black studies program, more black faculty, and increased black student enrollments and scholarships. Confrontation was the basic mode of interaction at San Francisco State, as it was on most campuses by 1969. Black students and their supporters held demonstrations, occupied buildings, and eventually went on strike. In the midst of daily, angry political action, most classes did not meet for months. Relations between the students and administration were tense and bitter. By the spring semester, the administration had made a commitment to a black studies program, to admitting more black students and giving them scholarships, and to the appointment of a black administrator. But the toll was high. Hundreds of students had been arrested and expelled and numerous faculty members who had supported the strike were fired. It was a raw struggle that revealed and articulated racial polarization on the campus and in the cities. Racial conflict erupted on other campuses in 1969 and 1970. The most spectacular occurred at Cornell University, where armed militant black students, demanding a black studies program, occupied the student union.[12]

No account of the student movement and the end of the decade is complete without Kent State, where on May 4, 1970, four students protesting the war in Vietnam were shot and killed by Ohio National Guardsmen, making it the most devastating student antiwar demonstration of the decade. Only a few days earlier, on April 30, President Nixon, who had pledged to end the war, had announced that the United States had invaded Cambodia in order to defeat the North Vietnamese who had established bases there. The invasion of Cambodia aroused frustration and anger on campuses everywhere. Student demonstrations, bombings, trashing, and strikes exploded. At Kent State, days of unrest resulted in the town's mayor declaring a state of emergency and requesting the help of the National Guard to occupy the campus. By the middle of the day on

May 4, students and guardsmen were facing off. Students hurled taunts and rocks, and soldiers responded with tear gas. Then, with no warning, the guardsmen opened fire on the students, killing four and wounding nine. Shock, sorrow, and rage boiled over at colleges throughout the nation. That the National Guard, representatives of the U.S. military, would open fire on demonstrating white students shocked many Americans, especially students. Days after Kent State, two unarmed black students were killed and twelve wounded by police at Jackson State College in Mississippi. The deaths in Ohio and Mississippi proved another turning point for the student movement. Although demonstrations continued to take place, in a way the heart of the student movement had been broken. Horror and despair provoked by the war's mounting death toll, violence everywhere, and deaths on campus frightened and discouraged student activists. In addition, and not insignificant, were negotiations with the North Vietnamese to end the war. The government made gestures toward peace while continuing to wage war, most visibly by bombing North Vietnam. In January 1973, almost three years after Kent State, the Nixon administration finally signed a peace agreement in Paris. A combination of despair, hope that the government might negotiate an end to the war, and the Paris Peace Accords undercut the massive student antiwar movement.

Finally, a discussion of the 1960s must at least refer to the federal government's shocking assault on the movements. There is a good deal of evidence that destructive policies and internecine battles were provoked by the government. The clear goal was to discredit and destroy the radical movements, with a special hatred reserved for the Black Panther Party. The Nixon administration and FBI Director J. Edgar Hoover were obsessed with the movements, convinced they were linked to communism, and committed to obliterating them. Sabotage was required, they contended, because of the movements' supposed threat to national security. Policies of surveillance had begun during the Kennedy administration, with Martin Luther King, Jr., a central target of Hoover's FBI. But surveillance widened throughout the decade, eventually including the CIA as well. The bureau set up its COINTELPRO program of counterintelligence against the movements and "eventually employed 2000 agents that infiltrated, provoked disturbances, and began a massive program of 'disinformation,' a euphemism for spreading lies."[13] The FBI conducted illegal wiretaps, infiltrated groups, harrassed individuals and played the role of agent provocateur, using informers to encourage extreme and violent behavior and feuds among activists. Twenty-eight Black Panther Party members were killed in shoot-outs with police across the country, including two Chicago Panthers shot in their beds. The government's undemocratic and often illegal policies contributed to the decline of the movements by wreaking destruction and confusion. And they encouraged a paranoia about the government that, in retrospect, does not seem unfounded.

During the time the New Left was coming apart as a political force, other important political developments, influenced by the Black Power movement, unfolded. In 1968 young people became smarter about power and less naive and idealistic about U.S. society. But it was also the moment when women and blacks and Latinos and Asian Americans and, eventually, gays and lesbians "came out." Their movements—referred to as identity politics—of anger and pride and affirmation, of demanding equality and respect, burst on the American scene, and much of the action took place on college campuses. It was a joyous and hopeful moment but angry and cautious as well. These politics took hold on campuses in the late 1960s, leading to fuller expression and the establishment of women's studies and African American studies programs in the 1970s. Thus while SDS, the student movement, and the antiwar movement declined after 1970, they paved the way for other movements to develop on campuses. Students continued to be activists in the early 1970s, but their energies were splintered into separate organizations and issues, and they were no longer identified as the student movement.

Legacies

Many factors combined to create the conditions for the movements of the 1960s. Looking back at the New Left and student movement, one of the most noticeable differences between then and now is that most students had more time and fewer career and financial pressures. Postwar prosperity contributed to students' sense that they had time and space in their lives and could take the risks connected to protest. They were less anxious about and focused on their future careers, perhaps because those among them who were middle class felt they could land on their feet whenever they needed to. Costs and the standard of living were lower for them than for students today. Radical students rejected careers and comfortable lives, making it even easier to take risks. Baby boomers, including southern black students who sat in at lunch counters and founded SNCC, had high expectations about their lives and their rights. The New Left and early student movement were committed to American ideals. They assumed that they could create a society in which freedom and justice for all was real. They believed that government officials would change their policies about civil rights and the war in Vietnam when they realized the "truth." The distrust of politics that many of us feel today can be traced back, in part, to the 1960s, when idealistic young people discovered and exposed the deceptions of those in power and recognized that politics is as much about power as it is about ideals. Political suspicion is a 1960s legacy that has only been reinforced by the cynicism of subsequent administrations and corporate national politics.

But politics is about ideals and activism, too. These are more important legacies of the New Left and student movement than passivity and cynicism. Many people, including students, work today to turn the United States into a juster and more humane society. In fact, colleges are still the sites of much political activism. Activists are not part of a social movement, but change happens in different ways, sometimes quickly and dramatically, and other times slowly through local organizing and campaigns that eventually become national. It can be discouraging to compare today's organizing with the 1960s but, in fact, there are activists, on campuses and off, quietly working to create a more egalitarian society. Some are veterans of the New Left and student movement. If we look around, we can find people collectively making a difference.

The free speech movement made it possible to organize and solicit for political causes on college campuses. Ironically, we take this for granted now—it seems surprising that it was ever an issue. Students liberalized colleges. *In loco parentis* was eliminated, and students were recognized as adults with the ability to make choices about their lives. The freedom that college students have today is in large part due to the student movement of the 1960s. The new Left and student movement contributed to more student-centered institutions of higher education that included an emphasis on good teaching. One of the more enduring influences has been on curriculum and intellectual life—a process of democratization that has been under way for thirty years. "Outsiders" demanded that academic disciplines be opened to include voices of those who had been excluded, primarily women, people of color, and homosexuals. Curricula nationwide began to reflect excluded people, experiences, and approaches. Through interdisciplinary approaches and the questioning of science, and of status and hierarchy in the university, radical intellectuals changed the academy.

But the New Left did not prevail in its basic critique of the university. Students struggled against the tide of consolidation of major institutions in late capitalist society. They argued that the university was contaminated by its close connections to the military and the corporate world, that those relationships entered campuses, even classrooms, to skew the world of learning. As universities and their personnel became increasingly financially dependent on corporations and the government, the idea of the university as a neutral place for the free exchange of ideas could not prevail. Today, of course, SDS's ideas seem quaint. We accept, even encourage, a close connection between the university, business world, and government. We recognize that universities *are* businesses. Unlike new leftists, students today often expect their colleges to link them to the corporate world. So the New Left ideal of the university as a pure ivory tower committed to the life of the mind, separate from the world of money and power, is no longer entertained. It is not a bad idea to hold on to, however, when attempting to understand the politics of higher education.

As for another of the New Left's critical beliefs, it appears that capitalism and conservative forces have won. Throughout the world, capitalism thrives. One rarely hears a discussion of socialism, although there is anticapitalist resistance around the globe. People continue to suffer everywhere—women and men, workers and employees, children, people of color. Despite the triumph of global capitalism, however, the New Left's analysis was not wrong. The Port Huron Statement is as relevant today as it was almost forty years ago. New Left concerns about participatory democracy and bureaucracy, meaningful work and fairness, concentrated power, and the right to a decent and meaningful life have never been addressed. We are left with a disturbing, and puzzling, picture of a society even more unequal than when SDS was founded, but with no major oppositional movements. Perhaps the sense of abundance and of a promising future that students in the 1960s implicitly relied on is no longer available and this inhibits Americans from critical political action. Power has become more concentrated, and that, too, may discourage activism. The New Left and student movement articulated a sense of powerlessness and lack of community that have only deepened in the last thirty years. It may be, too, that the movements sensed an historical moment in which America in the second half of the twentieth century was on the cusp of a postmodern society in which the concentration of capital and media would render the individual almost irrelevant and ineffectual. If this is true, then the New Left was prescient about what was to come and, successful or not, inspiring in its determined efforts to change the course of history.

I considered myself a member of the New Left, although I never belonged to SDS, and was active in the antiwar movement. In the late 1960s, I joined the early women's liberation movement. Many early young feminists had come through the movements of the 1960s. They applied the lessons of equality and democracy to themselves and recognized, with some amazement, that they had been participating in groups that discriminated against women. The New Left and student movement were male-dominated and insensitive to gender issues. Women decided they needed to organize themselves against sexism. But they learned many of their political ideas and gained enormous experience in the civil rights, New Left, student, and antiwar movements. There are deep links between the movements, particularly women's liberation with the civil rights movement and New Left.

Looking back, I believe it was enormously important to begin to understand politics, to recognize the operation of "the system" in all parts of life—economic, political, social, cultural, and personal—to feel a part of history, to believe that I/we could have a part in changing society. I recollect the hopes and illusions, dedication and dignity, disillusionment and despair. We were not passive. But we were often too arrogant, violent, and contemptuous. The white movement repeatedly faltered in its relations with the black movement. It was male chauvinist. But despite all the mistakes, students were part of a rupture with a repressive and hierarchical world in the name of democracy, equality, self-determination, and peace. We grappled with big issues and won some of them. We questioned authority and launched a cultural debate that has accompanied all of us into the twenty-first century.

NOTES

1. Terry H. Anderson, *The Movement and the Sixties: Protest in America from Greensboro to Wounded Knee* (New York: Oxford University Press, 1995), p. 95; Kenneth J. Heineman, *Campus Wars: The Peace Movement at American State Universities in the Vietnam Era* (New York: New York University Press, 1993), p. 77.

2. See Heineman, *Campus Wars*, chapter 1, "'Bastions of Defense': Cold War University Administrators," pp. 13–19.

3. It is important to point out, before proceeding further, that while the New Left and student movement were primarily white movements, black students were in motion too, primarily in the civil rights and black power movements. Students of all races were active in the 1960s but movements of students of color are usually identified as ethnic and racial movements, not as student movements. Whites, as usual, get the generic appellation—in this case, "student."

4. There were some activist elders. For example, A.J. Muste, Bayard Rustin, Ella Baker, Dorothy Day, and David Dellinger were older activists, and sometimes mentors, but rupture rather than continuity was the rule between the young and older radical traditions, with, perhaps, the exception of the Communist Party and their children, often called red diaper babies.

5. On an ominous note, in his farewell address to the nation in 1960, President (and General) Eisenhower, military war hero, warned of the dangers posed to democracy in the United States by the power of the military industrial complex.

6. For more on this, see Wini Breines, *Young, White, and Miserable: Growing Up Female in the Fifties* (Boston: Beacon Press, 1992), and Doug Rossinow, *The Politics of*

Authenticity: Liberalism, Christianity, and the New Left in America (New York: Columbia University Press, 1998).

7. Jim Miller, *"Democracy Is in the Streets": From Port Huron to the Siege of Chicago* (New York: Simon and Schuster, 1987), p. 13

8. For more on ERAP, see Wini Breines, *The Great Refusal: Community and Organization in the New Left* (New Brunswick, N.J.: Rutgers University Press, 1989), chapter 7; Sara Evans, *Personal Politics: The Roots of Women's Liberation in the Civil Rights Movement and the New Left* (New York: Alfred A. Knopf, 1979), chapter 6; and Miller, *Democracy Is in the Streets*, chapter 10.

9. Alexander Bloom and Wini Breines, eds., *"Takin' It to the Streets": A Sixties Reader* (New York: Oxford University Press, 1995), p. 112.

10. W. J. Rorabaugh, *Berkeley at War: The 1960s* (New York: Oxford University Press, 1989), p. 33.

11. See Heineman, *Campus Wars*, 79 ff., for a discussion of the class basis of student antiwar movement. He suggests that affluent students at elite schools were considered more newsworthy than were the working- and lower-middle-class Jews, Catholics, and Protestants who were more likely to be found in state universities. Thus the impression was created of an upper-middle-class student movement. Also see the introduction to Rossinow, *The Politics of Authenticity*.

12. Anderson, *The Movement and the Sixties*, pp. 294–300.

13. *Ibid*, p. 324.

Vietnam War Mythology and the Rise of Public Cynicism

Christian Appy
Alexander Bloom

When the Mongols rode into the country like thunder on horseback, the people . . . devised a plan. Everyone in the country painted, on each leaf of each tree, the following message with a brush dipped in honey: "It is the will of Heaven. The invaders must leave." When the caterpillars and ants ate the honey, they engraved and seared this message onto the leaves, holy tablets wrought from the heart of the land itself. The words looked supernatural, a spontaneous declaration by the forces of nature that terrified the Mongolians. Like ghosts conquered by an even greater spirit, they fled across the border and disappeared into the night.

Lan Cao,
Monkey Bridge (1997)

I had never visited Indochina, nor did I understand or appreciate its history, language, culture, or values. . . . When it came to Vietnam, we found ourselves setting policy for a region that was terra incognita.

Robert McNamara,
In Retrospect (1995)

ong before the American War, Vietnamese children learned the glo-
rious tales of ancient resistance to foreign domination. History and legend
are alive with the deeds of Vietnamese patriots. Rebel heroes are the central
figures in the Vietnamese pantheon. The Trung sisters led the first insurrection
against Chinese rule in 40 c.e. One of their soldiers, Phung Thi Chinh, was said
to give birth in the middle of battle and strap the newborn on her back to continue the fight. Another woman warrior, Trieu Au, rode to war in 248 atop an
elephant. In 938, Ngo Quyen lured Chinese warships into a spike-filled river so
the lowering tide would impale the enemy vessels. Under the command of Tran
Hung Dao, the Vietnamese routed three hundred thousand Mongolians in 1288.
More than a century later a giant tortoise rose from the bottom of Hoan Kiem
Lake with a magic sword in its mouth, and Le Loi grasped the weapon and led
Vietnam to victory over the Chinese. For two millennia the Vietnamese fought
for national unification and independence—against China for well over a thousand years, against France for a hundred, against Japan during World War II,
and eventually against the United States. In the face of such unrelenting resistance, many foreign soldiers came to believe that "the heart of the land itself"
opposed their presence.[1]

In 1968, Robert S. McNamara resigned as United States secretary of defense.
For seven years he had been such a key architect of American military intervention that many people called it "McNamara's War." As early as the fall of 1965,
McNamara privately concluded that the United States could not win the war. But
he continued to defend U.S. escalation for two more years and left office without voicing a word of public protest. The war went on for seven more years and
killed an additional thirty-five thousand Americans and at least one million more
Vietnamese. In the end, the United States failed in its thirty-year effort to crush
communist-led revolutionary nationalism in Vietnam (1945–75). During the years

CHRISTIAN G. APPY is the author of *Working-Class War: American Combat Soldiers and Vietnam* (1993)
and the editor of *Cold War Constructions: The Political Culture of United States Imperialism, 1945–
1966* (2000). Formerly an associate professor of history at MIT, he is now an independent
scholar working on an oral history of the Vietnam War. Appy also edits "Culture, Politics, and
the Cold War," a book series published by the University of Massachusetts Press. He lives in
Sharon, Massachusetts.

ALEXANDER BLOOM is professor of history and American studies at Wheaton College in Massachusetts. He was involved in civil rights causes in high school and was an antiwar activist at the
University of California, Santa Cruz. He is the author of *Prodigal Sons: The New York Intellectuals and Their World* (1986); coeditor of *Toward a Balanced Curriculum: Integrating Woman into
the Curriculum* (1985); coeditor, with Wini Brienes, of *"Takin' It to the Streets": A Sixties Reader*
(1995); and is currently working on a study of the way the Vietnam War experience has shaped
American life.

of direct United States combat (1961–73), at least two million Vietnamese lives were lost, and more than fifty-eight thousand Americans. Almost three decades after leaving the government, McNamara published a memoir declaring that U.S. policy makers had been "terribly wrong" to intervene in Vietnam. He attributed some of the failure to ignorance about Vietnamese history and culture. To McNamara and other officials, Vietnam was "terra incognita."

This belated admission of ignorance is as accurate as it is appalling. Just sample some of the official documents in the seven thousand-page Pentagon Papers, a history of official decision making that McNamara had his staff compile during his final year in office. The memos and reports tell us a good deal about the values and assumptions of U.S. policy makers, but almost nothing about Vietnam. To the Americans who planned and executed the war, Vietnam was merely a tactical area of operations in the Cold War. Official language was a kind of abstract code, full of icy, bloodless euphemisms, mind-numbing acronyms, and meaningless statistics. Unimaginable destruction was hidden behind phrases like "sustained reprisal" and "maximum remunerative rate."[2]

When policy makers put aside their technospeak, even their metaphors buried complex Vietnamese realities beneath ludicrous Americanisms. For example, in 1963, when CIA director John McCone advocated the continued support of South Vietnamese ruler Ngo Dinh Diem, he said: "Mr. President, if I was manager of a baseball team, and I had only one pitcher, I'd keep him in the box whether he was a good pitcher or not." As it turned out, the United States soon found a "relief pitcher," and Diem was assassinated in a military coup sanctioned by the United States. South Vietnamese client governments came and went, but U.S. self-absorption characterized the entire history of the war and revealed itself even in the names of military operations ("Paul Revere," "Speedy Express," "Linebacker"). United States policy makers took heart whenever they thought they saw their own reflection in a Vietnamese mirror. In 1966, for example, President Johnson met in Honolulu with Vietnamese leaders Nguyen Cao Ky and Nguyen Van Thieu. It was the first time since 1955 that a U.S. president had met with the leaders of South Vietnam—a government that Americans had already spent billions of dollars to install and sustain. Ky spoke of his desire to transform South Vietnam into a democracy with economic opportunity for all people, although it was, and would remain, a brutally repressive military oligarchy. When Ky had finished his speech, Johnson leaned over the table and said, "Boy, you speak just like an American."[3] Ky understood that Johnson meant this as the highest praise.

Failure to understand Vietnam has become a popular explanation for why the United States suffered its first defeat in eight major foreign wars. The argument takes various forms. If only we had known more about Vietnam, some say, we might have avoided an unwinnable and unjustified war; or we might have extracted ourselves earlier and more honorably; or we might have found a way to win. Such claims are appealing because it is easier to admit a failure of understanding than a failure of ideology, policy, or morality. McNamara and other policy makers certainly lacked a great deal of knowledge about Vietnam, but mere ignorance does not adequately explain why the United States intervened in Vietnam, fought there for so long, and lost. The heart of the explanation is that policy makers were wedded to a cold war orthodoxy and a vision of American power that rejected any information that posed fundamental challenges to the legitimacy and necessity of U.S. intervention. Indeed, they routinely dismissed critics of the war as ill informed and disloyal. They pursued war in Vietnam because they were convinced that a communist victory in Vietnam would be an intolerable blow to American power and prestige—and, naturally, to their own power and prestige.

During the key years of American escalation (1954–67), U.S. policy was grounded in a particular Cold War orthodoxy based on a set of powerful, though misguided, assumptions: (1) communism is an international movement, controlled by the Soviet Union and China, that seeks world domination; (2) all Third World communist-led revolutions are, by definition, controlled by Moscow and Peking; and, (3) a successful communist revolution anywhere in the world will enhance the power and reputation of international communism and represent a corresponding loss of strength and status to the United States and its allies. These assumptions made knowledge of Vietnam largely irrelevant except insofar as it served the overriding goal of containing the Soviet Union and China. To American policy makers, the revolutionary guerrillas in South Vietnam were merely the pawns of Hanoi, who, in turn, were the pawns of Beijing and Moscow. Because the main enemy was always outside of Vietnam, the lives, opinions, and history of the Vietnamese were of little, if any, importance. So convinced were policy makers of these basic truths that they did not think it significant that Vietnam had a long and bitter history of opposition to Chinese domination. Nor did the evidence of a growing rift between the Soviet Union and China do much to alter the assumption that communism was a global threat. And even when Nixon became fully aware of tension between the Soviet Union and China in the late 1960s (and tried to exacerbate those tensions), he still clung to the belief that a communist victory in Vietnam would be disastrous to U.S. credibility. In reality, by continuing the war, year after year, the United States did far more damage to its international reputation than ever could have been produced by an earlier withdrawal.

Cold War orthodoxy was fueled, in part, by imperial arrogance. Policy makers and military commanders never imagined that a small, largely agricultural nation could resist America's overwhelming military and technological power. Surely, they argued, steady increases in U.S. firepower would break the will of the enemy to fight on. In fact, heavy bombing and shelling only stiffened the resolve of the North Vietnamese and their southern allies, the National Liberation Front. Yet, Lyndon Johnson and Richard Nixon both believed Hanoi could be pounded into accepting a treaty favorable to U.S. objectives. Johnson, who raised the number of American troops in Vietnam from fourteen thousand in 1963 to five hundred fifty thousand in 1968, regarded Vietnam as a "raggedy-ass, little fourth-rate country."[4] Such a poor country, Johnson believed, would not only buckle under American bombs, but would surely be attracted by American promises of plentiful postwar aid. At one point LBJ held out the prospect of building a giant system of dams and power plants on the Mekong River and could not understand why Hanoi would not trade political control of the South for such a giant piece of American pork.

Nixon also believed he could make Hanoi cry "uncle." At the beginning of his first term, in 1969, Nixon confided to an aide that he wanted to convince North Vietnam that he was a "madman" who "might do anything to stop the war." "We'll just slip the word to them that, 'for God's sake, you know Nixon is obsessed about Communists. We can't restrain him when he's angry—and he has his hand on the nuclear button'—and Ho Chi Minh himself will be in Paris in two days begging for peace."[5]

American leaders persisted in these beliefs despite many indications that their policy would not work. Throughout the war, policy makers were privy to extremely pessimistic forecasts about the prospects of building a separate, anticommunist state in South Vietnam. In 1962, for example, three years before the enormous U.S. military escalation, the Pentagon commissioned a war game from a California think tank. Played by key policy makers, "Omega I" simulated a ten-year war in Vietnam. According to William Sullivan, one of the players and later ambassador to Laos, the game was remarkably prophetic. When it ended, the communist "Red Team" occupied virtually all of Laos, Cambodia, and South Vietnam. Upset with the result, officials decided to change the rules. In "Omega II" they made U.S. bombing a more effective instrument of war. But the American "Blue Team" lost the second war game as decisively as the first. United States policy makers escalated and prolonged a war not because they naively "knew" it could be won, but because they insisted that it had to be fought even if it failed.[6]

Arrogant confidence in American power, when added to the ideological rigidity of Cold War orthodoxy, blinded Washington officials to the steady stream of bad news about the war. No matter that one Saigon regime after another failed to earn the support of the South Vietnamese people; no matter that the enormous enemy body counts failed to diminish the will or capacity of the North Vietnamese and Viet Cong to continue fighting; no matter that the American public was ever more divided and demoralized by the war. Eventually the devastating use of power would prevail.

Underpinning this hubris was a potent and widespread strain of racism that viewed the Vietnamese, at best, as children in need of tutoring, and, at worst, as savage, subhuman "gooks." Many American soldiers learned as early as basic training that they would be fighting against "gooks." And when they arrived in Vietnam they were often told by more experienced men that all Vietnamese, even the supposed allies, were untrustworthy. The official position was that they were in Vietnam to help the people of South Vietnam. In practice, the military routinely treated Vietnamese as inferiors and referred to them as "slopes," "dinks," "zipperheads," and "gooks." When William Westmoreland, U.S. military commander from 1964 to 1968, tried to explain the will of the enemy to fight so hard for so long he claimed that "Orientals do not place the same high price on life as Westerners."

Still, Cold War orthodoxy, an excessive faith in the right and ability of the United States to assert its power, and a racist underestimation of the Vietnamese, do not fully explain the willingness of American policy makers to prolong the war for so long. Here the key explanation is the enormous weight policy makers put on maintaining national and personal "credibility." Once committed to waging war in Vietnam, Johnson and Nixon believed that even if they could not achieve a victory, they must, at all costs, avoid a defeat. In the early years of intervention, fear of defeat was linked to genuine concern that it might represent a blow to U.S. national security and a boost to the Communist bloc. But as the war went on, policy makers were more concerned merely with the effect of a defeat on the U.S. image as a world power. As Nixon put it, failure in Vietnam would foster the view that the United States had become a "pitiful, helpless giant."

Behind this stubborn refusal to admit error and change course was the long history of U.S. triumphalism. No one was willing to be the first president to lose a war, regardless of the cause or the cost. United States leaders were also plagued by the memory of how prior administrations had been attacked whenever communism came to power in another country. In the early 1950s, just a decade before the Vietnam escalation, Truman and the Democratic Party were deeply hurt by the charge that they had "lost " China to communism in 1949. It did no good to say that China was not our country's to lose, or that nothing could have preserved the corrupt and unpopular noncommunist government, or that it wasn't worth preserving. In the days of Senator Joe McCarthy there was a widespread and ruthless effort to purge anyone suspected of being "soft" on communism.

While the anticommunist witch hunt of the 1950s had lost a great deal of support by the 1960s, the federal government was still deeply affected by its memory. Johnson and Nixon were not about to be called soft on communism. In fact, they carried with them a profound strain of Cold War suspicion—bordering on clinical paranoia—that their personal power was being undermined by communists at home as well as abroad. Both presidents used the FBI, the CIA, and prowar front groups (secretly funded by the government) to harass, attack, spy on, infiltrate, and sabotage the antiwar movement. "The communists are taking over the country," LBJ ranted in 1967. Johnson and Nixon viewed the war abroad and dissent at home as fundamental challenges to their ideology, policy, power, and credibility. They became so personally invested in the outcome of the war, they would surely have seen anything smacking of defeat as the ultimate humiliation. As early as 1966 Assistant Secretary John McNaughton wrote a memorandum summing up U.S. war aims: "The present U.S. objective in Vietnam," he wrote, "is to avoid humiliation." Publicly, of course, officials continued to talk about fighting for freedom and self-determination and to repel communist aggression.

Over time, however, the vast disparity between official claims and historical reality became ever clearer. The result was a "credibility gap"—the growing awareness of U.S. citizens of the distance between what policy makers said about the war and the battlefield realities. Opposition to the war expanded as a growing number of Americans came to believe that their leaders were not merely sugarcoating the war news, but blatantly lying about the nature and success of American intervention. Many long-suspected lies were confirmed and new ones exposed by the 1971 publication of the Pentagon Papers by the *New York Times* and other newspapers. These top-secret documents were turned over to the *Times* by Daniel Ellsberg, a former State and Defense Department official who had once been a fervent supporter of American intervention. By the late 1960s Ellsberg had turned against the war and was willing to sacrifice his career in the hope that the public exposure of a long history of public lies, deception, and treaty breaking would somehow help to end the war. The documents themselves did not damage the Nixon administration (since they pertained only to the years prior to 1968), but Nixon considered Ellsberg's antiwar activism as a potential threat to his own war policies. So Nixon formed a group of hired thugs called "the Plumbers" (so named because he hoped they would stop "leaks") to ransack the offices of Ellsberg's psychiatrist in search of damning information. Nixon's efforts to silence antiwar dissent was the first link in the chain of illegal activities that became known as Watergate.

The Pentagon Papers that Ellsberg turned over revealed that American policy had been based on deception all the way back to the late 1940s. Some of the lies were overt, others merely deceptive, others lies of omission. But the overall record contributed to a profound distrust of the government. Here, then, is a compilation of major official claims followed by a discussion of the historical realities.

(1) *The Myth of "Clean Hands."* United States policy makers claimed that U.S. intervention in Vietnam, unlike that of the French, was free of self-interest and colonial ambition. As Secretary of State John Foster Dulles put it in 1954, "We have a clean base there now without a taint of colonialism." Accordingly, Americans thought the Vietnamese would welcome them as genuine allies.

In fact, the United States supported the French reconquest of Vietnam from 1946 to 1954. The Vietnamese perceived this support as a fundamental betrayal of the promises made during World War II, when Ho Chi Minh had been a wartime ally whose Viet Minh troops were trained by U.S. members of the Office of Strategic Service. The Atlantic Charter signed by Roosevelt and Churchill in 1941 promised a postwar world of self-determination for all nations. When, in 1945, Ho proclaimed Vietnamese independence, he modeled the declaration on the U.S. Declaration of Independence, yet the United States refused to recognize the new government. Instead, the United States, eager to gain French support for the Cold War alliance in Europe, supported France in its war to regain Vietnam. By 1953, the United States was paying for almost 80 percent of the French war. American leaders insisted that they were not supporting French colonialism but the state of Vietnam in its war against communist guerrillas. However, the state of Vietnam was merely a puppet regime of the French, not an independent government. Given U.S. support of France, it is not surprising that many Vietnamese came to view the United States as an imperialist power, a perception that only gained further currency when the United States directly intervened after 1954.

(2) *The Myth of South Vietnamese Nationhood.* Every president from Eisenhower to Nixon claimed that the Geneva Accords of 1954 had divided Vietnam into two separate nations and that the United States was defending South Vietnam from attacks by the North. But the Geneva Accords *did not* divide Vietnam into separate nations. Rather, the victorious, communist-led Viet Minh (under pressure from all the great powers, including the Soviet Union and China) agreed to a *temporary* division of Vietnam into two military regroupment zones.

Those who had fought with the French could move south while those who fought with the Viet Minh could move north. In 1956 the nation was to be reunited by a national election. But the United States brought in Ngo Dinh Diem to rule South Vietnam. When it became clear that Ho Chi Minh in the North would easily win a nationwide election, the United States and Diem called off the promised vote. It was the United States, not the Geneva Accords, that sought to establish a permanently separate South, denying an opportunity for democratic reunification and self-determination to Vietnam.

(3) *The Myth of South Vietnamese "Freedom and Democracy."* From 1954 to 1975 American officials claimed to be defending freedom and democracy in South Vietnam. However, every one of the regimes supported by the United States in South Vietnam was repressive, dictatorial, and riddled with corruption. They imprisoned tens of thousands of political prisoners, staged rigged elections, distributed or sold military and political posts to loyal supporters, and presided over an extensive system of graft, kickbacks, real estate scams, and drug profiteering. United States officials would sometimes rebuke their clients, but withdrew their support only when there were doubts about their ability to pursue the anticommunist crusade. The United States supported the overthrow of Ngo Dinh Diem because he was oppressing his people and failing to gain popular support. In addition, the Kennedy administration feared that his influential brother might try to negotiate a settlement with Hanoi and the NLF. The United States was not supporting freedom and democracy; it was supporting authoritarian regimes and pushing them to be more aggressively anticommunist.

(4) *The Myth of South Vietnamese "Independence."* United States policymakers wanted American citizens to believe that South Vietnam was clinging to its independence against communist aggressors from the North. In fact, South Vietnam was largely created by the United States and utterly dependent on it. Without massive injections of U.S. aid and, eventually, troops and heavy bombing, the Saigon regime would have collapsed. Depending on the timing of United States withdrawal of all support, the collapse might take place within days or months.

(5) *The Myth of "External Aggression."* Official explanations cast the war as an invasion of the independent and democratic South by the Communist North. While it is certainly true that North Vietnamese communists led the war in the South, it is also the case that the South itself was full of Viet Cong guerrillas determined to overthrow the U.S.-backed regime in Saigon. The Viet Cong were southern revolutionaries fighting for Vietnamese independence and reunification in alliance with the North Vietnamese Army. "Viet Cong" was a pejorative name meaning something like Vietnamese "commies"; they called themselves

the People's Liberation Armed Forces under the political leadership of the National Liberation Front. Until the end of the war in the 1970s, U.S. troops outnumbered North Vietnamese soldiers in South Vietnam. In reality, U.S. support of Saigon was vastly greater than the military and economic aid provided to Hanoi by the Soviet Union and China.

(6) *The Myth of "Unprovoked Attack" and the Gulf of Tonkin Resolution.* In August 1964 President Johnson announced that U.S. ships had been the victims of two unprovoked attacks by North Vietnamese patrol boats. In response he ordered retaliatory air strikes against the North and asked Congress to pass a resolution giving him broad powers to wage war in Vietnam. The "Gulf of Tonkin Resolution" was passed overwhelmingly (there were only two dissenting votes), and Johnson believed it provided him with all the constitutional authority he needed to escalate the war. In fact, the United States had been sponsoring covert attacks on North Vietnam that provoked the North into sending patrol boats after U.S. destroyers. Johnson also greatly exaggerated the minor North Vietnamese attack (indeed the second alleged attack never occurred). The congressional resolution that Johnson pushed for, supposedly written in response to the attacks by the North, had in fact been written months in advance of this trumped-up incident.

(7) *The Myth of Military "Assistance."* The U.S. military command in South Vietnam was called Military Assistance Command Vietnam. This was to preserve the fiction that the United States was merely offering secondary support to a war primarily waged by the South Vietnamese army—the Army of the Republic of Vietnam. However, for most of the war U.S. troops did the bulk of the fighting, and the South Vietnamese Army was almost entirely paid for and equipped by the United States. The myth of assistance also disguised the combat role of the United States in the early years of escalation. Throughout the first half of the 1960s Kennedy and Johnson insisted that U.S. troops in Vietnam were merely "advising" Vietnamese forces. In fact, they were actively engaged in combat missions. Even during the enormous buildup of early 1965, LBJ tried to preserve the fiction that U.S. forces were merely holding "defensive" positions. He also deceived the public about the size and rate of U.S. escalation. In July 1965 President Johnson made the fateful decisions that committed the United States to an open-ended course of large-scale military escalation. While privately agreeing to a deployment of one hundred thousand troops in 1965 and another one hundred thousand in 1966, in public LBJ merely announced a commitment to raise U.S. forces to fifty thousand and hid the fact that U.S. troops were already fully engaged in combat missions.[7]

(8) *The Myth of Progress, or "There's Light at the End of the Tunnel."* Through-out the war, policy makers assured the public that progress was being made in Vietnam, that the tide was turning, that soon the war would be won and the United States could withdraw. Throughout the war, the U.S. command routinely misled the public about the effectiveness of bombing and ground actions. While the United States usually killed more people than it lost, body counts were a meaningless measure of success. At no point in the war did the United States seriously threaten the will of the enemy to continue fighting and only periodi-cally did it threaten to undermine its ability to fight. The movement of troops from North Vietnam to the South was never effectively blocked. General Westmoreland reported in 1967 that the United States was winning the war of attrition, that enemy forces had declined. Yet some intelligence reports placed enemy forces at two and three times Westmoreland's figure and growing. The commander simply excluded whole categories of Viet Cong militia from his count. The daily press briefing in Saigon conveyed such a lunatic optimism that journalists began calling it the "Five o'clock Follies."

(9) *The Quagmire Myth.* A widespread view of the war argues that the United States got "stuck" in a bad war because of unwarranted optimism and naiveté. According to this interpretation, U.S. intervention in Vietnam was a well-intentioned but naive effort to do good in a place too alien to welcome American solutions. American leaders optimistically believed that each new escalation would bring success. Failure in Vietnam is thereby attributed not to deliberate policy, but to a combination of American innocence and Vietnamese inscruta-bility. Policy makers simply got unwittingly sucked into a foreign quagmire. But the historical record makes clear that policy makers were not at all naive about the poor chances of American success in Vietnam. They knowingly chose to prolong the stalemate even when they realized that the odds of victory were bad. Despite public assurances, policy makers never really believed that victory was near at hand. At every major stage of U.S. escalation of the war, most mili-tary analysts and policy makers were skeptical about the odds for success. In 1969, after years of warfare, the State Department circulated a top-secret ques-tionnaire to top policy makers and military officers designed to solicit their frank opinions about how the war was proceeding. As Seymour Hersh writes, "Even the most optimistic assessment from staunchly prowar military officers was that it would take a minimum of 8.3 years more to completely pacify and control the Vietcong areas of the South."[8] The United States did not inadvertently slip into a quagmire; it dug the pit, filled it with mud, and dove in headfirst.

(10) *The Myth of Economic Modernization.* Officials often claimed American intervention was bringing great economic opportunity to South Vietnam. While

the flood of American economic aid did lead to the creation of a larger elite, it exacerbated inequalities and made the economy far more dependent. Ultimately, South Vietnam had to begin importing rice because of the destruction of farmland and the willful creation of refugees by U.S. military policy. Former peasants moved to the cities or to shantytowns near U.S. bases, where prostitution, drugs, and a black market flourished.

(11) *The Myth of "Hearts and Minds."* Officials routinely claimed that the war could be won only if the government of South Vietnam succeeded at winning the "hearts and minds" of the Vietnamese people. But this was just lip service. In reality, the United States did very little to earn the political allegiance of the population. The overwhelming obsession of U.S. policy in Vietnam was to use massive firepower to crush the Viet Cong and the North Vietnamese Army. Indeed, the ruthless pursuit of attrition did more to galvanize political opposition to the U.S. war than it did to weaken the enemy, provide security to the population, or win the allegiance of the Vietnamese. At the end of the war, a U.S. colonel said to a former opponent, "You know, you never defeated us on the battlefield." The Vietnamese colonel replied, "That may be so, but it is also irrelevant."[9]

(12) *The Myth of Withdrawal and Vietnamization.* While Nixon publicly promised to end the war by withdrawing American troops and replacing them with Vietnamese (called "Vietnamization"), Nixon actually escalated the war by initiating the secret bombing of Cambodia (1969–73) and launching a ground invasion in 1970. The United States waged a secret war in Laos from 1962 to 1973, dropping more than two million tons of bombs on a country with a population of only four million people. This war relied on the recruitment of many tribal peoples, especially the Hmong, who were ultimately devastated by the war. Nixon also increased the bombing in Laos and launched a ground invasion in 1971. In Cambodia, American bombing and support for the unpopular government of Lon Nol (who overthrew the neutralist Sihnaouk in 1970) helped the Cambodian communists—the Khmer Rouge—recruit new members. From a small and largely ineffective force of four thousand, it grew quickly to forty thousand. When the Khmer Rouge took over Cambodia in 1975 it committed one of the worst genocides in world history, killing 1.5 million to 2 million of its own people out of a population of 8 million.

(13) *The Myth of "Peace With Honor."* President Nixon promised peace in Vietnam, but only if it could be achieved with "honor." The U.S. commitment to South Vietnam, Nixon insisted, required that the United States ensure its survival. However, by the fall of 1972, National Security Adviser Henry Kissinger negotiated a settlement that called for unilateral American withdrawal and al-

lowed the North to keep its troops in South Vietnam. When the negotiations broke down, Nixon insisted that the North had reneged, and he used this as his justification for launching the massive "Christmas bombing" of 1972. In fact, the major obstacle to the settlement was presented by Nguyen Van Thieu, premier of South Vietnam. The bombing's primary aim was to reassure Thieu that the United States would continue to protect his regime. When the peace accords were signed in January 1973, the terms were essentially the same as they had been in October. And indeed, the terms finally agreed to by the United States might have been the basis for a similar settlement at almost any point in the past, thereby averting the loss of millions of lives. Had Nixon not been politically destroyed by Watergate he might have tried to renew bombing in 1975 to forestall South Vietnamese defeat. But the Nixon-Kissinger "peace with honor" had a purely cynical underlying goal. If the South could not be saved, the accord might at least provide a "decent interval" between U.S. withdrawal and the ultimate collapse of Saigon.

Some of the myths summarized above were outright lies. Others were lies of omission. All were flagrant distortions of reality. United States soldiers who fought in Vietnam experienced many of those contradictions firsthand. Told that they had been sent to Vietnam to help the people of South Vietnam, they very quickly realized that most Vietnamese did not regard them as liberators or even as welcome allies. More often than not, they viewed Americans with some combination of suspicion, fear, and hostility. Many Vietnamese became economically dependent on the military presence and viewed the GIs as crucial customers, but rarely did they volunteer useful intelligence about the Viet Cong.

In the villages, it was obvious that most civilians resented the U.S. soldiers who bullied them, rifled through their belongings, and sometimes burned their homes. While policy makers talked about "saving" Vietnam, it soon became clear that U.S. military policy was doing far more to destroy it. Even the South Vietnamese rulers, whose very survival depended on U.S. support, were often ambivalent about the enormous size and scale of U.S. intervention.

Attrition was the central U.S. strategy; search-and-destroy was the principal tactic; and the enemy body count was the primary measure of progress. Every other pursuit paled in comparison with the effort to "find, fix, and finish" the enemy. There was little effort to gain and hold territory or to provide permanent protection to civilian populations. Nor was the "other war"—the campaign to win the political support of the South Vietnamese—ever more than window dressing. Far from holding communism behind a clear boundary, the U.S. military launched ground and air assaults throughout South Vietnam, acknowledging by their actions, if not their words, that the enemy could not be contained, much less defeated.

For many U.S. soldiers the official explanations of the war proved essentially meaningless. It was quite obvious that the war was not "helping" the people of South Vietnam, nor was it "containing" communism. When one grunt heard a discussion of the domino theory he said, "All that's just a *load*, man. We're here to kill gooks. Period."[10] The pressure for ever higher body count productivity provided an incentive to shoot first and ask questions later. According to GI slang, "If it's dead and Vietnamese, then it's VC." Most Vietnamese civilians who died in the war were killed by U.S. bombing, gunships, and artillery. Some of it was random "harassment and interdiction" fire, shot into "free fire zones" where all Vietnamese were regarded, by definition, as the enemy. Sometimes, however, bombing was ordered directly on populated areas. According to the rules of engagement, U.S. forces had the authority to destroy any village from which they received hostile fire. Thus, a single sniper's bullet from a nearby treeline might result in the American napalming of an entire hamlet. Throughout the war, the United States destroyed more than six thousand hamlets, a fact that helps explain why so many rural villages joined the National Liberation Front.

A military policy based on rooting out guerrillas from a population that largely opposed U.S. intervention was a prescription for atrocities. At times, some U.S. soldiers would not even try to distinguish civilians from combatants. The most horrific example occurred on March 16, 1968, when a company of U.S. infantrymen from the Americal Division slaughtered more than five hundred Vietnamese civilians in the village of My Lai. Virtually all the victims were women, children, and old men. The massacre was not a spontaneous convulsion of violence; it went on for several hours, during which many of the GIs took breaks to eat C-rations and smoke cigarettes. On that day they did not receive a single round of hostile fire. United States commanders reported the day's events as a successful firefight in which 128 Viet Cong had been killed in action. This cover-up endured for twenty months.

When photos of the atrocity appeared in *Life* on December 5, 1969, the magazine was inundated with letters. Some people denied that the massacre had occurred, or blamed it on the Vietnamese enemy, or insisted that the media had exaggerated, maybe even fabricated, the story. Others regarded the killing as a predictable by-product of an unjust war or, as some would have it, the inevitable reality of all wars. But in virtually every response, perhaps most of all in the tortured evasions and justifications, there was an almost desperate need to reestablish some secure sense of national identity.

Never before had that identity, based so much on a claim to exceptional virtue and morality, been more beleaguered. By the end of the 1960s, perhaps more than at any time in our history, Americans had to contend with the charge that their country's behavior in the world was not "ill advised" or "naive" or "overly ambitious," but criminal. This, increasingly, was the charge of the antiwar movement, and the presence of that claim began to emerge in ordinary public discourse. In 1971, the *New York Times* published a long article by Neil Sheehan titled "Should We Have War Crime Trials?" Taking what was once an unthinkable position, Sheehan raised the idea of putting *U.S.* leaders on trial, not Vietnamese.

In January 1973 the last U.S. troops pulled out of Vietnam. But the South Vietnamese government had little chance to survive in the absence of massive U.S. support. A kind of phony peace, punctuated by ongoing fighting, endured until the North began its final offensive in early 1975. Despite a few pockets of resistance from the South, the communist offensive was a rout. By early April, eighteen North Vietnamese Army divisions had moved to within a forty-mile radius of Saigon.

American ambassador Graham Martin, unwilling to accept the inevitable defeat, refused to call for a full-scale evacuation. Saigon was awash in rumor, fear, and panic. At the end of April, the United States managed to evacuate thousands of Vietnamese; but many thousands more who wanted to get out were left behind. Some U.S. Marines used tear gas to keep their former allies from clambering onto the last helicopters leaving the U.S. embassy.

This scene was the crowning betrayal of a dishonorable war. Yet the suffering did not end there. In addition to the three million Vietnamese who had died during the war, hundreds of thousands of South Vietnamese officials and military officers were sent to "reeducation" camps where they faced years of hard labor, imprisonment, and political indoctrination. Since 1975, about one million Vietnamese have emigrated to the United States. A great many made desperate escapes in the late 1970s and early 1980s. More than fifty thousand of these "boat people" died in flight from their country—a total almost equivalent to all U.S. fatalities in the war.

The fighting had stopped. The rationalizations and technospeak ceased. But the specter of the Vietnam experience persisted.

Graffiti on the wall of a Saigon latrine:

- America lost her virginity in Vietnam
- (And she caught the clap, too.)
- That's nothing—so did I
- I did too, but now I watch who I go out with
- So should America![11]

Something much deeper than U.S. foreign policy intentions or military strategy failed in Vietnam. In the post–World War II years, U.S. policy had been
hailed as the bearer of a better way of life. Contrary to its communist adversar-
ies, the United States stood for democracy, embodied in democratic institutions,
especially free elections. Vietnam awakened many Americans to the fact that
U.S. foreign policy supported virtually any government, no matter how dictatorial, so long as it allied itself with America in the Cold War. By the time the
Vietnam War ended, public trust in the government had plummeted, from a
high of 76 percent in 1964 to a low of 37 percent. Attitudes about government
duplicity with regard to Vietnam were compounded by a sense of betrayal
around other key events, most notably Watergate. Disbelief in the words and
disapproval of the actions of government officials caused a deep sense of loss
and a growing cynical attitude on the part of American citizens.

In the first outpouring of comment after the war's end, the Vietnam experience was depicted in apocalyptic terms across the political spectrum. In the
deeply conservative *National Review*, one commentator concluded, "America
has become a simpering, defeatist, isolationist nation. The damage done to
America by the Vietnam debacle is inestimable. It is going to work a spell on
America for 25 years. America is going into a national eclipse, and it is going
away willingly. . . . America has lost its honor." Christopher Lasch, writing in
the Left-leaning *New York Review of Books*, observed, "Any lingering illusions
that this was to be the American century have been shattered by the collapse
of anti-communism in Southeast Asia."[12]

And these sentiments weren't only expressed by political or cultural analysts. In May 1975, a *CBS News* reporter visited Bardstown, Kentucky—a town
that sent many of its sons to Vietnam. The local mayor told him the war had
not been worth the costs. A middle-aged couple, parents of a soldier who had
been killed in action, asked, "If we had won it, if we had won the war, what
would we have?" Or, as one interviewee summarized the impact, "There is no
way I'll buy the American dream again."[13]

Americans have often learned much of their history, especially their history of
wars, from the movies. Vietnam proved no different. Indeed, once the fighting
had stopped, films about the war began not only to reflect attitudes, but to shape
them. Increasingly, Americans were drawn to fictionalized and symbolic depictions of the war and its aftermath.

During the 1960s, the only major Hollywood film about Vietnam was John
Wayne's *The Green Berets*. This film, whose structure mirrored World War II films
and not Vietnam, drew ridicule from both the antiwar segment of the popula-

tion, who laughed at its unthinking patriotism, and from American soldiers in Vietnam, who laughed at its wrongheaded depiction of the actual warfare and the ludicrous final scene in which Wayne walks off into a sunset that was geographically impossible in Vietnam.

John Wayne personified the World War II spirit in the postwar era, becoming a symbol of American military success. Many young men went off to war with the image of John Wayne in their minds. This was not just a national agenda but a personal identity. When writer and Vietnam veteran Philip Caputo was a boy, he writes, "I saw myself charging up some distant beachhead, like John Wayne in *The Sands of Iwo Jima*."[14]

But the Vietnam experience revised these cinematic associations. One vet observed: "There was no doubt that they had tricked us, deceived us—them with their John Wayne charging up Mount Suribachi, with their Gary Cooper as Sergeant York rounding up half the German army and sharp-shooting to death the other half. . . . We had imagined a movie. . . . What we got was a garbage pail." Another recalled that after killing an enemy, "I felt sorry. I don't know why I felt sorry. John Wayne never felt sorry." One veteran put it succinctly after returning home: "I believed in Jesus Christ and John Wayne before I went to Vietnam. After Vietnam, both went down the tubes."[15]

During the 1970s, Vietnam films reflected these ambivalent or antagonistic views. The most famous Vietnam films of the era—*The Deer Hunter, Coming Home,* and *Apocalypse Now*—painted images of a grueling war and a disrupted home front. Even *The Deer Hunter*, which created considerable debate over its depiction of Viet Cong torture and its "God Bless America" finale, never attempted to paint the war in heroic terms and was unflinching in its portrayal of the impact of Vietnam on the young soldiers. None of these films were the kind of movies that made young boys anxious to enlist.

Even more so than movies, the most revealing example of the way in which the U.S. public dealt with Vietnam was its attitudes toward and treatment of the Vietnam War veterans. Upon their homecoming, the vets found themselves ignored, unable to elicit interest in their problems, and facing a cutback in government funding for veterans programs. This contrasted sharply with what was done for World War II veterans, for whom the GI Bill provided free college educations, low-interest mortgages, and other benefits believed to be the tickets to postwar prosperity and security. Hoping to escape memories of Vietnam, no one wanted to hear from or about the vets. The attempt to put Vietnam behind us meant putting the Vietnam veterans out of sight.

This lack of attention led to simmering hostility, as well as enormous personal problems. From divorce to substance abuse and suicide, personal problems afflicted vets at a much higher rate than the general population. By the 1980s, veterans' counselors estimated that the number of suicides of Vietnam veterans equaled the number killed in the war. Even the majority of vets who returned home, entered the workforce, and established families generally kept quiet about Vietnam except when talking among themselves.

Instead of seeing this diverse population of individuals, the depiction of vets in the popular culture of the 1970s narrowed to a few unflattering stereotypes. As one veteran put it, "The message sent from national leadership and embraced by the public was clear: Vietnam veterans were malcontents, liars, wackos, losers." In popular culture, the vet came to be viewed as someone who was dangerous, not heroic. Movie and TV writers, this vet continued, "discovered a marketable villain. *Kojack, Ironside,* and the friendly folks at *Hawaii Five-O* confronted crazed, heroin-addicted veterans with the regularity and enthusiasm Saturday morning heroes once dispensed with godless red savages."[16]

These depictions of the vets as "wackos" and "losers" served to distract the nation from different conclusions. "Because we see the Vietnam veteran as crazy, inadequate, second-rate, feeble," a vet put it directly, "we never have to face Vietnam. Or face what was required of him. We can keep our distance." And keep our distance we did. It was not until the early 1980s that the psychological diagnosis post-traumatic stress syndrome was added to the roster of identifiable maladies. Until then, vets suffering these problems were often labeled schizophrenics, sometimes heavily sedated in Veterans Administration hospitals, and frequently characterized as weaker than their World War II counterparts. As one veterans counselor summarized, "The government had 'ripped him off' by sending him to Vietnam; society had called him a 'baby-killer' on his return; and then the VA (which he called the 'green machine' like the army) was finishing 'the job.'"[17]

Beginning in the late 1970s, veterans groups began to organize both to aid the vets and to reaffirm their place in American life. The movement to establish a Vietnam Veterans Memorial was the centerpiece of this effort. The memorial lists the names of all those who died in Vietnam—a kind of "tomb of the known soldiers"—and became a place to remember, to honor, and to weep. In marked contrast with the heroic memorials for the dead of past wars, nothing at the veterans memorial suggests that these dead did not die in vain. It is, however, not a national monument, but a veterans monument, paid for by private fundraising efforts. Vets take a highly proprietary attitude toward it. As one recently put it, "It is ours, as in the veterans', not ours, as in America's."[18] In a very real way, this was in keeping with the attitudes of the 1970s about the war, with the vets' own ambivalence about not having been told the truth, and with America's sense of trying to overcome both its military and social frustrations and failures.

The move to relegitimize the Vietnam veterans, however, was drawn into a larger effort to remythologize the war itself. An alternative, constructed vision of the role of the United States in Vietnam and even the outcome began to emerge. Richard Nixon argued in a 1980 book that "we won the war"—something few Americans agreed with—while Ronald Reagan declared Vietnam "a noble cause" in his presidential campaign of that year. In a 1982 press conference Reagan re-wrote history, rearranging the events leading to American entry; claiming that Vietnam had always been divided into two nations and that Ho Chi Minh (rather than the United States) had sabotaged the reunification election promised by the Geneva Accords of 1954. Reagan also backdated North Vietnamese troops cross-ing into South Vietnam by nearly a decade and portrayed the U.S. "advisers" of the early years of the war as essentially unarmed civilians workers.[19]

The combat phase of the war produced equally mythic reconstructions, paralleling the myths spun by the government in the 1960s. One analyst has chronicled the new attitudes that emerged in the 1980s as another series of myths, "the myth that the United States intervened to defend a free people against outside aggression; the myth that the domino theory was correct; and (*most compellingly*) the myth that American troops would have been victori-ous if they had been unleashed by Washington, rather than stabbed-in-the-back by Democratic doves, disloyal media, and a pro-Hanoi antiwar movement."[20] The last myth, that American "could have won," took on the most power within the culture. Individuals inside and outside of government reiterated this theme. "The war in Vietnam was won four times on the River Mekong; it was lost on the River Potomac," Reagan's ambassador to Costa Rica, Lewis Tambs, argued.[21] Though these views were often pure fiction, they became incorporated into the popular mythology of the 1980s.

Revising the history of the Vietnam War and the Cold War image of the United States as the leader of the free world fed directly into 1980s foreign policy. We had failed in Vietnam because we did not have the will to stand up to com-munism, the new thinking went. We would not fail in Nicaragua and elsewhere. With the 1983 U.S. overthrow of a leftist government in Grenada, Reagan de-clared, "Our days of weakness are over. Our military forces are back on their feet and standing tall."[22] That the president would make so much of a dubious military intervention, lasting only a matter of hours, against the tiniest of Car-ibbean islands, illustrates just how devastating the loss in Vietnam had been to many Americans. Lee Atwater, chairman of the Republican National Commit-tee, claimed that the 1989 invasion of Panama "knocked the question about being timid and a wimp out of the stadium." And columnist David Broder concluded that "Panama represents the best evidence yet that, 15 years after the Vietnam War ended, Americans really have come together in recognition of the circumstances in which military intervention makes sense."[23]

George Bush claimed that with U.S. efforts in the gulf, "we've kicked the Vietnam Syndrome once and for all." Drawing on the postwar revision of the war's history, Bush had promised that U.S. forces "will not be asked to fight with one hand tied behind their back."[24] He, like Reagan, perpetuated the false idea that the United States had simply not used the full might of the American military. In fact we fought our longest war, dropped three times more bombs than had been used in World War II, defoliated four million acres of the Vietnamese countryside, and killed three million people. Just about the only weapon the United States did not use in Vietnam was the atomic bomb.

Bush also proclaimed that the United States would not become involved in a quagmire. He promised that he would gain congressional approval before engagement and that the veterans would not be abandoned once they returned home. At war's end, yellow ribbons flowered across the country as a show of national support. The military's victory was widely depicted as decisive and with incredibly low U.S. casualty figures. The returning soldiers were feted with parades, entertainment extravaganzas, and public accolades.

Others echoed this sense of a new day. Charles Krauthammer, in *The New Republic*, prophesied that "with a dazzling display of American technological superiority, individual grit and, most unexpectedly for Saddam, national resolve—we will no longer speak of post-Vietnam America. A new, post-gulf America will emerge, its self-image, sense of history, even its political discourse transformed." America would regain "the legacy of the last good war, World War II, a legacy lost in the jungles of Vietnam." "It's almost like the whole burden of Vietnam has been lifted off everyone's shoulders," said Clayton Yeuter, Lee Atwater's successor as chairman of the Republican National Committee. "Americans have pride again."[25]

The Iraqis were driven out of Kuwait, but the Vietnam syndrome continued. All the attention heaped upon the returning forces often only added to the Vietnam veterans' sense of frustration. Americans may have felt better because they treated the Gulf War veterans well. Vietnam veterans often felt worse because of the comparisons with their own treatment. In fact, in recent years an echo of Vietnam has entered the Gulf War discussion, that of a debilitating "Gulf War syndrome," paralleling the Agent Orange controversy. Once again, veterans believe that the government put them in harm's way, has not told them the truth about their exposure, and is unresponsive to their needs.

Despite initial waves of enthusiasm among the U.S. public in general, the Bush administration's high approval ratings after the Iraqi surrender plummeted as many Americans came to doubt the value of the war, the heralded precision of our technology, and whether the overall aims of the United States had been achieved. As the economy turned sour in 1991, a bumper sticker began to appear in primary states: "Saddam Still Has His Job, But I Don't."

Regardless of the justifications for any U.S. military actions during the 1980s and 1990s, what was demonstrably false was the argument that "we could have won the war" in Vietnam, at least as the revisionists articulated the position. It became much easier to achieve victory in Vietnam in one's imagination, after the fact, than to actually fight the war on the ground in the 1960s and 1970s. We were not engaging in this self-deception to fight a real war but to expunge bitter memories and restore national pride. And again the movies reflected the new vision and, in addition, helped to mold it.

While films such as Oliver Stone's *Platoon* and *Born on the Fourth of July* continued to paint harsh images of Vietnam and its effect on American soldiers, new film themes reflected the growing revision of the war and the new mythology under construction. Vietnam veterans as troubled outsiders unable to reconnect with American society gave way to the individual hero who overcomes government unwillingness to achieve victory. For example, in *First Blood*, released in 1982, the initial appearance of Sylvester Stallone's John Rambo, the main character is a Vietnam veteran abused by the authorities and running amok. By 1985, in *Rambo: First Blood Part II*, the character is hired by the government and sent back to Vietnam to rescue prisoners of war our government cannot or will not save. The Rambo character of this second film became a common symbol for the notion that we could have won the war had the government not tied the hands of the military. Receiving his orders, Rambo asks, "Sir, do we get to win *this* time?" Where World War II films had heroically recreated the great moments of the war—Iwo Jima, D-Day, Guadalcanal, the Battle of the Bulge—these Vietnam films either chose moments of individual heroism disconnected from overall strategy or, more likely, sent U.S. soldiers back to Vietnam, post-1975, "to do the job right, this time."

This vision did more than revisit the past, it helped frame the present. Ronald Reagan was the perfect president to lead this effort. It was not that he was a former movie star but, as he later admitted, "Maybe I had seen too many war movies, the heroics of which I sometimes confused with real life."[26] He phrased his solution to the problem of Libyan terrorists by observing, "I saw *Rambo* last night, and now I know what to do." Current international problems could be viewed through the new prism of Vietnam revisionism, at least at the movies. In *The Year of the Dragon*, a New York police detective and Vietnam veteran (played by Mickey Rourke) is thwarted by both Asian organized crime and the politics of his department. "This is a fucking war," he declares, "and I'm not going to lose it, not this one. Not over politics. It's always fucking politics. This is Vietnam all over again. Nobody wants to win this thing. Just flat-out win."

The newly revised images of Vietnam appearing at the movies offered Americans an alternative vision from the disheartening and frustrating one they had experienced in the actual war. If we couldn't win the war in Vietnam on the ground, at least we could win it at the cineplex. Though escapism in entertainment is nothing new, what grew problematic was the manner in which the entertainment message supplanted the historical one. As Americans confronted problems in the world, the response often came from the new, mythologized view of Vietnam. Watching Rambo single-handedly wipe out hundreds of Vietnamese might have made Americans temporarily feel better. It did little to provide realistic answers for a more complicated world than the movies presented.

Other problems festered in the national consciousness about the Vietnam experience. The reintegration of the Vietnam veterans into the fabric of U.S. society was tempered by ongoing concerns about the government's actions over Agent Orange and prisoners of war, two issues that continued to haunt the nation. The controversy over the effects of exposure to Agent Orange proved a sad and frustrating experience for many veterans and their families. Since the war, individual veterans and veterans' groups have battled the U.S. government in an attempt to prove the connections between illness and the use of the defoliant and to receive compensation for its effects. Beyond the medical and legal issues, even beyond the pain suffered by the individual veterans and their families, was the reprise of feelings about the government's lack of honesty with regard to its soldiers' lives.

The story of Admiral Elmo Zumwalt, Jr., and his son serves as a kind of parable for this issue, if not for the war and its aftermath. As Navy commander in Vietnam, Admiral Zumwalt had ordered the use of Agent Orange and other chemicals of war. His son, Lieutenant Elmo Zumwalt III, was a field commander on the ground in Vietnam, exposed to the defoliants. After the younger Zumwalt's death from a rare form of lymphoma in 1988, the senior Zumwalt, while steadfastly defending the U.S. role in Vietnam, became one of the government's severest critics, arguing that his son's death was caused by exposure to Agent Orange. He charged before a congressional subcommittee that the work on Agent Orange done by the Centers for Disease Control had been "a fraud" and that the work of one of its senior officials prevented "the true facts from being determined." Zumwalt was not alone. The subcommittee's chair later claimed the CDC analysis was "rigged."[27] And then there is the veteran who told a congressional committee he had "five screwed-up kids." One had three kidneys, one a defective heart, one a brain dysfunction, one an immunological problem, and the last had skin problems. And he told the panel that the VA "treated him like dirt" when he asked for help.[28]

Throughout the war in Vietnam, the issue of prisoners of war took on a character unlike any previous wartime experience. In fact, in the last years of the war, the POWs were often held up as the reason for continuing to fight the war, even though past experience had shown that at the conclusion of a war prisoners were routinely released. The POWs who returned to the United States in 1973, after Nixon's "peace with honor," were feted at the White House and in hometown parades, one of the few genuine celebrations offered returning soldiers from Vietnam.

Cold War images of communist torture and "brainwashing," reinforced in movies, novels, and on television, helped paint a picture in the minds of many Americans of a ruthless enemy keeping U.S. soldiers as prisoners even after the war's end. The very nature of warfare in Vietnam, with guerrilla raids, search-and-destroy missions, and planes and helicopters shot down throughout the countryside and over water, all led to a great number of bodies never having been recovered. Finally, the lack of any diplomatic relations between the United States and the government of Vietnam made it difficult to resolve the questions of the MIAs and to disprove the fantasized claims of remaining POWs well into the 1980s. The number of soldiers unaccounted for in Vietnam is, however, actually much smaller than previous U.S. wars. There remained 78,750 Americans unaccounted for from World War II, 8,177 from the Korean War. And of the 2,255 Americans missing from Vietnam, 1,804 were airmen lost at sea and thus very difficult to recover.[29]

Nevertheless, in the 1980s, attempts to overcome our sense of loss about Vietnam included fictionalized heroic Americans returning to Vietnam to free comrades left behind in the war. American audiences watched as Sylvester Stallone, Chuck Norris, and others returned to "backlot" Vietnams and rescued "soldiers" our government had deserted. These films only reinforced the growing claims of POW-MIA groups that the government had abandoned their loved ones and was keeping the information a secret. Even though a Defense and State Department report issued in 1989 concluded there were no living POWs in Vietnam,[30] an advertisement for Chuck Norris's *Missing in Action* proclaimed: "It ain't over until the last man comes home."

Once again, a painful and poignant issue was taken up by political aspirants seeking to use the pathos as both a means for personal advancement and to symbolize individual frustration with a callous government. In addition, unscrupulous confidence men exploited and then dashed the hopes of families that their loved ones might still be alive. Both the POW-MIA issue and the questions about the effects of Agent Orange continued to haunt veterans, their families, and the nation, keeping issues from the war and cynical attitudes about our government's policies animate well after the last shots had been fired.

Finally, the reintegration and relegitimization of the vets into U.S. society left a complicated question to resolve. What was the place of the antiwar activists? If the war was wrong or a mistake, as Americans overwhelmingly believed, then the position of the antiwar voices had been accurate. Nevertheless, the antiwar activists and those who avoided going to Vietnam went through a reverse pattern from that of the Vietnam veterans. The conservative ascendancy of the 1980s transformed the public memory of the antiwar movement into a bizarre caricature of self-absorbed hippies who spat on the returning veterans. Virtually forgotten in this reconstruction was the fact that the antiwar movement had been at the forefront in criticizing the inequities in the draft that made working-class men disproportionately vulnerable to military service. In fact, activists typically directed their venom at the political and military authorities and not at ordinary soldiers.

Buried as well during the Reagan years was the fact that many veterans themselves participated in the antiwar movement. When they returned home, thousands of veterans joined Vietnam Veterans Against the War, the most significant veterans' antiwar movement in U.S. history.

Despite all the efforts to reconstruct Vietnam as a honorable effort, Americans remained profoundly troubled by the war and skeptical of all politicians. Vietnam veterans, although glad to have their role rehabilitated, frequently spoke of never allowing their children into the situation in which they had been placed. "The American people can go to hell before I or my sons fight another war for them," one wrote.[31]

For Americans, the twin symbols of World War II and Vietnam kept conflicting models in the minds of policy makers and citizens. While many still believed that the United States was a force for good in the world, with a responsibility to protect our economic interests, they remained skeptical that the United States could serve as policeman to the world. They were also extremely wary of any engagement that might not be quick, decisive, and with little loss of American life. During and after World War II, we had couched our self-interest in our verbal commitments to spread the beneficence of American life to the four corners of the globe. After Vietnam, self-interest took a firmer place at the center of foreign policy debates.

This conflict over symbolic models—World War II and Vietnam—was never so clear as in 1995, when the United States celebrated both the fiftieth anniversary of the end of World War II and the twentieth anniversary of the fall of Saigon. While the World War II celebrations were louder and more self-congratulatory, the Saigon memories had a more powerful hold on the American psyche and, thus, our policies. Caution about Bosnia and, then, Kosovo, despite evidence of mass murder and ethnic cleansing—activities that resonate of World War II—suggests that it is our losses and fears, rather than our triumphs and virtues, that still drive U.S. foreign policy. Critics, fearing of another Vietnam, warned about sending U.S. troops into harm's way or ending up in a stalemated quagmire. In an ironic turnabout, conservative critics of Bill Clinton reminded him that he once demonstrated against Vietnam and therefore should be cautious about sending U.S. troops to the Balkans.

In the spring of 1995, former Defense Secretary Robert McNamara published his memoir *In Retrospect: The Tragedy and Lessons of Vietnam*. Admitting years after the fact that the government had no real strategy to win the war in Vietnam, McNamara's book prompted a national outpouring of pain, anger, and disbelief. Vietnam veterans showed up at public appearances by McNamara and angrily berated him for sending their comrades off to die without a clear plan. Former supporters of the war who had believed in the government's position statements felt a renewed sense of cynicism and frustration. Until 1995, McNamara had refused to answer questions about the Vietnam War. Why did he, at long last, break his silence? He explains in his preface that he hopes it will restore faith in U.S. government: "I have grown sick at heart witnessing the cynicism and even contempt with which so many people view our political institutions and leaders." But nowhere does he seem to realize how fully it was the war in Vietnam that sowed the seeds of that cynicism.

What the debate on his memoir demonstrated is how deeply the issue of Vietnam remains rooted in the American soul. More than a quarter of a century after the last American soldier left Southeast Asia, the outer scars remain and psychic wounds have not healed. We are still fighting with the war. We know we lost. We know that fifty-eight thousand Americans died in a futile engagement. We know we lost something more than just a war.

Gone was the post–World War II sense of idealism—a feeling that flowed through both the defenders of the postwar United States as the best of all possible worlds and the reformers who came forth in the late 1950s and the 1960s to fulfill the promise of U.S. life. Instead, Americans emerged wary, cynical, and pessimistic—untrusting of our leaders and unsure about the future of the nation. At the end of the nineteenth century, the novelist Henry James noted the way the Civil War had affected Americans. Something had happened to "the national consciousness," he wrote; the war had "left a different tone from the tone it found." Vietnam, too, changed the "tone of our national consciousness." And like the Civil War, the Vietnam experience may continue to haunt the generation that planned it and the one that fought it, until they themselves pass into history.

NOTES

1. In addition to *Monkey Bridge*, see Le Ly Hayslip, *When Heaven and Earth Changed Places* (New York: Doubleday, 1989), esp. p. 30.

2. These examples are taken from McGeorge Bundy's memos of 7 February 1965 and 6 April 1965. *The Pentagon Papers: The Senator Gravel Edition* (Boston: Beacon Press, 1972), vol. III, pp. 687, 703.

3. McCone's comment is in Robert S. McNamara, *In Retrospect* (New York: Vintage Books, 1995), pp. 81–82. The Johnson-Ky exchange is in Nguyen Cao Ky, *Twenty Years and Twenty Days* (New York: Stein and Day, 1976), p. 81. It may be that Ky sounded "just like a American" because his speech was written by a U.S.official. See Chester L. Cooper, *The Longest Crusade: America in Vietnam* (New York: Dodd, Mead, 1970), p. 299.

4. David Halberstam, *The Best and Brightest* (New York: Random House, 1972), p. 512.

5. Bob Haldeman, *The Ends of Power* (New York: Dell, 1978), p. 122.

6. The Omega games are discussed by Roger Warner, *Shooting at the Moon* (South Royalton, Vt: Steerforth Press, 1996), pp. 88–90.

7. George C. Herring, *America's Longest War* (New York: McGraw-Hill, 1996), pp. 152–55.

8. Seymour Hersh, *The Price of Power* (New York: Summit Books, 1983), p. 50.

9. Harry G. Summers, Jr., *On Strategy: A Critical Analysis of the Vietnam War* (Novato, Calif.: Presidio Press, 1982), p. 1.

10. Michael Herr, *Dispatches* (New York: Alfred A. Knopf, 1977), p. 20.

11. Cited in John Clark Pratt, *Vietnam Voices: Perspectives on the War Years, 1941–1982* (New York: Penguin Books, 1984), p. 639.

12. Anthony T. Bouscaren, "All Quiet on the Eastern Front," *National Review* 27, 20 June 1975, p. 658; Christopher Lasch, "The Meaning of Vietnam," *New York Review of Books* 22 12 June 1975, p. 28.

13. Gloria Emerson, *Winners and Losers* (New York: Random House, 1976), pp. 62, 374.

14. Philip Caputo, *Rumor of War* (New York: Henry Holt, 1977), p. 6.

15. First vet quoted in Pratt, *Vietnam Voices*, p. 649; second vet quoted in James William Gibson, *Warrior Dreams: Violence and Manhood in Post-Vietnam America* (New York: Hill and Wang, 1994), p. 24; third vet quoted in Walter H. Capps, *The Unfinished War: Vietnam and the American Conscience* (Boston: Beacon Press, 2nd ed., 1990), p. 99.

16. Quoted in George Sweirs, "'Demented Vets' and Other Myths—The Moral Obligation of Veterans," in *Vietnam Reconsidered: Lessons from a War*, ed. Harrison E. Salisbury (New York: Harper and Row, 1984), p. 198.

17. Shad Meshad, "The Treatment of Vietnam Veterans: From Rap Groups To Counseling Centers," in Salisbury, *Lessons from a War*, p. 203.

18. Derek Price, interview with Alexander Bloom.

19. Richard Nixon, *The Real War* (New York: Warner Books, 1980), p. 114; Ronald Reagan, news conference of April 1982, in Pratt, *Vietnam Voices*, p. 3.

20. Harvard Sitkoff, "Vietnam Revisionism," *A History of Our Time*, 3rd ed., ed. William H. Chafe and Harvard Sitkoff (New York: Oxford University Press, 1991), p. 330.

21. Quoted in Gibson, *Warrior Dreams*, p. 168.

22. Quoted in Tom Engelhardt, *The End of Victory Culture: Cold War America and the Disillusioning of a Generation* (New York: Basic Books, 1995), p. 282.

23. Quoted in Gibson, *Warrior Dreams*, p. 291.

24. Quoted in Engelhardt, *End of Victory Culture*, p. 299.

25. Quoted in Gibson, *Warrior Dreams*, p. 293, 294.

26. Ibid., p. 268.

27. "A Cover-Up on Agent Orange?," *Time* 136, 23 July 1990), p. 27.

28. Quoted in George Ewalt, Jr., "Agent Orange and the Effects of the Herbicide Program," in Salisbury, *Lessons from a War*, p. 195.

29. Bruce Franklin, *M.I.A or Mythmaking in America* (New Brunswick, N.J.: Rutgers University Press, 1993), pp. 11–12.

30. Ibid., p. 16.

31. Quoted in Bob Greene, *Homecoming: When the Soldiers Returned from Vietnam* (New York: G.P. Putnam's Sons, 1989), p. 29.

Running Battle

Washington's War at Home

Tom Wells

Like most of my friends, my evenings were
spent listening to my wife and children
screaming about how awful the war was.
former Pentagon official

I felt like throwing up. There they are
demonstrating against me.
William Watts,
National Security Council staffer,
on seeing his wife and children
marching against the Vietnam War

There has got to be a lot of guilt and
depression inside my father about Vietnam.
Craig McNamara, son of
Defense Secretary Robert McNamara

The Vietnam War gave rise to opposition unprecedented in U.S. history. Never before had so many U.S. citizens defied their government during wartime. And yet officials often feigned disregard of antiwar protest. They made it known that foreign policy would not be made in the streets, certainly not by people who lacked the same inside information on the war that they had, or by those who were too emotional and perhaps not even rational. "Under no circumstances will I be affected whatever by it," President Nixon declared.[1] Nixon made a point of announcing that he would spend part of the afternoon of one large demonstration in Washington watching college football on television.

But the reality inside the government was rather different. From the time the antiwar movement took off in earnest in the spring of 1965, U.S. officials followed the movement closely. Presidents Johnson and Nixon paid keen attention to the movement's activities. The movement was a serious matter. Officials considered it a particularly visible and persistent sign of domestic dissatisfaction with the war, a threat to public support for the war and even domestic social stability, and encouragement to the enemy in Vietnam. They recognized that the protesters were the cutting edge of domestic antiwar sentiment as a whole. "They were noisy and they squeaked a lot, and when the wheel squeaks that's the one you pay attention to," one of those officials, Lawrence Eagleburger, would recall.[2] The government could ignore the movement only at its peril. Officials were increasingly disturbed by the growth of this opposing force and spent many hours devising ways to contain it and undercut the antiwar movement.[3]

Rising Tensions

In the spring of 1965, following the start of a sustained U.S. bombing campaign against North Vietnam, "teach-ins" on the war were held on college campuses across the country. Some were debates, others essentially antiwar forums. Professors, students, and others questioned the wisdom and morality of the war at the teach-ins, awakening much of the academic community to these issues. That

TOM WELLS earned a Ph.D. in sociology from the University of California, Berkeley. He is the author of *The War Within: America's Battle over Vietnam*, and has taught at the University of San Francisco, San Jose State University, and Mills College. He is currently writing a biography of Daniel Ellsberg for St. Martin's Press, and for which he received a National Endowment for the Humanities Fellowship. As a junior and senior high school student, he largely missed the Vietnam War, only coming to consider it after the fact.

spring the first national antiwar demonstration, sponsored by Students for a Democratic Society (SDS), was held in Washington. President Johnson was unhappy with anything that focused public attention (or at least the wrong kind of attention) on the war at this time; he wanted to keep the growing U.S. intervention in Vietnam quiet. He also worried that the country as a whole would not rally behind the war; public support for it, he recognized, was wide but not deep. Teach-ins and demonstrations wouldn't help. The administration thus sent officials out to select locations to challenge antiwar speakers at the teach-ins and attempt to blunt their arguments. But the officials typically found themselves on the defensive, and their comments often incited the protesters. At the University of Wisconsin, when one administration official denied that the United States "runs the show" in South Vietnam, students shouted, "Aw, c'mon. Let's be honest."[4] Officials soon decided to participate only in "responsible" forums on the war.[5] The government also attempted to tarnish the movement's public image (for instance, by linking it to communism, i.e. "red-baiting" it) and to infiltrate the movement. In addition, officials covertly fostered expressions of public support for the war. For example, they built up a prowar group called the American Friends of Vietnam (AFV). So close were the White House's relations with the organization that one official who helped build the group could tell colleagues that "we have an instrument for public information on Vietnam."[6] The public, however, was kept unaware of the connection.

During 1966 and 1967, the antiwar movement expanded, attracting growing support off-college campuses. The movement's tactics were diverse, ranging from congressional lobbying to legal demonstrations to militant civil disobedience, occasionally even political violence. In addition, there were protests by U.S. servicemen, campaigns to provide medical aid to civilians maimed by the war in Vietnam, and draft resistance. Prominent opponents of the war were growing in number. In 1967 Martin Luther King, Jr., came out against the war, and that fall Senator Eugene McCarthy, encouraged by the movement's growth, announced he would challenge Johnson for the presidency. McCarthy's strong showing in the New Hampshire Democratic primary several months later was a serious political blow to Johnson and his war policies. Demonstrations were growing in size. Whereas twenty thousand had turned out for the SDS demonstration in the spring of 1965, more than three hundred thousand people protested the war in April 1967 in New York, making it the largest demonstration in U.S. history up to that date. Six months later, fifty thousand people besieged the Pentagon.

In response, Washington stepped up its surveillance of antiwar activists and red-baited them, organized a prowar parade in New York, and promoted a report written by scholars defending the war. Through leaks to the press, it also forecast violence at the Pentagon protest to inhibit attendance and discredit the movement. What's more, it covertly organized another national prowar committee, dubbed the "Citizens Committee for Peace with Freedom in Vietnam," which boasted a number of heavyweight members (including former Presidents Eisenhower and Truman). President Johnson, who knew that public disclosure of the White House's role in organizing the committee would undermine its effectiveness, personally approved the effort while cautioning an aide who spearheaded it, "But don't get surfaced."[7] Three weeks before the demonstration at the Pentagon, Johnson demanded daily reports from the Justice Department on the planning of it and on Justice's responses. "Have in my office before 8:00 P.M.," he tersely directed U.S. Attorney General Ramsey Clark.[8] These reports included detailed descriptions of the antiwar activities scheduled for the weekend of the demonstration, the protest leaders, and the administration's preparations. Johnson received frequent reports throughout the day of the demonstration while simultaneously acting unconcerned and discussing other matters with reporters. The Johnson administration also indicted five prominent supporters of draft resistance, including the world-famous pediatrician Dr. Benjamin Spock, for conspiracy.

Meanwhile, general public support for the war was declining considerably. Public opinion polls in the fall of 1967 showed that, for the first time, more people thought U.S. intervention in Vietnam had been a mistake than did not. Only 35 percent approved of Johnson's handling of the war. Blacks and women were the most dovish social groups.[9] One study subsequently found antiwar sentiment was inversely correlated with Americans' socioeconomic level.[10] "Public discontent with the war is now wide and deep," McGeorge Bundy, the recently departed national security adviser, wrote Johnson that November. Most officials likely agreed with Bundy that the war's "principal battleground" was now "in domestic opinion."[11] When Johnson announced he was partially halting the bombing of North Vietnam in late March 1968, he was hoping to reverse the political tide at home and take steam out of the antiwar movement.

The Federal Bureau of Investigation played important roles in the government's efforts to undermine the antiwar movement. It infiltrated and wiretapped the movement, for example, and recruited others to report on it. In the spring of 1968, the FBI launched an extensive COINTELPRO program to discredit, divide, and otherwise hamper New Leftists and other antiwar protesters. Besides infiltration, the FBI's methods included forging poison-pen letters and literature and leaking false information to the media. It also set up protesters on drug charges and painted some movement leaders as government informants or homosexuals. J. Edgar Hoover, the director of the FBI, instructed FBI agents that "ridicule is one of the most potent weapons that we can use" and that COINTELPRO "must be approached with imagination and enthusiasm if it is to be successful."[12]

The antiwar movement crested during the Nixon administration. In October 1969, more than two million people participated in diverse Vietnam Moratorium protests around the country in another display of dissent unprecedented in U.S. history. Many were protesting the war for the first time; prominent Establishment figures such as veteran diplomat Averell Harriman, celebrities including Woody Allen, and businessmen joined the Moratorium protests. That same month in Chicago, the Weatherman, an ultraleftist youth group, held much narrower (and, some would say, suicidal) "Days of Rage" demonstrations in which they attempted to "bring the war home" by fighting the police in the streets; most were injured or arrested. "It didn't make sense—although we did it," one leader of the group reflected years later.[13] The Weatherman had originated as a splinter group when SDS fractured the previous June, to the delight of the Nixon administration: "The sectarianism is staggering, even by leftist standards, as the SDS divides, amoeba-like, into less and less significant cells," one Nixon aide observed.[14] Other forms of militant protest, mainly youthful, and including building occupations and bombings, were spreading. Talk of armed revolution was common. Legal, peaceful demonstrations continued to grow in size. In November protests organized by a national "Mobilization" coalition, more than five hundred thousand people demonstrated in Washington, one hundred fifty thousand in San Francisco. Broad public discontent with the war continued to mount.

Senior Nixon administration officials logged long hours "agonizing over" youthful protest (as one wrote later), assessing its roots and potential, and devising schemes for blunting it.[15] "The youth problem" was the topic of numerous White House memos.[16] President Nixon himself was a close student of the problem. At his request, White House aides collected data, readings, and even an annotated bibliography on student protest for his perusal. Nixon also asked an aide to solicit the views of university professors around the country on the nature of the youth problem. Nixon's top aides desired maximum intelligence on the antiwar movement and further heightened the surveillance. Close Nixon aide John Ehrlichman loved intelligence operations and was attracted to antiwar demonstrations like "a firehouse Dalmatian at a blaze," White House Chief of Staff H. R. Haldeman once remarked.[17] "John got quite absorbed in that on a personal basis—much more so, really, than the president did," Haldeman later recalled.[18] "Field Marshal Ehrlichman," as White House counsel John Dean dubbed him, set up an elaborate command post in the bomb shelter of the White House during large demonstrations in Washington to better monitor them.

To defuse domestic dissent on the war and buy time for developing a viable Vietnam strategy, Nixon began slowly withdrawing U.S. troops from Vietnam in 1969. The president also signed a reformed draft law that limited draft liability to one year. "This will take care of a lot of the draft dodgers," he remarked to aides, one recounted.[19] And the administration showed it meant to play tough: in March 1969 it indicted eight protesters (the "Chicago Eight," later reduced to seven) for conspiracy to incite a riot during raucous demonstrations at the 1968 Democratic Convention in Chicago. Nixon, an anti-Semite, later seemed focused on the Jews among them. "Aren't the Chicago Seven all Jews?" he asked Haldeman amid antiwar protests in 1971.[20]

The Nixon White House worried that the large Moratorium and Mobilization protests in the fall of 1969 would exert significant political influence at home and further weaken Nixon's negotiating position with the North Vietnamese. The White House knew the protests also reflected growing public impatience with Nixon's war policies: something "was boiling up around the country," one official perceived.[21] Nixon asked John Ehrlichman to come up with a "game plan" to counteract the Moratorium one week before Moratorium leaders had even publicly announced their plan to hold the protest.[22] (That's good intelligence.) The key element of the game plan was to politically isolate the protesters by rallying support for Nixon's policies, a key element of the Johnson administration's strategies as well. Nixon believed this approach had greater political advantages than trying to win his critics over, which he was viscerally averse to anyway. Officials mobilized supporters of all stripes (including legislators, businesspeople, veterans, police officers, and students) and helped set up more prowar front groups (including one led by comedian Bob Hope), again allegedly "citizens committees." They arranged to have proadministration bumper stickers and buttons made up for supporters and helped organize more prowar rallies. The White House bombarded congressional supporters of the Moratorium and the media with prowar letters, purportedly from private citizens. For this it utilized a discreet "Nixon Network" (as Nixon himself called it) for manufacturing such letters and calls to the media. "Clobber commentators, especially NBC," Nixon directed in a meeting with Haldeman. "Load the switchboard—crack them."[23] Nixon wanted the "maximum game planning cranked up" for surfacing political support.[24] To further foster the impression of support, the administration even sent prowar letters and telegrams to itself, then invited the media to take pictures of them stacked on Nixon's desk.

Simultaneously, the FBI and Central Intelligence Agency targeted and reported on Moratorium and Mobilization organizers. "We got two FBI agents up there now," a Moratorium activist told a reporter outside the group's national headquarters one day. "They're pretending to be students. But we spotted them right away. Everybody knows who they are."[25] The Justice Department put together "Daily Intelligence Summaries" on Moratorium and Mobilization activities well in advance of the protests.[26] The FBI disrupted bus transportation to the Mobilization. The day of the Moratorium, Ehrlichman tracked protest activities around the country.

The administration also tried to split the moderate demonstrators from the radicals. "The trick here is to try to find a way to divide the black sheep from the white sheep within the group that participated in the Moratorium yesterday," Haldeman wrote Secretary of State William Rogers in October, following a discussion with Nixon. "The problem is to find a way to divide the good guys from the bad guys in the demonstration movement without discouraging the people who have backed us all along."[27] Vice President Spiro Agnew derided antiwar leaders as an "effete corps of impudent snobs who characterized themselves as intellectuals," and declared, "We can also afford to separate them from our society with no more regret than we should feel over discarding rotten apples from a barrel."[28] But as Nixon administration officials learned more about the antiwar leaders, their organizational skills impressed them. "We knew that these people were good at coordinating and planning," Haldeman recalled. "John [Ehrlichman] did his intelligence. . . . They used walkie-talkies, and we had their frequencies. You could listen to their command post and all their stuff going through. I mean, they were well-staffed and skillfully operated."[29]

The militant antiwar protests also concerned administration officials. While streetfighting, bombings, and general unruliness hurt the antiwar movement's public image, officials knew these events also raised the specter of uncontrollable social disorder while suggesting to the public that the government was in dubious command. Moreover, they fed public concern that the war was causing too much turbulence at home. Although the administration tried to use the militants to its political advantage (by smearing Democrats with them and using them as foils at hard-line speeches by Nixon), officials believed their net political impact was harmful. "In the overall perspective, I wouldn't say that *any* facet of that [movement] was good for us," Haldeman analyzed.[30] Following a wave of bombings by militants in the winter of 1970, Nixon ordered a review of U.S. intelligence-gathering methods that led to development of the infamous "Huston Plan." The plan included a wide assortment of criminal acts, including mail openings, burglaries, and phone taps, to combat the protesters.

All of this would be directed from the White House. Although Nixon approved the plan, FBI Director J. Edgar Hoover's strong opposition forced him to abandon it. However, elements of the plan were implemented, indeed had been used against protesters for some time. The plan later became part of the Watergate scandal.

Like their predecessors in the Johnson administration, Nixon administration officials typically encountered protesters when they ventured out for public appearances. In an April 1970 visit to Johns Hopkins University, Nixon's national security adviser, Henry Kissinger, was greeted with dissent and consequently decided to junk his prepared speech and open the floor to questions. "Dr. Kissinger, do you consider yourself a war criminal?" was the first. Kissinger walked out.[31] The threat of protests forced officials to restrict their public appearances. Here too the movement's efficiency impressed them, even as it frustrated and angered them. In November 1967 the Johnson White House ordered the FBI to "discreetly" determine "how and why demonstrators are so well organized and so efficient in getting to locations where the President is speaking and whether there is any proof that there is a prearranged policy to prevent the President from speaking."[32] Officials' houses were picketed and even vandalized. "People came up and urinated on my front door and threw bricks through the windows," Melvin Laird, Nixon's secretary of defense, remembered.[33] Some staged mock combat on Laird's front lawn and hung a National Liberation Front flag on his porch. Robert McNamara, Johnson's defense secretary, frequently attracted demonstrators while vacationing in Colorado. One woman came up to him in a ski lodge and yelled that she hoped that the ketchup on his hamburger reminded him of blood.

In May 1970, the U.S. invasion of Cambodia and the killing of four student demonstrators by National Guardsmen at Kent State University sparked the greatest display of protest on college campuses in U.S. history. A national student strike shut down more than five hundred campuses. Perhaps half the nation's students participated in protests, whose variety "seemed to exhaust the entire known repertoire of forms of dissent," Clark Kerr, the chairman of the Carnegie Commission on Higher Education, observed.[34] Many were moderate or conservative students protesting for the first time. "The general effect of May was one of radicalizing as well as politicizing student opinion across the board," one university chancellor subsequently told Nixon. "The meaning of May [was] a big shove Leftward."[35] Other citizens protested the invasion and killings in cities across the country. More than one hundred thousand demonstrated in Washington, despite only a week's prior notice. Many union leaders spoke out against the war for the first time, and workers participated in antiwar protests in unprecedented numbers. The United States seemed as divided as it had been since the Civil War; it was on the verge of a "physical breakdown," New York Mayor John Lindsay remarked.[36]

The Nixon administration and the president himself were shaken by the May protests. Seeming to side with the protesters, Congress passed legislation prohibiting funding of U.S. ground forces and advisers in Cambodia. Nixon struck a conciliatory stance in public and announced the withdrawal of all U.S. troops from Cambodia by the end of June. (In private his distaste for antiwar protesters continued to show no bounds.) Nixon, who was having trouble sleeping and seemed on the verge of a nervous breakdown, ventured over to the Lincoln Memorial before dawn one morning for a surprise visit with protesters gathered there. His visit brought to sharp and comic relief the divisions separating him from his young critics. In an attempt to "lift them a bit out of the miserable intellectual wasteland in which they now wander aimlessly around" (as he put it afterward), Nixon talked mainly about sports and travel, very little about "the war thing." "It was a surreal atmosphere," a White House aide on the scene remembered. "I hope it was because he was tired, but most of what he was saying was absurd," one student told a reporter afterward. "Here we had come from a university that's completely uptight, on strike, and when we told him where we were from, he talked about the football team."[37] Kissinger aide Anthony Lake later commented with a smile, "If you look at Nixon's behavior after Kent State, it was not a true Alan Alda-ish, sensitive male performance."[38] Nixon followed his meeting with the protesters by taking his valet on an early-morning tour of the Capitol, highlighted by speechmaking in an empty House Chamber. All in all, it was a strange episode, with the president of the United States wandering sleeplessly about Washington before dawn, psychologically ajar.

Nixon's mental state aside, behind-the-scenes efforts to build support for the war continued that spring. The White House helped labor union leaders stage proadministration rallies. It also had a hand in an assault by two hundred construction workers on peaceful student demonstrators in New York.[39] The workers used their fists, crowbars, and metal wrenches on the protesters, injuring seventy, some brutally. "It had a sobering effect on the demonstrators," Haldeman would recall. "It wasn't too bad a result. . . . Kind of nice to see our side dishing some of it back."[40] During an antiwar protest a year later, Nixon and Haldeman discussed utilizing the talents of some "thugs" in the Teamsters. "They've got guys who'll go in and knock their heads off," Nixon remarked. "Sure," Haldeman responded. "Murderers. Guys that really, you know, that's what they really do. . . . They're gonna beat the shit out of some of these people. . . . And hope they really hurt 'em. You know, I mean go in . . . and smash some noses."[41]

In April 1971, despite a flagging antiwar movement increasingly hampered by internal divisions (which were always a serious problem for the movement), five hundred thousand demonstrated against the war in Washington and two hundred thousand in San Francisco. The Vietnam Veterans Against the War (VVAW), who three months earlier had held a "Winter Soldier Investigation" into U.S. war crimes in Vietnam, staged dramatic and emotional protests in Washington. After the father of a young man killed in Vietnam blew taps on a bugle, the veterans threw their war medals over a fence surrounding the Capitol, bringing onlookers and veterans alike to tears. The White House responded to VVAW's protests by smearing the veterans and mobilizing friendly vets. It generated letters to the media urging they "expose" VVAW leader John Kerry (later a U.S. senator) as "a fraud."[42] Other protesters that spring engaged in a mass civil disobedience action known as "May Day," designed to shut down Washington; it engendered a police dragnet and twelve thousand arrests over three days (seven thousand the first day, the most for any event in U.S. history).

While all these spring protests were unwelcome to the Nixon administration, May Day—with its ominous and seemingly realizable goal of paralyzing Washington—attracted special concern in the White House. "It doesn't take that many terrorists to block all the traffic arteries," one official remarked later.[43] Nixon was determined that the protest be thwarted, and with some success the government went to considerable lengths to do so. Nixon received multiple reports on May Day on each of the three days it occurred.

By that spring, polling showed for the first time, that most Americans felt the war was "morally wrong."[44] In June, the *New York Times* and other newspapers published a top-secret history of U.S. policy in Vietnam. Released by Daniel Ellsberg, a former Pentagon aide, the "Pentagon Papers" provided evidence of considerable duplicity by the Johnson administration on the war. Ellsberg's disclosure angered and panicked the Nixon White House, which feared he might release other classified documents and that he was part of a conspiracy, possibly even a Soviet spy ring. The administration moved to destroy Ellsberg's public image and to send him to prison for many years. Operatives hired by the White House also attempted to assault him physically.

Meanwhile, dissent among U.S. soldiers had grown enormously. In the United States, antiwar coffeehouses and GI newspapers were widespread. Many GIs openly protested, at great personal risk. Some were imprisoned. In Vietnam, the morale and discipline of U.S. soldiers was "deteriorating very seriously," as one columnist observed. The entire U.S. Army there was "in danger of going plumb to hell." Drug abuse was "out of control."[45] Some U.S. soldiers were mutinying or even murdering ("fragging," as with a fragmentation grenade) their own officers. They placed bounties on the heads of unpopular officers. Some commanders consequently restricted access to grenades and rifles. One infantry officer commented, "You can't give them an order and expect them to obey immediately. They ask why, and you have to tell them." A member of a platoon who refused an order to advance against heavy enemy fire explained, simply, "the reason given wasn't a very good one."[46] A retired Marine colonel wrote in the June 1971 issue of *Armed Forces Journal,* "The morale, discipline and battleworthiness of the U.S. Armed Forces are, with a few salient exceptions, lower and worse than at any time in this century and possibly in the history of the United States. By every conceivable indicator, our army that now remains in Vietnam is in a state approaching collapse, with individual units avoiding or having refused combat, murdering their officers and noncommissioned officers, drug-ridden, and dispirited where not near-mutinous."[47] Conditions in Vietnam worried the Nixon administration and provided additional impetus to U.S. troop withdrawals.

As the troops returned between 1971 and 1975, the antiwar movement gradually declined. However, many Americans continued to protest U.S. bombing of North Vietnam and Cambodia, the existence of political prisoners in South Vietnam, and U.S. funding of the Thieu regime in Vietnam and the Lon Nol regime in Cambodia. Protests continued to run the gamut of forms, from mass demonstrations to lobbying Congress.

Shirkers, Spoiled Children, and Communist Dupes

Despite its close monitoring of the antiwar movement, the U.S. government misunderstood the protesters in significant ways. Many officials ascribed the causes of dissent to psychological problems, emotionalism, and outside influences rather than rational thinking. While their theories had some merit, they mainly fell wide of the mark, suggesting a government somewhat out of touch with its critics. Some officials believed antiwar students felt guilty or were emotionally disturbed about their decision to avoid the draft and, consequently, their militancy and radicalism were demonstrations of "their manhood" in the face of questions about their courage.[48] Many officials felt draft resisters were simply cowards. Nixon believed numerous protesters wanted "to keep from getting their asses shot off."[49] At one meeting, President Johnson referred to FBI reports claiming that many of those who had burned their draft cards "were crazy people who had previous history in mental institutions."[50] Johnson explained the opposition of college professors to the war by saying their salaries and status were historically low, and that "they were now feeling power for the first time."[51] Admiral Thomas Moorer, the chairman of the Joint Chiefs of Staff during the Nixon administration, said he thought professors felt guilty about avoiding military service, "so they tried to teach their students to do the same thing they did to show that it was all right."[52] Key Johnson adviser Walt Rostow told other cabinet officials in 1968 that a "very significant" factor in student dissent was "the high number of dissident leaders and followers who come out of sociology and the soft subjects. They are accustomed to dealing in generalities and abstractions. The hard-subject people, economists and engineers, do not seem to have the same trouble fitting in. They can find their place." Rostow, who was an economist and historian, also opined that many youths were "impatient" and thus having difficulty figuring out "how to get from here to there" in this "period of great and complex transition in the world."[53]

Some officials felt student protest was partly a reflection of youthful alienation or a desire for fun and games. Young people typically find circumstances "intolerable" until age twenty-five, presidential adviser Daniel Patrick Moynihan told Nixon. Then they learn to adjust.[54] H. R. Haldeman perceived that "there are people who want to get excited about something, and they don't really give much of a darn what it is they're excited about. And they move from one cause to the next. They get fired up on civil rights, then on antiwar, then on ecology, and it moves from one thing to another. Antinuke and so forth." Haldeman believed that "there were a lot of people in that movement, especially the younger segments of it, that were simply motivated by the desire to get out and raise hell, without the slightest concern of what they were raising hell about. You know, they had some concern about it, but their motivation really was to get out and do something—it wasn't to stop the war."[55] Another Nixon aide told the president that nice weather tended to stir students up. "Most large campus disruptions, whether political or otherwise, have tended historically to develop in the first warm days of Spring," he wrote. "Such disruptions are generally spontaneous and usually reflect a widespread restlessness caused by a combination of factors including the warm weather and the tedium of the daily class routine. . . . Such disruptions are generally not issue-oriented."[56]

Ray Price, a Nixon speechwriter, felt protest "was in fashion at the time. . . . It became the latest hula hoop."[57] He considered it a thoughtless fad. "Each time I talked with a group of students, I was dismayed anew at how abysmally ignorant most of them were," he later wrote. They were "unaware of even the most elementary facts about whatever issue they were currently inflamed about. They rushed to embrace any rumor, as long as its effect was to discredit the war or the 'Establishment.' And, sadly, they had no idea of how little they knew." They were "strangers to linear logic," Price perceived. They saw "'truth' not in terms of observable, hard facts . . . but rather in terms of emotional 'truth'—what seemed right because it felt right, what felt right because it made them feel good, what pleased the senses, what excited the libido or gratified their hungers." They were engaging in "an orgy of right-brain indulgence."[58]

Price said that one of the "key elements" of youthful protest "might well be a pervasive fear which they [the protesters] themselves neither articulated nor even explicitly recognized." He advanced this view in a memo to Kissinger and other officials in October 1969:

> The most overwhelming characteristic of our society today is its complexity. To those just entering on the mysteries of adulthood, this complexity is not merely a phenomenon to be observed; it is a direct, personal threat to their capacity to manage their own futures, to their achievement of "manhood," to their sense of identity, to their place in a world they yearn to call their own. . . .
>
> I suggest that a lot of today's young see the complexity of modern life not as a challenge, but as a barrier, precisely because they see no way . . . by which they can master it; and thus, instead of expending the energy needed to meet the "challenge," they rebel against the system. . . .
>
> Rebellion can be many things—and one of those things is a crutch for those who fear they can't make it. . . . By rebelling against the "system," the youth sets up an excuse for failure; by rejecting its values, he rejects in advance the anticipated negative judgment of the society that embraces those values.
>
> It's no coincidence that so much of the youthful rebellion . . . is focused on the search for simple answers, simple relationships, simple truths. Or that in its inarticulateness, this same set . . . reduces communication to little more than simple grunts and code phrases. . . . It's as though, by instinct, the herd is running from the thunder, seeking shelter: and its shelter is the simple, even the primitive.[59]

Henry Kissinger theorized that permissive child-rearing practices were partly responsible for the protest. Antiwar students, he wrote in his memoir, "had been brought up by skeptics, relativists, and psychiatrists; now they were rudderless in a world from which they demanded certainty without sacrifice. My generation had failed them by encouraging self-indulgence and neglecting to provide roots."[60] Amid the Moratorium and Mobilization protests in the fall of 1969, one of his aides later recalled, Kissinger spoke acidly of "the neurotic character of the demonstrators." "They don't know who they are," Kissinger said. "They need fathers, not brothers. . . . This is like dealing with thumb-sucking."[61] Another Kissinger aide remembered, "He saw them as spoiled children."[62] Kissinger told Nixon that most protesters were "casualties of our affluence." "They have had the leisure for self-pity, and the education enabling them to focus it in a fashionable critique of the 'system.'" The protesters' upbringings had conditioned them to scorn their affluence, he analyzed. "Stimulated by a sense of guilt encouraged by modern psychiatry and the radical chic rhetoric of upper middle-class suburbia," Kissinger wrote, youths were rebelling against a society that had proved to be "a spiritual desert." They were suffering from "metaphysical despair."[63]

Kissinger aide Anthony Lake accurately described Nixon officials' flawed understanding of the roots of antiwar protest when he remarked, "They were so clueless as to what was going on that Kissinger was their resident expert, and would write memos on what students think—which is silly."[64] Still, the notion that the protesters were spoiled, self-centered shirkers would attract many adherents in the United States during the Reagan 1980s.

Another theory floating around the government was even further off the mark. Many officials believed foreign communists, particularly the Soviet Union, were aiding and abetting, if not actually directing, the antiwar movement. "Some were pretty paranoid over there [at the White House] about that," Melvin Laird later chuckled.[65] The Soviets simply *had* to be involved, officials reasoned; the Soviets would have to be foolish, even derelict in their duty, not to try to fan the flames of dissent. "I think most of the radicals were more duped in that regard than they were conspirators," Nixon press secretary Ronald Ziegler later argued.[66] Some officials perceived that the efficiency with which the protesters organized their demonstrations required the involvement of an outside force. George Christian, Johnson's press secretary, remembered:

> I think there was always a question of what was spontaneous and what wasn't. I know in Johnson's travels around the country he became convinced, based on what the Secret Service told him, and the FBI, that he could not even announce such a thing [his travel schedule] off the record to the press, or let me announce it off the record to the press, because there were reports made straight from the White House to somebody to get something started. And I think that was very true. We had an open White House, we had a lot of people accredited. We also had [representatives of] Eastern bloc countries. We had foreign reporters of one kind or another. We had some domestic reporters who may not have been security risks but at least could have been targeted by somebody. And I think we learned a bad lesson. We really did learn that you couldn't really say much about what Johnson was going to do in traveling, or you were guaranteed a demonstration. . . .
>
> You know, there's no way some of these things were spontaneous. I don't care what anybody says, some of the demonstrations were not spontaneous!

. . . They had an efficient network of some kind. And I think one of the things that really bothered us at that time about some of the campus activities in particular were the people that were on the campuses stirring things up—they weren't students. They were not students.[67]

Officials believed that money had to be coming from communists overseas. "You know damn well that if you charter fifty or sixty buses, and you're spending all your time rioting, you're not going to be able to [fund] it yourself," observed Thomas Moorer. "These people always accused me of seeing a communist under every bush. Well, that's because there *is* a communist under every bush."[68]

It is difficult to overstate the degree of paranoia about communist subversion inside the U.S. government during the war. President Johnson told one aide in 1965 that "the communists are taking over the country." He gloomily remarked to a group of his staffers weeks later, "I'm going to be the one who lost this form of government. The communists already control the three major networks and the forty major outlets of communication."[69] During a discussion with top advisers in November 1967, two weeks after protesters surrounded the Pentagon, a White House memo records,

The President turned his attention to the troubles [i.e., protests] at home and said "I'm not going to let the Communists take this government and they're doing it right now." The President pointed out that he has been protecting civil liberties since he was nine years old, but "I told the Attorney General that I am not going to let 200,000 of these people ruin everything for the 200 million Americans. I've got my belly full of seeing these people put on a Communist plane and shipped all over this country. I want someone to carefully look at who leaves this country, where they go, why they are going, and if they're going to Hanoi, how are we going to keep them from getting back into this country."[70]

This type of thinking led two Johnson aides to consult with psychiatrists, who diagnosed Johnson with "a textbook case of paranoid disintegration."[71]

Presidents Johnson and Nixon both craved hard evidence of foreign communist involvement in the antiwar movement. They pressured the CIA and FBI to obtain such evidence, but both agencies came up empty-handed. A lengthy CIA report titled "International Connections of the U.S. Peace Movement," submitted to the White House in November 1967, stated, "We see no significant evidence that would prove Communist control or direction of the U.S. peace movement or its leaders."[72] Two other CIA reports on the movement's international connections also failed to find any evidence of foreign communist subversion. When CIA Director Richard Helms informed other cabinet officials in 1968 that yet another CIA report on student protest, this one titled

"Restless Youth," had found "no convincing evidence of Communist control, manipulation, or support of student dissidents," his listeners were incredulous. Johnson was contemptuous. "I just don't believe this business that there is no support," he declared. "I've seen it in my own school. I've seen them provoke and aggravate trouble. I know that Students for a Democratic Society and the DuBois Clubs are Communist infiltrated, Communist supported and aggravated."[73] As Helms recounted, "When we would come back with reports that we couldn't find any evidence of this, that hardly changed his mind. He still felt that there was a strong foreign influence in all of this." Johnson was "after us all the time" to obtain documentation, Helms said.[74]

Yet other officials would have nothing to do with the notion of a foreign communist conspiracy. "You've got to be a real dummy to believe that!" Paul Warnke, a senior Pentagon official, later exclaimed.[75] U.S. Attorney General Ramsey Clark, who considered such theories "bunkum," found having to "constantly" listen to them "really nauseating."[76]

Family Troubles

Another source of concern about the antiwar movement to U.S. officials was the participation of their relatives in it. Many officials had children who opposed the war. "*All* of us . . . had sons or daughters who were involved in this," Marshall Green, a senior State Department official during the Nixon administration, fervently recalled. "I mean, everybody did. I had a son who was poised to go to Canada. I had to keep arguing, 'For God sakes, *don't*,' you know, and trying to pull him back. All of us were torn in our own family lives." After the 1970 U.S. invasion of Cambodia, Green's son "said, 'I don't want to see you again.' And he left," Green recounted. "And we didn't see him again for weeks. . . . You were driven to the brink of suicide, you really were."[77] Other children of officials also unequivocally expressed their opposition to the war to their fathers. Some wives of officials argued with their husbands, too. One senior Pentagon official remembered, "Like most of my friends, my evenings, when I did get home, were spent listening to my wife and children screaming about how awful the war was."[78]

Craig McNamara and his father, Robert McNamara, suffered a particularly painful split over Vietnam. Craig, who was a student in prep school at the time, felt the war "was absolutely wrong" and tacked a small flag of the National Liberation Front (also known as the Viet Cong) onto one wall of his bedroom in his parents' home. On the opposite wall, he hung an American flag—turned upside down. His dad was angry. "It must have just really hurt my folks," Craig reflected afterward. "It must have been devastating."[79] Craig was emotionally torn by his father's role in the war; he developed a stomach ulcer at age seventeen. Compounding his distress, his father wouldn't discuss the war with him. He protested the war extensively when attending Stanford, where Susan Haldeman and Peter Ehrlichman, children of H. R. Haldeman and John Ehrlichman, also demonstrated. "We had a need for a lot of communication," the senior Ehrlichman would recall.[80] Frustrated with his father and his country, Craig McNamara moved to Chile (site of Marxist President Salvador Allende's socialist experiment) in 1971.

Senior Defense Department official Paul Nitze was the government's self-proclaimed "mastermind of the planning of the defense of the Pentagon" against the fifty thousand demonstrators who besieged the building in October 1967.[81] At least three of Nitze's four children were among the crowd of protesters that day, as were the children of other officials. One of Nitze's kids associated with the radical leadership of Columbia University's SDS chapter. "Caught between love for my father and the growing horror of Vietnam," Richard Rusk, son of Secretary of State Dean Rusk, would ultimately suffer a nervous breakdown.[82] Anthony Lake, who served as an aide to Under Secretary of State Nicholas Katzenbach during the Johnson administration, would remember going to dinner at Katzenbach's house and "hearing his kids really mau-mau him" on the war. "His back would be against the wall."[83] William Watts, an aide to Henry Kissinger, While working on a bellicose presidential speech during a Moratorium march in October 1969, walked over to the White House gate to get a better look at the marchers. There he saw his wife and children walking by. "I felt like throwing up," Watts recalled. "There they are demonstrating against me, and here I am inside writing a speech." Watts also commented, "It was very painful to be on the other side of the fence. . . . It was astounding."[84] Lake's wife, whose differences with her husband over the war sometimes led her to question whether their marriage could survive, was also among the marchers that day.

Opposition to the war inside officials' families contributed to the sense of besiegement many felt and heightened their awareness of the war's unpopularity. It may even have altered some of their perceptions of the war's merits. Paul Warnke said of Robert McNamara (at least one of whose two daughters also opposed the war), "I'm quite sure that the strong opposition of his own children to the war had a very definite impact on him. I think Craig in particular. He was very opposed to the war and very disapproving of his father."[85]

Asked if his own son's views affected him, Marshall Green exclaimed, "Of course!"[86]

The Movement and the War

The course of the Vietnam War cannot be understood without taking into account the U.S. war at home.[87] During the Johnson administration, the movement played a substantial role in constraining the war. It was one of the primary factors restraining the U.S. bombing of North Vietnam and the level of U.S. troop deployments, and inhibiting U.S. invasions of North Vietnam, Cambodia, and Laos. Officials recognized that if they substantially escalated the war, it would further incite the protesters and thereby worsen their public opinion problems as a whole. The movement also fed the growing unease with the war of key Johnson administration officials. Clark Clifford, who succeeded Robert McNamara as secretary of defense in early 1968 and who played the most influential role in the administration's policy reversal that year (when it partially halted the bombing of North Vietnam and effectively capped U.S. troop deployments), was affected by the opposition to the war. "I didn't like what I was seeing going on at the time," he remembered later. "It was a period of the deepest concern because of the very sharp divisions among our people. It was very distressing."[88] Clifford wrote, "I was more conscious each day of domestic unrest in our own country. Draft card burnings, marches in the streets, problems on school campuses, bitterness and divisiveness were rampant."[89] Johnson aide Harry McPherson, another important player in the administration's policy reversal, "saw that the vast majority of liberal intellectuals were violently opposed to the war. And that had a very large effect on people like me," he recalled.[90] The movement also had a significant influence on a group of influential, private Johnson advisers known as the Wise Men. The Wise Men, an elite cast of former officials and military leaders who had previously supported the war, were "shaken by the opposition in this country," Richard Helms observed.[91] And while it was largely public opposition as a whole that led the Johnson administration to reverse its course in Vietnam in 1968, the antiwar movement was the most important manifestation of that opposition. It was visible, influential, disruptive, and persistent. Had antiwar sentiment not been expressed through active, vocal dissent, it is unlikely Johnson would have reversed direction, as the domestic pressures he faced would have been considerably weaker.

During the Nixon administration, the movement fueled U.S. troop withdrawals from Vietnam while continuing to inhibit the air and ground wars in Indochina. Nixon realized that unleashing the war would incite angry protests.

The movement exerted a critical influence on his decision in the fall of 1969 not to carry out a threat he made to North Vietnam of massive military escalation; he felt the Moratorium protests had undermined the credibility of his threat and worried about mounting protest, he revealed later. The tremendous upswelling of dissent that followed the invasion of Cambodia and the Kent State killings in 1970 shaped Nixon's decision to withdraw U.S. troops from Cambodia earlier than he desired. "I think it's quite clear that he felt that domestic political pressure obliged him to curtail that operation before it really was finished," Helms commented.[92] Antiwar activists organized among U.S. soldiers, fostering the decline in troop discipline and morale in Vietnam, which also fueled U.S. troop withdrawals. Moreover, the movement put pressure on the administration to negotiate a settlement of the war, and it nourished congressional legislation that ultimately cut off U.S. funding of the war.

The movement accomplished none of this by itself. Its power was always bound up with broader political forces. As officials realized, it was the cutting edge of domestic antiwar sentiment as a whole. The movement also promoted wider opposition. Though public disillusionment with the war was probably mainly a product of the war's length and cost, the movement fed public questioning of it, including among influential elite figures. "It would be crazy to argue that that kind of thing didn't have any impact on my mind and on the minds of my associates," John Oakes, who was the editor of the *New York Times* editorial page, commented. "I would have had to have been deaf, dumb and blind not to have felt . . . an impact."[93] That the war "was tearing apart American society" contributed to the *Times'* calls for an end to it. "We certainly were concerned about what this was doing to American society," Oakes recalled.[94] Of course, many Americans hated the protesters, and some may have supported the war longer and more strongly as a result. But others grew so tired of the protests that they wanted the war to end so the disorder would end.

In addition, the movement fostered the Watergate scandal, a series of abuses of governmental power that also played a key role in ending the war. The movement shaped Nixon's decision to bomb Cambodia secretly starting in 1969 and then to lie to Congress about it, a consideration in the later proceedings to impeach him. Public disclosure of the bombing prompted the administration to illegally wiretap eighteen officials and reporters, another abuse of power. The movement and Nixon's belief that foreign communists were involved in it gave rise to the "Huston Plan" for combating the protesters. Also, antiwar activists influenced Daniel Ellsberg, whose release of the Pentagon Papers inspired the White House to set up a secret intelligence unit that became known as the Plumbers. The Plumbers' illegal acts were a major part of Watergate, including spreading derogatory information about Ellsberg, breaking into the office of his former psychiatrist to gain intelligence about him, and attempting to assault him physically. Ellsberg's leak further inspired a plan for a break-in at the Brookings Institution, where Nixon thought Ellsberg's coconspirators were harboring other classified documents. The movement also fed the White House's paranoia about its political enemies, a major factor in the Watergate break-ins themselves. And the Watergate revelations undermined Nixon's authority in Congress and thus his capacity to continue prosecuting the war.

Aftermath

Following the Vietnam War, many Americans were disillusioned with U.S. military interventions overseas. America's defeat in Vietnam and the turmoil at home left them uneasy about the use of force abroad, particularly the sending of U.S. ground troops into situations not amenable to quick resolution. That uneasiness is with us still, though applications of concentrated military force (particularly from the air) evoke wide public support. Americans don't want to get bogged down in "another Vietnam." Influential figures in the media and Congress bolster that sentiment. Many Americans are also more likely to question the rectitude of such military interventions than before Vietnam. A Gallup poll in 1990 found that 72 percent agreed with the statement that the Vietnam War was "more than a mistake; it was fundamentally wrong and immoral." A majority of respondents "strongly" agreed.[95] Had there been no antiwar movement, that poll question would probably never have even been asked. And should the U.S. government undertake another lengthy combat involvement overseas, its domestic opponents will have the example of a successful antiwar movement to look to.

The Vietnam War left many Americans distrustful of their government. The numerous revelations of official lying during the war, many unearthed or publicized by the antiwar movement (the Pentagon Papers study being a major source of them), left large segments of the public feeling betrayed and skeptical of their leaders. The Watergate scandal greatly increased the public's distrust. But their skepticism is healthy and beneficial for democracy. Some of the same arguments U.S. officials used to justify the Vietnam War, such as keeping Americans free and defending democracy, would not draw as many people today as in the 1960s. That Americans are more skeptical of the U.S. government's motives in interventions overseas is partially the result of the antiwar movement.

United States officials are also mindful of Vietnam. When faced with the prospect of large-scale military action in a foreign land, they worry about provoking widespread public opposition again. The specter of mass protest gave the government cause for restraint, for example, in Central American policy during the 1980s. United States leaders favor quick, massive, decisive military strikes, rather than the gradualist approach used in Vietnam, hoping that victory can be achieved before public support declines and the country devours itself again. If the fighting drags on, they know, domestic opposition will only grow, and probably more quickly than during Vietnam. They have a shorter time limit and thus more cause for restraint.

But another lesson of Vietnam to U.S. officials is that the government should control as much as possible what Americans see, hear, and read of U.S. military actions overseas. The U.S. government censored the press during interventions in Grenada, Panama, and Iraq in the 1980s and 1990s. To those who believe in informed debate, indeed democracy, this is a disturbing lesson from Vietnam.

The widespread protest over the Vietnam War generated a protracted and intently fought political struggle in the United States, forcing the U.S. government to conduct the war while simultaneously keeping a close eye on its domestic rear and ultimately restraining U.S. foreign policies. Its political aftereffects linger on.

NOTES

1. *New York Times*, 27 September 1969.

2. Lawrence Eagleburger, interview.

3. For fuller discussion and sources of events and issues discussed in this essay, see Tom Wells, *The War Within: America's Battle over Vietnam* (Berkeley: University of California Press, 1994; reprint, New York: Owl/Henry Holt, 1996).

4. Louis Menashe and Ronald Radosh, eds. *Teach-ins: U.S.A.* (New York: Praeger, 1967), pp. 133–34.

5. Chester Cooper memo on 23 August 1965, meeting of Public Affairs Policy Committee for Vietnam (National Security File, Country File, Vietnam, box 197, LBJ Library).

6. Gordon Chase memo "August 4 Luncheon Meeting on the Information Problem," 1965 (National Security File, Country File, Vietnam, box 197, LBJ Library).

7. John Roche to Lyndon Johnson, 26 May 1967 (White House Central Files, Confidential File, ND, box 73, LBJ Library). Johnson wrote his comment on Roche's memo.

8. Johnson to Ramsey Clark, 3 October 1967 (Diary Backup, box 80, LBJ Library).

9. Sidney Verba and Richard A. Brody, "Participation, Policy Preferences, and the War in Vietnam," *Public Opinion Quarterly* 34 (fall 1970): 329; Sidney Verba, Richard A. Brody, Edwin B. Parker, Norman H. Nie, Nelson W. Polsby, Paul Ekman, and Gordon S. Black, "Public Opinion and the War in Vietnam," *American Political Science Review* 61 (June 1967): 325–26.

10. Harlan Hahn, "Correlates of Public Sentiments about War: Local Referenda on the Vietnam Issue," *American Political Science Review* 64 (December 1970): 1190–92.

11. McGeorge Bundy to Johnson, 10 November 1967 (Vietnam Reference File, box 1, LBJ Library).

12. Ward Churchill and Jim Vander Wall, *The* COINTELPRO *Papers: Documents from the FBI's Secret Wars Against Domestic Dissent* (Boston: South End Press, 1990), p. 184.

13. Jeff Jones, interview.

14. Stephen Hess to John Ehrlichman, 28 July 1969 (White House Special Files, Krogh, box 60, Nixon Project).

15. Raymond Price, *With Nixon* (New York: Viking, 1977), p. 154.

16. On official discussions on "the youth problem," see particularly boxes 57, 66 and 69 of Egil Krogh's files in the White House Special Files, Nixon Project.

17. John Dean, *Blind Ambition: The White House Years* (New York: Pocket Books, 1977), p. 19.

18. H. R. Haldeman, interview.

19. William Watts, interview.

20. *New York Times*, 24 September 1981.

21. Ray Price, interview.

22. Action Memorandum to John Ehrlichman, 24 June 1969 (White House Special Files, Krogh, box 57, Nixon Project).

23. Haldeman's notes of 3 November 1969, meeting with Nixon (White House Special Files, Haldeman, box 40, Nixon Project).

24. Lawrence Higby to Jeb Magruder, 21 October 1969 (White House Special Files, Haldeman, box 208, Nixon Project).

25. Paul Hoffman, *Moratorium: An American Protest* (New York: Tower Publications, 1970), p. 34.

26. See White House Special Files, Dean, box 81, Nixon Project.

27. Haldeman to William Rogers, 16 October 1969 (White House Special Files, Haldeman, box 130, Nixon Project).

28. Jonathan Schell, *The Time of Illusion* (New York: Vintage Books, 1976), pp. 56–57.

29. Haldeman, interview.

30. *Ibid.*

31. Seymour Hersh, *The Price of Power: Kissinger in the Nixon White House* (New York: Summit Books, 1983), p. 196n.

32. Joseph Califano to Johnson, 15 November 1967 (White House Central Files, HU, box 60, LBJ Library).

33. Melvin Laird, interview.

34. Richard Peterson and John Bilorusky, *May 1970: The Campus Aftermath of Cambodia and Kent State* (Carnegie Commission on Higher Education, 1971), p. xi.

35. Alexander Heard to Richard Nixon, 19 June 1970 (White House Special Files, Confidential Files, HU, box 36, Nixon Project).

36. *Washington Post*, 8 May 1970.

37. Bruce Oudes, ed., *From the President; Richard Nixon's Secret Files* (New York: Harper and Row, 1989), pp. 128, 133; *Washington Post*, 10 May 1970; "Nixon," PBS television program.

38. Anthony Lake, interview.

39. Nick Akerman to Files, 26 July 1973 (Watergate Special Prosecution Force records, Fielding break-in, box 20, National Archives).

40. Haldeman, interview.

41. *New York Times*, 24 September 1981.

42. Charles Colson to Dick Howard, 4 May 1971 (White House Special Files, Colson, box 129, Nixon Project).

43. Ray Price, interview.

44. *Washington Post*, 3 May 1971.

45. *Newsweek*, 7 December 1970; Colonel Robert D. Heinl, Jr., "The Collapse of the Armed Forces," *Armed Forces Journal*, 7 June 1971 (reprint), p. 9.

46. Heinl, "Collapse," p. 14; David Cortright, *Soldiers in Revolt: The American Military Today* (Garden City, N.Y.: Anchor Press/Doubleday, 1975), p. 37.

47. Heinl, "Collapse," p. 3.

48. Paul Nitze, interview; Daniel Moynihan to Nixon, 19 August 1969 (White House Special Files, Krogh, box 57, Nixon Project).

49. Curt Smith, *Long Time Gone: The Years of Turmoil Remembered* (South Bend, Ind.: Icarus Press, 1982), p. 217.

50. Jim Jones to Johnson, 31 October 1967 (Meeting Notes File, box 2, LBJ Library).

51. Lady Bird Johnson, *A White House Diary* (New York: Holt, Rinehart and Winston, 1970), p. 714.

52. Thomas Moorer, interview.

53. Minutes of 18 September 1968, cabinet meeting (Cabinet Papers, box 15, LBJ Library).

54. Moynihan to Nixon, 19 August 1969 (White House Special Files, Krogh, box 57, Nixon Project).

55. Haldeman, interview.

56. Robert Brown to Nixon, 17 March 1969 (White House Special Files, Krogh, box 69, Nixon Project).

57. Price, interview.

58. Price, *With Nixon*, pp. 143, 151, 152.

59. Ibid., p. 154; Price, "Thoughts on Dealing with Youthful Unrest," 2 October 1969 (White House Special Files, Krogh, box 66, Nixon Project).

60. Henry Kissinger, *White House Years* (Boston: Little, Brown, 1979), p. 510.

61. Roger Morris, *Uncertain Greatness: Henry Kissinger and American Foreign Policy* (New York: Harper and Row, 1977), p. 169; Morris, interview.

62. Lake, interview.

63. Kissinger, *White House Years*, pp. 297, 299, 301–302.

64. Lake, interview.

65. Melvin Laird, interview.

66. Ronald Ziegler, interview.

67. George Christian, interview.

68. Moorer, interview.

69. Richard Goodwin, *Remembering America* (Boston: Little, Brown, 1988), pp. 402, 404.

70. Jones to Johnson, 4 November 1967 (Meeting Notes File, box 2, LBJ Library).

71. Goodwin, *Remembering America*, p. 403.

72. CIA, "International Connections of the U.S. Peace Movement," 15 November 1967 (National Security File, Intelligence File, box 3, LBJ Library).

73. Minutes of 18 September 1968, cabinet meeting (Cabinet Papers, box 15, LBJ Library).

74. Richard Helms, interview.

75. Paul Warnke, interview.

76. Ramsey Clark, interview.

77. Marshall Green, interview.

78. *Washington Post*, 15 September 1971.

79. Craig McNamara, interview.

80. John Ehrlichman, interview.

81. Paul Nitze, interview.

82. Dean Rusk as told to Richard Rusk, *As I Saw It* (New York: Norton, 1990), p. 420.

83. Lake, interview.

84. Hersh, *Price of Power*, p. 131; Watts, interview.

85. Warnke, interview.

86. Green, interview.

87. For fuller discussion of the antiwar movement's impact on U.S. policies in Vietnam, see Wells, *War Within*, pp. 4–5, 105, 151, 152–53, 154, 155–57, 158, 252, 254–57, 288, 289, 290, 308, 326, 345, 377–79, 397, 415, 434–35, 463, 470, 512–13, 535, 541, 562–63, 579–80.

88. Clark Clifford, interview.

89. Clifford, "A Viet Nam Reappraisal: The Personal History of One Man's View and How It Evolved," *Foreign Affairs* 47 (July 1969), p. 612.

90. Harry McPherson, interview.

91. Helms, interview.

92. *Ibid.*

93. John Oakes, interview.

94. *Ibid.*

95. "American Public Opinion and U.S. Foreign Policy" poll sponsored by Chicago Council on Foreign Relations.

Lyndon Johnson and the Roots of Contemporary Conservatism

Tom Wicker

In 1990, several surviving members of Lyndon Johnson's White House staff met at the LBJ Library in Austin, Texas, to commemorate the twenty-fifth anniversary of his inaugural as president in his own right. As a correspondent who had covered the Johnson White House and knew most of those attending, I took a minor part—though never feeling quite comfortable in that devoted company.

One night a group of us gathered in a hotel lobby to talk about—naturally—the inimitable LBJ. Douglass Cater, by then a college president but formerly a journalist and a member of Johnson's White House staff, expressed puzzlement at what we all knew to be plain fact.

"Why do so many people hate him so much? After all he did for this country. Why do they hate him?"

I broke the ensuing silence with a conventional answer. "Doug," I said, "it's the war. They hate him because of the war."

No one in the group disputed this, but the words hardly were out of my mouth before I sensed their inadequacy. Not that they were wrong. In the 1960s, when young people dogged the president everywhere he went with

> Hey, hey, LBJ!
> How many kids
> did you kill today?

many Americans did hate "Johnson's war," as in the last years of his five in office they had called the carnage in Vietnam. American participation in the war in Vietnam actually had begun, with national approval—or indifference, interpreted in Washington as approval—during the Kennedy administration. But few, then or now, blamed JFK, while many hated Lyndon Johnson.

By 1967, as the body count rose on both sides and the body bags piled up in America, the president's promise of eventual victory seemed empty to millions of his countrymen, and his insistence that the war had to go on appeared stubborn, senseless, and, in a favorite word of the time, "unresponsive." Nor did he or any of his associates ever make an adequate, coherent, believable case as to why the war had to be fought and an elusive victory endlessly pursued. By the end of his term, the man who just four years earlier had won an epic landslide over Barry Goldwater and who had confidently considered himself the heir to Franklin Roosevelt was so unpopular that he risked public embarrassment and even physical attack if he spoke anywhere but on a military base, where discipline could be enforced.

Many Americans opposed the war, and many did hate Lyndon Johnson because of it. Probably an equal number, however, continued to *support* the war—some because they could not conceive of the most powerful country on earth *losing* to a Third World country, others because they remembered the supposedly applicable lesson of World War II that "aggression" had to be stopped at its start, and quite a few because they were loyal if unhappy Democrats standing by their party and their President. And of course there were those who had sons, brothers, husbands, or fathers risking their lives in the rice paddies.

By 1969, moreover, when Johnson left office, the "sixties" culture—represented by chanting, long-haired, dope-smoking, draft-dodging "kids" (as an older generation and Johnson himself usually saw them)—was beginning its long fade into age and futility and reluctant acceptance of the world as it was, and is.

Despite the costs in money and popularity of a divisive and ill-understood war in Vietnam, Johnson's victory in 1964 and the great Democratic liberal majorities he carried into Congress were responsible for the Voting Rights Act of 1965, which transformed the country. Within three weeks of the passage of the act, for instance, federal registrars put tens of thousands of southern

---

TOM WICKER was the White House correspondent of the *New York Times* during the Kennedy administration, and covered the murder of the president in Dallas in 1963. He became the *Times*'s Washington bureau chief in the years after Lyndon Johnson's election as president. From 1966 until his retirement at the end of 1991, he was a political columnist for the *Times* op-ed page. He has written for all leading American magazines and is the author of ten novels and five books of nonfiction, including *Kennedy without Tears; JFK & LBJ: The Influence of Personality upon Politics;* and *One of Us: Richard Nixon and the American Dream.* He lives in Rochester, Vermont, with his wife, Pamela Hill, a former television executive with ABC-TV and CNN.

blacks on voting rolls from which they had been excluded by force and guile for decades. Within three years, black voter registration in Mississippi, the most repressive southern state, increased from 6 precent to 44 percent. Lyndon Johnson's Voting Rights Act alone, changing U.S. politics forever, represented a social and statistical success hard to deny. But that was not all.

LBJ's War on Poverty, though underfunded from the start and plagued by political disruption in the cities, nevertheless sharply reduced in its short-lived existence the number of people living in poverty in the United States—from a shocking 18 percent in 1960 to about 12 percent in 1969. By 1972, that figure would be down to 9 percent, as a Republican administration continued some Great Society programs—though, sadly, this progress later slowed and was reversed.

Cutting through a legislative logjam that dated back to the Truman administration of the late 1940s, Johnson and his majorities even effected a veritable revolution in American health care, implementing Medicaid and Medicare. Other programs started in the Johnson years resulted in more money for education, cleaner air, purer water, more consumer protection, the rescue of endangered species, federal aid for the arts and humanities (which did not become a target of conservative ire until recent years)—even highway beautification and the retreat, at least in some areas, of the ubiquitous advertising billboard.

So why *did* Americans hate a president who had accomplished so much, changed the country so remarkably? Why did they hate him more in 1990, when Doug Cater asked his question, than they had in 1969, when LBJ went home to die in Texas, leaving the White House to Richard Nixon—a man who would be hated, too, for far different reasons. And why do they hate Lyndon Johnson still?

That night in Austin and on many later occasions, I reflected on Cater's question and on Johnson's war as well as his successes. Finally, it came to me that—paradoxically, perhaps even tragically—Johnson's splendid achievements, particularly in gains for African Americans, had carried also the seeds of his fate. In the transformation he sought for the United States was to be found solid evidence why Lyndon Baines Johnson—who had seemed a giant astride the earth in 1964 and 1965, but who became a mere mortal driven from office in 1969—remains today one of the least popular presidents in memory (including Richard Nixon), and perhaps the least popular of all strong presidents of great achievement.

It is not an unusual presidential story—landslide reelection brings overconfidence, hence trouble. Roosevelt's forty-six-state victory over Alf Landon in 1936 led him to the ill-fated court-packing plan that almost ruined his administration. Nixon's huge reelection victory over George McGovern in 1972 caused him to underestimate and thus to "stonewall" the threat of the Watergate offenses that forced his resignation in 1974. Had Ronald Reagan not so decisively defeated Walter Mondale in 1984, it's arguable that Reagan would not have lowered his political guard against the near-fatal "Iran-Contra scandal" of his second term.

A "squeaker" election in 1964 might have restrained even Lyndon Johnson's ebullience. As it was, the passage of the Civil Rights Act in 1964—a feat that it was widely believed John Kennedy could not have achieved—followed by LBJ's huge victory over Goldwater undoubtedly encouraged him, as he headed into a term of his own, to push a program even the title of which—the "Great Society"—was characteristically grandiose. But it was not, as the civil rights victory had been, a response to significant public demand. The Great Society was, instead, the product of the president's own vision, dreams, and political ambition to surpass or equal his model, Franklin Roosevelt, in improving the lives of the American people.

After a successful year in office as Kennedy's successor, and his landslide victory over Goldwater, Johnson was in 1965 at the pinnacle of his power. A big man physically, Johnson also had a Texas-sized ego, which was actually a form of compensation for an innate sense of inferiority derived from an inadequate education, a western impression of eastern intellectual dominance, and the damaging comparisons frequently made between him and the sophisticated Kennedy. But no one questioned the political brilliance—some called it mere craftiness—which Johnson often had demonstrated in his years as Senate majority leader. And no one doubted his powerful will and ambition.*

As president elected in his own right, with vast experience in the ways of Washington, Johnson still was a driven, somewhat insecure westerner, openly contemptuous, of and secretly envious of all things Ivy League. He believed he had much to prove, not just that he could do the job, but that he could do it better than JFK, perhaps even better than Franklin Roosevelt. He believed he could not only win the war Kennedy had started, but he could also complete the national transformation unfulfilled by Roosevelt's New Deal. The nation

---

*Old Democrats, like Sam Rayburn, another Texan and for many years the respected Speaker of the House, were amazed when LBJ accepted second place on Kennedy's ticket—but later Johnson was given credit for carrying the South in the 1960 election and making possible a Democratic victory. During the new young president's "thousand days" in office, LBJ kept himself cautiously—and uncharacteristically—in the background.

could have "guns and butter" and Lyndon Johnson was determined that he would be the president to prove it.

The Great Society was to become a major factor in the public image of an imperious, often arrogant president single-handedly trying to remake the nation. Unfortunately, Lyndon Johnson's paternalistic specifications for the re-making of the nation—particularly in racial matters—took perhaps too cautious a note of American antipathy to precipitate change. Even so, his vision did not always represent how the country wished to remake itself. Worse, the Great Society deeply offended those who saw no pressing need for the country to be remade at all.

Another fateful consequence of his 1964 landslide for LBJ was that it may have aided—it certainly did not impede—the election of Robert Kennedy as a Democratic senator from New York. Many of those who had supported his slain brother shifted their political allegiance to the younger Kennedy and followed him unquestionably. Lyndon Johnson—as sensitive as a virgin about his po-litical flanks—therefore was confirmed in his only slightly paranoid view that Robert Kennedy was a sworn enemy out to reclaim the presidency so brutally stripped from his brother in 1963.

Robert Kennedy was a charismatic man whose grief and growth in the years following John Kennedy's murder brought him an almost fanatic following, devoted not only to a "restoration" of the rightful heir to the White House but also to "Bobby" himself. His passionate commitment to poor and disadvantaged Americans was seen by his followers as more genuine than LBJ's ballyhooed Great Society. Commitment, personality, and family heritage came together to create Robert Kennedy's army of aficionados. Nor was he ever, in Johnson's vice presidential *or* presidential years, personally devoted to LBJ, his brother's old rival. The animosity—amounting sometimes to hatred—between Robert Kennedy and Lyndon Johnson and their partisans divided Democrats and diluted the party support a president usually could have expected.

The split was, in fact, already made and waiting to widen. In 1960, John F. Kennedy had not been the universal choice of his party. An indifferent sena-tor, young and relatively untried, a Roman Catholic at a time when no one of his religion ever had won the White House, suspect (by Eleanor Roosevelt and the *New York Times*, among others) as a closet supporter of Joe McCarthy, the son of an unpopular father, and not well known personally to party veterans, JFK had at one time been opposed by Harry Truman, challenged by Adlai Stevenson and Lyndon Johnson (who had aroused Robert Kennedy's lasting resentment), and viewed without enthusiasm by Speaker Sam Rayburn. Yet, John Kennedy bested the old-line Democratic Party and seized its presidential nomination mostly by his personal attractiveness and by running well in selected state primaries (a relatively new tactic in 1960). Then, in 1961, the new president surrounded himself with faces unfamiliar to old-line Democrats, including those of his brother Robert as attorney general and Robert McNamara as secretary of defense, rather than rewarding party regulars.

Despite these affronts, victory, as JFK liked to say, has "a thousand fathers," and the Democrats quickly adopted a victorious son. Especially because he had defeated the despised "Tricky Dick" Nixon and was personally appealing, Kennedy became a popular party leader as well as president. Still, most of the Democrats who came to Washington with JFK in 1961 bore little resemblance to the party of Roosevelt and Truman, which had been out of power for the eight Eisenhower years and whose chosen leader would have been Lyndon Johnson of Texas.

After Kennedy's assassination in 1963, when LBJ did ascend from the vice presidency to the White House, many more traditional Democrats, while sincerely mourning Kennedy, felt that they and their real leader finally had assumed their rightful positions. As the *Times* Washington Bureau chief in 1965, I was implored by a group of the wives of these traditional Democrats to use my supposed influence to persuade the former Margaret Truman to overcome her dislike of Washington and attend Johnson's inaugural, as a sort of celebration of the return of the old Democratic Party. She was the wife of the *Times* managing editor, my boss. She finally did attend with her elderly father, Harry Truman—but not because of anything I did.

To Robert Kennedy, however, and to his legions of followers, LBJ was perceived as the usurper, and a crude and unworthy one at that. By 1966, the personal and party split was real and virulent, as Johnson pushed his Great Society bills through Congress and Kennedy sought a political role of his own. Though at first resisting frequent suggestions that he run against Johnson in 1968, Kennedy sharply questioned some details of the president's policies—for instance, whether the federal money that Great Society legislation would make newly available to schools really was the key to improved education.

In retrospect, we now can see that by 1966 Lyndon Johnson was in deep political trouble, which had little to do with Robert Kennedy and went largely unrecognized by the American public, the press, and perhaps even by the seemingly powerful president himself. Even the monumental Voting Rights Act, in a sense, had quickly rebounded against him. On August 11, 1965, just five days after he signed that measure, racial riots exploded in Watts, a largely black section of Los Angeles. Its poor black residents did not riot or loot because of the Voting Rights Act; but with the racial outburst coming so soon after the ceremony in the East Room, millions of shocked whites associated the two. The act somehow, it seemed, must have freed the impulse of the mob—the black mob.

Reporters particularly remember the Watts riot as a sharp change from the violence they had become accustomed to in the South. In Birmingham, for instance, shelter from danger would be offered to journalists by blacks, but in Watts, refuge for the press, if any, was to be had mostly from whites. Reporters' observations are symbolically significant, because violence, once the tactic of white segregationists, seemed to become in Watts the new resort of blacks, who had once followed the nonviolent ethic the Reverend Martin Luther King, Jr., had borrowed from Gandhi. Daniel Patrick Moynihan, the social science professor who later became a Democratic senator from New York, has written that Watts "shattered, probably forever, the image of non-violent suffering" by blacks. However justified the riots may have been—and many studies concluded that racial disturbances in Watts and elsewhere were caused primarily by black rage boiling over in white-imposed, white-dominated black slums—Watts caused whites to see blacks less as long-suffering victims than as threatening invaders of what had been a privileged white world.

Nor was Watts an isolated incident. That riot began a veritable war in the United States, little better understood and even more visible than the one in Southeast Asia. Combat troops were sent to both; television images of each dominated the home TV screen, and many illusions survived neither Vietnam nor the so-called "long hot summer" (actually several summers) of race riots in hundreds of American cities.

By the late 1960s urban warfare was a familiar facet of American life. So was the Black Power movement, reinforcing with its clenched-fist symbol and defiant rhetoric growing white fears of black violence. Both riots and rhetoric alienated whites who had appeared sympathetic to the non-violent civil rights movement in the 1950s and earlier 1960s—whites who had voted in 1964 for Lyndon Johnson and the Democrats. A common white complaint of those times was that Negroes, as blacks still were most often called, showed no "gratitude" for all that been "given" them, as if their civil and voting rights were gifts within the power of white citizens to grant. "They haven't moved an inch," a *Times* colleague told me resentfully. He had been and still considered himself a strong supporter of the civil rights movement. Hadn't he and others done what was asked of them? What more did these people want?

Only a year after Watts, in the summer of 1966, Martin Luther King, Jr.— for the first time taking the civil rights movement to the North—met defeat in his campaign for open housing reforms in Chicago. Mayor Richard Daley was in no mood to make concessions to his city's huge black population, most of whose leaders he had co-opted, and he had the political power and a tough police force to back up his determination. That year, too, Lyndon Johnson's open housing bill, though it passed the House, was stonewalled in the Senate—the first of the Great Society bills to meet strong resistance. Significantly, that opposition was led by Illinois Republican Everett McKinley Dirksen, the same smooth-tongued Dirksen (known as "the wizard of ooze") who in 1964 had mustered the conservative support that assured passage of the Civil Rights Act in the teeth of a southern filibuster. In September 1966, signaling that he had felt a change in the public mood, Dirksen helped kill the open housing bill in a Congress no longer subservient to LBJ. The brief triumph of the civil rights movement was coming to an end.

It was not only Watts and the succeeding "long hot summer" riots that brought the movement's demise; nor was it King's invasion of Chicago, or even the shock and fear with which whites viewed the militants of the Black Power movement. It was all these developments, together with perhaps the single most important cause: the failed national expectation—unrealistic and even naive but widespread—that only the formerly segregated South would be much affected by civil rights legislation.

By the autumn of 1966, Gallup poll figures depicted a swiftly rising "white backlash." In 1964, 72 percent of non-southern whites had told Dr. Gallup's questioners that the Johnson administration's pace in establishing civil rights for blacks was "about right" or too slow. Two years later, in an astonishing reversal, more than half of all whites responding to a Gallup poll believed Lyndon Johnson and the Democrats were pushing blacks' civil rights too far, too fast. Other opinion surveys found as many as three-fourths of white voters sharing the view that blacks were being "given" too much, too soon, and too often at the expense of whites.

That was the real answer to Doug Cater's sorrowful question. Virtually every important element of Lyndon Johnson's Great Society—following on the Civil Rights and Voting Rights acts—had come to seem part of a program of aid and comfort for the black minority, rather than an effort to lift Americans of every race onto a higher social and economic plane. Johnson's great consensus, the "great tent" under which he had proposed to shelter the people of America and advance their welfare, was splintering into antagonistic factions on the ancient rock of the race question—as ever-present and dangerous under the deceptive surface of the 1960s as any reef under the smooth waters of an apparently innocent sea.

It only remained for the backlash to be officially certified at the polls, and it didn't take long, after Dirksen and other conservatives gave evidence of backlash pressures in the Senate in September 1966. In the nonpresidential elections that November, resurgent Republicans gained forty-seven House and three Senate seats, and elected eight new Republican governors—including the old movie actor Ronald Reagan in California. Johnson and the Democrats retained control of Congress, but the great liberal majorities that had enacted the Voting Rights Act of 1965, the Elementary and Secondary Education Act, Medicare and Medicaid, had been shattered. Like Humpty-Dumpty, they could never be put together again.

The Republican recovery of 1966 that destroyed the Johnson majorities and brought Ronald Reagan to the national stage was also an important "comeback" step for Richard Nixon. The narrowly defeated presidential candidate of 1960 had designated himself leader of the Republican Party's 1966 national campaign, led it effectively, and gained a strong position from which to seek the Republican presidential nomination in 1968.

The Republican gains did *not*, however, result mostly from the war in Vietnam, as is often and too glibly asserted. In 1966 the war *was* unpopular, as by then was the imperious Johnson himself, though neither had reached the depths of unpopularity that lay ahead. Both were political handicaps for the Democrats and especially for those old-line liberal candidates who out of party loyalty or ritual patriotism, or both, doggedly supported the president and his war.

That war was not, however, in 1966 the bloody monster it was to become. Opposition to it would not have caused as stunning a defeat as the Democrats suffered unless most Republican candidates and the party itself had offered the clear alternative of a quick end to an unpopular war. In fact, most Republicans in 1966—notably Nixon, Reagan, and New York Governor Nelson Rockefeller— supported the war. They took only the quasi-"me too" position that they could manage it better and win it sooner than Lyndon Johnson and the Democrats. Few Republicans even came near to pledging an immediate end to or a quick withdrawal from the war.

Nixon, for example, made it clear that he was for outright military victory. He did say he had a plan (not, as popularly remembered, a "secret plan") to "end the war and win the peace"—but he was clearly understood to mean that he opposed Johnson's policies ("suggesting that we only want peace," he said, "that we want to negotiate, has the effect of prolonging the war rather than bringing it to a close"), not the necessity for waging and winning the war. Only five days before the 1966 election, Nixon also declared that a "communist victory would most certainly be the result of 'mutual withdrawal'"—which a Johnson statement had seemed to suggest might someday be forthcoming. Republicans—certainly their leader—clearly were not offering peace; they seemed, rather, to be promising a continued, perhaps intensified, war.

No doubt enough Americans already opposed a struggle that seemed endless and unjustified, and resented the president who waged it, to contribute a number of votes to the Republican victory—rebuking Johnson and the Democrats even if they had been given little reason to prefer the Republicans. But it seems plausible to conclude that the major cause of the remarkable Republican recovery, only two years after Goldwater's devastating defeat, was the white backlash—the growing resentment of the many white voters to whom it appeared by November 1966 that Lyndon Johnson's Great Society was designed primarily to "give" black Americans equality with whites. Few were prepared for that.

Americans had been willing to accept the notion that blacks should have equal *opportunity*. Many considered it only fair, for example, that Jackie Robinson should be able to play in the major baseball leagues if he could hit, run, and throw well enough, or that black children in Alabama and Mississippi should be able to attend decent schools. But Robinson was not taking an infielder's job away from most whites, and he had only been allowed what he deserved—a chance, not a guaranteed starter's job. And to the average white American, allowing those black kids in the South to enter decent schools did not mean they would attend them in Cleveland or Indianapolis or Chicago or "my neighborhood."

That was the rub. Civil rights, equal opportunity, voting rights—all that was well enough, even desirable, as long as the only whites to be disturbed were southern segregationists, who no doubt deserved what they got. But few whites outside the South expected that their schools were to be integrated, that their neighborhoods might not remain all white, that their property values would be endangered, or that their cities could be burned by ungrateful blacks.

Nor had they meant for the "equality of opportunity" they had been persuaded to "give" (after denying it for centuries) to be interpreted by "pointy-headed bureaucrats in Washington" (a phrase George Wallace was to make familiar) as promising equality of results. The hulking leader of the pointy-headed bureaucrats, however, had personally proclaimed to Congress in his Texas accent that "we shall overcome," identifying himself indelibly with black and white civil rights activists who had made those words their hymn. And he had made his further intentions all too clear in his Howard University commencement address in June 1965: "It is not enough just to open the gates of opportunity. All our citizens must have the ability to walk through those gates. . . . We seek . . . not just equality as a right and a theory but equality as a fact and equality as a result."

Did that mean it was "not enough" for Jackie Robinson to have had his chance? Did the Dodgers have to guarantee him a place in the lineup even if he couldn't hit a major league curve ball?

Of course it did *not* mean that. But as the Great Society fell piece by piece into place, it began to look to more and more whites as a program not meant for everyone but instead to give African Americans social and economic *equality*. Just when rioting and Black Power talk were causing many whites to see blacks as threatening, Johnson and his Great Society seemed to be providing them with all sorts of unearned privileges—in effect, rewarding them for Watts and other violent acts of ingratitude, or perhaps bribing them not to riot again or to spout offensive Black Power rhetoric.

The so-called War on Poverty was prominent among those programs that whites believed to be designed for blacks, rather than for all Americans, and that, in the long term, proved more disruptive than fruitful. The "war" was formally declared by Congress in August 1964, when it approved the Johnson administration's Equal Opportunity Act, setting up, among other things, a Community Action Program. The CAP was to mobilize community resources to fight poverty, and thus called for the "maximum feasible participation" of the poor themselves in developing and directing antipoverty efforts. Though a good idea on paper and in committee, community action as it developed in the cities proved politically and racially divisive.

Community action not only empowered poor blacks and other minorities long without political power, it also provided a political base and federal money to community action agencies. Both functions threatened existing political institutions, such as mayors, boards of aldermen, and established social welfare agencies, and set up organizations that would be dominated by racial militants and even Black Power extremists. It was not long before intracity political warfare, stimulated not least by community action, was antagonizing mayors and other traditional Democratic Party mainstays. In effect, this encouraged the white public to see antipoverty efforts as mostly racial programs, and these were particularly resented in cities torn apart by racial violence.

While its programs resulted in white and married blue-collar workers' real median earnings rising by 15 percent between 1965 and 1969, the view persisted that the War on Poverty was essentially waged on behalf of blacks. Johnson had rejected an even more sweeping antipoverty program based on structural economic change to create more jobs and benefit *all* the poor, fearing that would have been impossible politically, owing to public resistance to radical change and congressional sensitivity to that resistance. LBJ's "war" instead targeted training and education for people who had little or no ability to get and keep jobs. Though more whites lived in poverty than blacks, those who most needed this kind of job training were among the urban, uneducated poor, who were heavily black. By 1968, blacks held 59 percent of Job Corps slots and 47 percent of those in the Neighborhood Youth Corps. No wonder these appeared to watchful whites to be programs *for* blacks.

The task of training the urban poor was more complicated than anticipated. Many training enrollees could not read at all; half could not read or do arithmetic above fifth-grade level. The disciplines of job holding were unknown to many, perhaps most. Graduates either didn't find jobs or couldn't hold them, leaving many disappointed blacks with the bitter impression that job training was just another white deception. Moreover, 1960s-style job training concentrated on skills needed in the already crowded service sector, so for those who did manage to find scarce jobs, wages tended to be low and their status lower. Support for job training fell with the failure rate of its heavily black trainees, and as its dropout rate increased. White prejudice about "shiftless blacks" seemed confirmed, and white resentment of the programs rose, at the same time as urban rioting was bringing new demands for "law and order" legislation.

The War on Poverty also had been projected as virtually cost free, since Johnson and his aides believed that economic expansion would underwrite the new programs. Even if that had proved true in the aggregate—it never did, owing much to expenditures for the war in Vietnam—economic growth tended to be uneven and to do the least for those who needed it the most. That was one reason the poverty war was so inadequately funded. In the three years 1965–68, the Office of Economic Opportunity spent an average of only $50 to $65 annually for each person in poverty, including administrative costs. In 1967 alone, in sharp contrast, it cost the United States $300,000 for each Viet Cong killed.

The public impression, nevertheless, was that the liberal Johnson administration was spending huge amounts, mostly on failing efforts to reward or bribe or uplift blacks, or all three. The truth was that the 1966 OEO budget, $1.5 billion, represented about 1.5 percent of the entire federal budget. OEO's first-year funding had been for half that, $800 million. That year, the War on Poverty touched less than 1 percent of the millions of Americans, white and minority, who actually lived in poverty. A truly effective "war," some experts have estimated, might have cost $30 billion a year. African American labor leader A. Philip Randolph's proposed (but never adopted) ten-year "freedom budget" to end poverty totaled $185 billion.

Worse than these statistics, particularly for Lyndon Johnson's lasting reputation, was the overexpectation in which he and many Americans indulged. One particularly egregious example was his repeatedly stated belief, shared by every civil rights leader I remember and by many in Johnson's congressional majorities, that political empowerment alone could bring about equality. Give blacks the vote, remove barriers to their political participation—so the argument went—and they could open their own path to economic success. That suggested that whites outside the South needed to do very little and certainly need not effect fundamental change in the economy. But thirty years later, black political empowerment has long been substantially achieved, yet more than half of American blacks still live below middle-class economic standards. Political power has been nowhere near enough.

Overpromising and underfunding plagued the Great Society in general. But linkage of Medicare and Medicaid to racial politics was less likely than in the case of antipoverty programs, even in a public mind grown wary, in the late 1960s, of black demands. Both programs were immensely popular, graphic testimony to the U.S. public's hunger for the adequate access to health care they had so long been denied. In both, benefits were available to all eligible Americans, without regard to race. But in the post-Watts atmosphere, even Medicaid and Medicare engendered racial aspects not appreciated by all whites, particularly those in the South. In three years, from 1966 (when Medicare and Medicaid took effect) to 1969, the number of minority patients in hospitals rose by 30 percent. The number of minority doctors and dentists on hospital staffs increased as well. In the South, Title VI of the Civil Rights Act, banning racial discrimination in federally assisted programs, effectively if slowly ended any form of segregation in federally aided hospitals. This undoubtedly contributed to the southern political trend toward the Republican Party.

Medicare and Medicaid were part of Social Security. Thus, the 1967 Social Security amendments affected both and indirectly associated them with the antipoverty efforts widely regarded as racially aimed. That year, President Johnson requested an increase in Social Security benefits to the elderly, saying that a 15 percent rise would lift 1.4 million people—of all races—out of poverty. He coupled this with a proposal to extend Medicare to 1.5 million disabled persons—of all races—under age 65. Thus, Social Security would be partially diverted from old-age assistance to an antipoverty program. These 1967 amendments provided for a 13 percent increase in benefits, financed by increased Social

Security payroll taxes. But Congress rejected inclusion in Medicare of under-65 disabled persons. More immediately important than either of these (though the rise in benefits accelerated the long-term drain on Social Security reserves) was an effort to curb the growth of Aid to Families of Dependent Children (AFDC), whose recipients had doubled in number during the previous decade. This represented another congressional recognition of white backlash—if not to specific Great Society programs, then to the growth of "welfare" among blacks. Despite this growth, a "welfare culture" came to be seen as an unwarranted result of the Great Society.

One nonracial, nonhealth aspect of Medicare and Medicaid effected lasting change. These programs, as conceived and approved in the 1960s, were designed to improve *access* to medical care. No effort was made to address the *costs* of health care, because Johnson knew that any degree of cost control would have been characterized by opponents, most notably the American Medical Association, as "government control." That charge had been the political kiss of death for previous health-care legislation, and he was determined to avoid it—with long-lasting consequences. Without cost control and with no incentives for hospitals and doctors to keep costs down, both took quick advantage of the programs. Federal outlays for health care rose tenfold in the 1960s, while individual out-of-pocket costs for health services *dropped* by 15 percent. The rising costs of even popular programs paradoxically but inevitably led to their being attacked as an example of "wasteful welfare bureaucracy." Consequently, in the late 1960s, there was an administrative shift from increasing access to efforts at managerial efficiency, ultimately including forms of cost control. Such efforts continue today.

Federal aid to education, embodied after many years of failed efforts in Lyndon Johnson's Elementary and Secondary Education Act of 1965, was finally achieved through two political stratagems. First, the usual church-state objections were avoided by a shift from offering aid to *schools* to providing aid to *children*, particularly poor children in slums and rural areas. Second, the formula for distribution of the money was to be based ostensibly on the numbers of poor children per state. This meant, in practical political terms, that wealthier states already spending heavily on education would be rewarded. Without these approaches the legislation probably would have foundered as had all preceding bills, including the one introduced during the Kennedy administration. But the price of the distribution formula, hence of the legislation, was high. Eighty-one percent of the nation's poor children were concentrated in only 32 percent of its school districts, but districts in about 95 percent of the counties in the nation ultimately received federal aid.

Thus, legislative success was not so much targeted at the poor as achieved on the old, familiar principle of spreading the gravy around. Poor children received nowhere near the financial benefit originally promised—an effect compounded by the response of many recipient districts who used the money not to help ragged urchins but instead for tax relief and other benefits for middle-class voters and their children.

Several studies even raised the question—as did Robert Kennedy in the Senate—whether greater infusion of money was, in fact, the key to improved education. The 1966 Coleman Report found that "family background and socio-economic factors" were more important than what happened, or didn't, in the classroom. In 1967, a government report determined that "massive integration" was more important than money, a hopeless prescription in the era of race riots, Black Power, and the shortcomings of the War on Poverty. Once again, LBJ and the Great Society had made simplistic promises on a complex matter that could not be kept. The Education act, despite all the new and mostly needed federal money it provided for states and communities, was not going to open a high road to education, hence to economic success, for the nation's poor children.

For a while, however, the education act did serve to materially aid the process of school integration in the South, progress which had been almost non-existent since the *Brown v. Board of Education* decision in 1954. In 1965–66, 94 percent of southern black children still were enrolled in segregated schools. The Elementary and Secondary Education Act, combined with Title I of the Civil Rights Act, which prevented racial discrimination in federally aided programs, gave Washington the power to withhold funds to the many school districts insufficiently desegregated. Some districts hastened to desegregate enough to comply with the education act's requirements, but money for more than 60 southern school districts had to be withheld for noncompliance. In Chicago, where *de facto* segregation had left the city's schools in flagrant noncompliance, $34 million was also withheld. Mayor Daley protested with such potent political force that LBJ quickly ordered the Chicago funds restored. Southerners no doubt watched this surrender with a certain bitterness.

Whether owing to such inequities, or to stiffening southern resentment of "forced" integration, by 1967 the threat of a federal funds cutoff had little further effect in speeding school integration. Almost surely, however, Title I cutoffs did hasten the already progressing conversion of the former "solid South" from a Democratic to a Republican political stronghold. That transformation, of course, had promising effect on the gathering conservative movement that was about to win the White House for twenty of the next twenty-four years.

Again, the success for Great Society legislation—the new education act's infusion of federal money into education—bore within it the seeds of future problems for its progenitor and his party.

After rolling over Goldwater in 1964, LBJ lost little time in turning to urban affairs. His huge new congressional majorities pushed through a big housing bill, for the first time providing rental subsidies for low-income families and authorizing the construction of two hundred thousand units of public housing (of which all too few were built). In September, a Department of Housing and Urban Development (HUD) was established at cabinet level.

Meanwhile, that ubiquitous symbol of LBJ-style government, a task force composed of "the best and the brightest" was at work on the "urban problem." By September 1965 the president sent Congress an unusual "Demonstration Cities Program," accompanied by the characteristic Johnson overstatement that "nineteen sixty-six can be the year of rebirth for American cities." It proved, as has any later year, to be far from that. With somewhat greater candor, the final bill opened with the declaration that "Congress finds and declares that improving the quality of urban life is the most critical domestic problem facing the United States." To address that problem, the bill authorized numerous demonstration programs in cities of various sizes, meant to address all aspects of the urban environment. The federal government would pay up to 80 percent of the cost of each approved program.

The urban riots, stimulating public concern about the cities, provided political muscle for passage of this "Demonstration Cities" measure. Those riots, together with the rumblings of Black Power militants, the focus on urban blacks in the War on Poverty, and, probably, LBJ's appointment of Robert Weaver, a black, as secretary of HUD, caused many to think that this was another program for African Americans. In fact, Johnson, always sensitive to political symbolism, later renamed his program "Model Cities," because race riots had so often been called "demonstrations."

Aside from its racial identification, Model Cities ultimately suffered from many other problems that had limited Great Society efforts. Too little money was provided and, as the "model cities" concept came under political pressure, what money there was had to be divided among too many competing cities. By 1972, for instance, only 18 percent of community development funds had actually gone to poverty neighborhoods. The final bill provided money for traditional but largely discredited "urban renewal." To head off charges of "federal control," so little supervision was mandated that cities could and did use grant funds for irrelevant "urban" projects that did little to solve or ease real urban problems. Most of the recipient cities were Democratic strongholds, which caused Republicans to charge partisanship in the distribution of federal money. And of 118 cities that had suffered serious rioting by 1968, 69 received Model Cities grants—thus appearing to support charges that federal money was being used to "reward" rioters or "bribe" them not to riot again.

Crucially, the program, though intended to be comprehensive, was not designed to generate new jobs, though the loss of manufacturing and other employment in urban areas was a major cause of urban poverty. This deficiency reflected Johnson's determination that Great Society reforms were not to be so radical as to deprive or disadvantage important interests. He wanted to offend as few groups as possible, in order to maintain the supposed national "consensus" supporting his program. Again, the fundamental changes sought by Johnson did not involve major structural modifications of the economy, which in his view would not have been approved even by a heavily Democratic Congress.

No subject more occupied or frustrated Great Society planners than housing and urban affairs—and nothing more occupies or frustrates the nation today than the plight of its cities and their largely black ghettos, those blighted pools of joblessness, crime, and despair. Nor has any element of the persistent race problem been more persistent than housing segregation in the cities. Unfortunately, nothing as ambitious as the Great Society program is likely to be proposed, much less achieved, in today's mood of pinched economic concerns and sullen, if muted, backlash.

Jobs were a problem in another sense. The Model Cities legislation required grant programs to hire local minorities, though it carefully set no precise "quotas"; they had been banned in the 1964 Civil Rights Act. This requirement nevertheless appeared to support the idea that Model Cities, too, was a program to aid blacks. And in some cities, like Philadelphia, where the building trades were lily white by tradition, the provision was highly divisive politically.

When the summer of 1967 brought riots in more than 160 cities, Americans began to ask, "What has happened to all those antipoverty funds? All those promises?" The worst and most destructive of the riots, probably the worst of the entire era, erupted in Detroit. The Motor City lagged only behind New York and Chicago in antipoverty funds received since passage of the Economic Opportunity Act in 1964. Despite the infusion of money, black anger in Detroit was *still* focused on *de facto* segregation, poor housing, and education, problems with hostile police and white merchants, inadequate recreational facilities, and of course the disappearance of jobs—precisely the problems the Great Society and its War on Poverty were supposed to be addressing.

Few Americans, under the spell of LBJ's claims, realized that the Great Society lacked adequate funding and that many of its planned operations did not have enough time to accomplish their objectives—even if, given time and money, they could have performed as expected. The Detroit riot, graphically contradicting expectations, struck a serious blow at political support for the Great Society, and for Lyndon Johnson and the Democrats, even among Americans who had believed in the president and his programs.

The report of the Kerner Commission on Urban Disorders, commissioned by the president and released in March 1968, disappointed both him and an already largely disillusioned public. It detailed the dangers of continuing urban problems and projected a hefty price tag for an effective, long-term program to deal with the situation. *More* had to be done, the report said, than even the generally praiseworthy Great Society reforms had attempted, because "white racism" was so pervasive that the nation was "moving toward two societies, one black, one white—separate but unequal."

The public—at least the dominant white public—liked neither the indictment of white racism nor the costly prescription for change. What about the *Brown* decision and the Civil Rights and Voting Rights acts and all the Great Society efforts? What had happened to the idea that economic expansion was going to pay for everything? Or that black political empowerment would solve all racial problems?

For his part, President Johnson was miffed by what he saw as inadequate praise for him and the Great Society, and he scoffed at the idea that Congress, in view of the riots and the costs of the war, would approve a program as radical and expensive as the Kerner Report recommended. That report, indeed, may have been something of a "last straw" for a president who already thought he had been ill used and unappreciated.

That "bitch of a war on the other side of the world," as he had described Vietnam to Doris Kearns Goodwin, the war he had inherited and on which he had expended so much money, lives, and political capital, was going badly, offering little hope for victory anytime soon, causing rising dissent at home, and clearly about to bring his archenemy Robert Kennedy into the Presidential campaign.

Now the president's own commission on urban affairs was reporting that the grand schemes of the Great Society, perhaps the most comprehensive vision for national progress ever conceived by a president, had been so thwarted and limited that the reality has fallen far short of the vision. And all that a politically skilled president had done and planned for blacks would not be enough to prevent the kind of national division that Lyndon Johnson feared and hated.

By that spring of 1968, most of the Left was alienated by the war and much of the Right resented the struggle to achieve "equality in fact" for those at the bottom of the social and economic scales. Even what was left of the center—and of support for the Johnson administration—was being crushed between the converging forces of resistance to the war and opposition to the Great Society.

Less than a month after the Kerner Report's dire warning, with the war no nearer success or even conclusion than it had been for years, late on the night of March 31, 1968, Lyndon Johnson announced to an astounded nation that he would neither seek nor accept renomination for President. To many Americans, even those who already hated him, it was as if a giant had fallen.

Still, the Great Society had one last gasp. On his third try, after failures in 1966 and 1967, LBJ succeeded in pushing an open-housing bill through Congress. It prohibited discrimination in the sale or rental of housing, making it the first legislation of its kind in this century—hence as badly needed, perhaps more needed, than any Great Society reform. But Congress was still listening, with at least one ear, to the backlash; it added several antiriot provisions and softened its impact by denying funds to enforce open housing. A subsequent housing construction bill authorized 1.7 million units over three years at a cost of $5.3 billion, but was so influenced by the banking lobby that it more nearly underwrote developers' risks than provided better access to housing. It also authorized subsidies for mortgage and other lenders, rather than assisting poor borrowers. The Great Society, like Lyndon Johnson himself, was a spent force.

The true value of the Great Society may be that it focused American attention, for a while at least, on long-standing problems of race issues and poverty, particularly in the nation's troubled cities. It also provided a needed counter, again for a while, to the endemic American belief that anything was possible to a people who already had accomplished so much. Two world wars had been won. Through NASA, we had explored space and were preparing to send a man to the moon. If a proud and adventurous people could do that, while developing nuclear warheads and intercontinental missiles with which to defend what Lyndon Johnson liked to call "the free world," at the same time defeating communist aggression in Vietnam—as he claimed for too long—surely such a people could end poverty at home.

Humanity is not technology, however, and reform is not warfare. The unexpected but massive sociopolitical difficulties of eliminating poverty and elevating American, particularly urban, life soon were evident and overwhelming. And even though Johnson had warned that there would be no quick results, much of the nation wanted and expected just that—an American trait that the extravagantly American LBJ probably shared, despite his own warnings. His public rhetoric simply promised too much, for his program and for U.S. capacities, and the listening public was only too eager to believe him—at first. Later, in all-too-human fashion, the nation's violated credulity made them equally eager to blame this president, who had fulsomely and confidently promised a Great Society, to be had for practically nothing but the application of brains and willpower. Blame him they did, for a failure in no small part their own. Not only did they hold him accountable for the perceived failure of the over-sold Great Society, but far more bitterly, they held him accountable for his pre-sumed efforts to force "equality as a fact and equality as a result" on a people who did not really want either.

Three decades later, white Americans, including those with only faint knowl-edge of Great Society days, pay little more than lip service to the idea of a "color-blind" society of whites and blacks living together in true social and economic equality. But many resent the lingering, mostly anecdotal, and not necessarily accurate image of an overbearing LBJ—never personally popular in his own time, and less so in legend—whom they believe to have done more than any other president to force such a society down their throats.

Just to make sure they wouldn't forget after the passage of thirty years, Newt Gingrich of Georgia pointed out in 1994, in his inaugural remarks as the Re-publican Speaker of the House, that Johnson-led Democrats had been "the great-est leaders in fighting for an integrated America. It was the liberal wing of the Democratic Party that ended segregation." Honeyed words—with the sting of a bee.

The failure of the Great Society, or even the limited success plausibly claimed for it by some researchers, has had great repercussions through the years. Fol-lowing almost immediately on Johnson's "abdication" speech came the assas-sination of Martin Luther King, Jr., attributable to the Great Society only by its most virulent critics, which removed the most effective black leader of nonvio-lent action from the scene. King's murder ironically sparked off another dam-aging spasm of urban riots, this time reaching even into Washington, D.C., where fires burned within sight of the Capitol.

Robert Kennedy, who emerged as one of the most articulate antiwar spokes-men, despite his own and his brother's role in the Vietnam War's inception, fulfilled one of Johnson's deepest fears by belatedly running for president in 1968. Some of his closest associates do not believe, in hindsight, that Kennedy could have won the Democratic nomination despite Johnson's party control; but he would have been the strongest challenger at the party convention had he not been assassinated in June, following his victory in the California pri-mary. Robert Kennedy's fanatic following had already split Johnson's party, probably fatally, and his death, five years after his brother's, strengthened the widespread sense that only murder had torn the presidency from their hands—and delivered it to the usurper from Texas.

In what was left of the 1968 campaign, both the Republican presidential candidate, Richard Nixon (subtly), and the swaggering third-party maverick, George Wallace of Alabama (loudly), emphasized "law and order." Both attacked and derided the Great Society, even though Johnson had taken himself out of the race. Both also denounced the president's conduct of the war in Vietnam—but neither repudiated it. Voters could not have chosen Nixon or Wallace reasonably believing that either would stop the war or pull out of it. No doubt some did vote for one or the other in the belief that they were rebuking Johnson and the Democrats for a bloody, seemingly unwinnable war, or even in misguided fealty to the late Robert Kennedy.

Wallace campaigned widely and effectively, especially in riot-torn cities like Detroit, using code, and sometimes plain, words and flamboyant oratory to stimulate white fears and to castigate Johnson, the mainstream parties, and the federal government. He finished a relatively distant third, and it's not clear whether he took more votes from Democrats deserting the old liberal warhorse, Vice President Hubert Humphrey (who was Johnson's candidate) or from Republicans, who preferred Wallace's tough talk to Nixon's less blatant appeals to white attitudes.

Regardless of his loss, Wallace's campaign—third party or no—may have been the most important of the year, and certainly was one of the most consequential of the postwar period. It was instrumental in moving the country to the right, in making racial fears seem legitimate, and in speeding the national retreat from integration that marked the post–Great Society years. Far more than anything later done by the Watergate-crippled Nixon or by his pardoner, Gerald Ford, the Wallace campaign of 1968 paved the way for the election of Ronald Reagan twelve years later, and the fruition of right-wing conservatism's long climb to power.

Nixon with his "southern strategy" won the presidency—barely defeating Humphrey—not least because of his disguised racial appeals to the conservative, anti-LBJ South on such issues as school segregation. He could win and Wallace could have such profound political impact—though both supported the war—because white voters recoiled from Johnson and the Democrats on the plausible assumption that they and Humphrey would further promote the racial equality at which so much of the floundering Great Society had seemed to be aimed. With the riots still in the headlines, the unspoken but ever-potent race issue pervaded the minds of the voters and, only four years after the Democratic landslide of 1964, began the great swing to conservatism that marked the 1970s and brought Ronald Reagan to the White House.

As early as 1967, polls suggested that the "number one concern" of most respondents was fear that black gains would damage the well-being of whites. As the 1960s turned to the 1970s, busing and affirmative action sharpened that fear. The first was resented by white parents and some black families, for taking their children from neighborhood schools and busing them long distances to improve racial balance throughout a school district; the second heightened concerns about black competition in jobs and school applications and caused anger at (often mythological) tales of outrageous "preferences" for African Americans. Few whites stopped to consider that centuries of black repression—whites-only admissions policies, for instance—actually had constituted *de facto* "preferences" for whites that had left blacks far behind. Affirmative action was seen, particularly by those who felt threatened, as an unfair, even unconstitutional reward for a people who had burned cities, shouted black-power slogans, and shown no gratitude for being "given" the vote.

Low-income whites who could not afford private schools for their children and who feared that blacks would now take their places in institutions of higher learning were particularly offended by the "forced integration" and "reverse discrimination" they perceived in busing and affirmative action. Crime was increasing, too, much of it perpetrated by poor urban blacks against other poor urban blacks, but all of it scarily dramatized on the living room television screens. Welfare rolls were rising rapidly, and in the cities the newly noticed "underclass" teemed with idleness, drug addiction, prostitution, family breakdown, and out-of-wedlock births. The old order of things seemed to be falling apart, and few doubted the fundamental reason.

"We have to simply, calmly, methodically reassert American civilization," Newt Gingrich asserted in 1994—before *they* began to despoil it, he was widely understood to be saying.

Twelve years of Ronald Reagan's and George Bush's presidencies were underpinned by the conservatism originally spawned by the urban riots, the Great Society, and the ultimate national reaction against an integration policy that only for a brief period in the 1960s had seemed triumphant. It's not entirely fair, of course, to blame Lyndon Johnson for the Reagan and Bush eras or for the national mood that sustained them, any more than it's fair for a president to be reelected or retired owing to some economic result that only happened on his watch and over which he had little control. But the state of the economy *does* dominate presidential elections. And much of today's conservatism *does* have its roots in the soil of the Great Society and the "long, hot summer" its reforms not only failed to prevent but perhaps stimulated—at least as some Americans saw it and still see it.

Johnson left the White House in 1969 a tired and bitter old man who in his last few years railed against "that bitch of a war on the other side of the world" which had ruined his lofty plans. The conventional view, the one I gave Douglass Cater in 1990, is that he was right—the war in Vietnam, draining off funds and killing public support as well as too many Americans, ruined Lyndon Johnson. That view isn't wrong, but it is insufficient. Had an admittedly unpopular war not had a substratum of animosity to build upon, might not the often demonstrated capacity of Americans to "rally round the flag" and "support our boys" have come to Johnson's rescue? Even though neither the opposition party nor any demonstrable voting majority ever turned fully against the war, the combination of the substratum of animosity combined with overt antiwar sentiment became decisive. That substratum was composed of elements: LBJ's overwhelming and paternalistic personality, a blustery "I know best" approach compensating for his basic sense of inferiority, and the contrast of that looming, Texas-sized presence with cool, confident, and handsome John Kennedy; the growing belief of so many Americans—recorded in polls of the time—that Johnson and the Democrats were pushing too hard and too fast for black economic and social equality, at the expense of white society; and the riots, which demonstrated not only that the Great Society was an overblown failure (perhaps like Johnson himself?) but that its attempted reforms might even have contributed to the impatience and ingratitude of blacks.

Not for the first time, good intentions had failed to bring good results. And probably not for the last time, Americans had demonstrated their fear of fundamental change in the accustomed order of things—so much so that even a president who could dream of a Great Society thought he knew better than to propose radical steps to reach it. Just as LBJ's downfall was rooted in his achievements, so his splendid vision was frustrated by the limits he believed he had to impose on it.

Negroes No More

The Emergence of Black Student Activism

Karen K. Miller

In following the NAACP's own lawyers and social scientists, the Court in *Brown* dealt blacks an unwitting slight. . . . For *Brown* implied first, that black schools, whatever their physical endowments, could not equal white ones; second, that integration was a matter of a white benefactor and a black beneficiary. . . . The whole gamut of integrationist ideals—from *Brown* to busing to affirmative action—would incorporate this same condescending assumption: that contact with whites was necessary for black students to improve.

J. Harvie Wilkinson,
From Brown to Bakke (1976)

Most black guys who come here are on their own for the first time, and when you're on your own it's the first chance you really have to develop any sense of self or self-consciousness. But when white people want to be tutored by you in terms of how you are related to them in the world situation, then it is a matter of you wasting your time. You realize it's hard enough to deal with yourself and other black people and to try to figure out your place in the world. . . . [T]his is the essence of black consciousness: figuring out in your mind what you are to yourself and what you mean to the world in terms of its black population.

Glenn E. deChabert,
"On Being Black at Yale" (1969)

During the decade immediately following the Supreme Court's *Brown v. Board of Education* decision in 1954, assimilationist integration dominated civil rights discourse as well as strategies adopted to overcome racial inequality in the United States. Implicit in integrationist discourse was a "color blindness" that belied the historical evolution of racial politics and policy. Assimilationist idealism projected an invisibility of race in image and in language that emphasized the common humanity of blacks and whites, but it overlooked the centrality of race in post-*Brown* civil rights conflicts. Symbolic images of blacks and whites playing, working, praying, and singing together, oblivious to skin color, conveyed optimism about the possibilities for an interracial harmonic future. Rather than speak in terms of black and white, assimilationist integration employed a racially neutered lexicon of "disadvantaged," "underprivileged," and "less fortunate" to articulate a vision of "minority" absorption into the "American mainstream."

Within higher education, such optimism fueled predominantly white college and university efforts to recruit black students during the mid-1960s. Integrationist impulses, generated by the pressures of civil rights activism and urban unrest, prompted a number of institutional resolutions to "do something" to make higher education more accessible to African Americans and American ethnic minorities. At Rutgers University, for instance, the 1963 arrest of a popular black alumnus involved in a southern black voter registration drive became a catalyst for black student recruitment. Campus historian Richard McCormick found that the effort "raised the number of black undergraduates from around 100 in 1965, to 266 in 1967, and 413 in 1968."[1] At Cornell University in 1967, a former student recalled, the Committee on Special Education Programs used regular and special admissions policies to bring in "two hundred of us, the largest class of blacks ever admitted at one time."[2] Nationally, educational opportunity and targeted recruitment programs in concert with federal, state, foundation, and private funding supported the push for increasing black and ethnic minority enrollment. Few envisioned the eruption of black student activism that would occur on several of the nation's campuses before the end of the decade.

This essay treats the interval between large-scale black student recruitment by predominantly white institutions in 1965 and the proliferation of demands

KAREN K. MILLER teaches African American history and is the associate director of Black Studies at Boston College. She has written several articles treating the institutionalization of black studies by predominantly white colleges and universities. She is currently working on a book-length project titled, *Overcoming, Overlooking, or Transcending Blackness: Discourses on Race and Identity in Twentieth-Century African American Life Narratives.*

for autonomous black studies programs in late 1968. Marked by the arrival of critical masses of black students on white campuses in unprecedented numbers, the formation of black student unions, and the competition between assimilationist integration and black nationalism for dominance as the ideological foundation for collective black student activism, the 1965–68 period set the stage for the convergence of complex institutional, public, and political pressures at work during the more strident 1968–69 phase of campus unrest. Black student agitation was both a part of and apart from other contemporaneous campus protests, though free speech and antiwar demonstrations usually receive more attention in treatments of the 1960s.

Integration was not the point of contention. The critical masses of black recruits who attended predominantly white colleges could have chosen historically black institutions instead. They might have opted to forgo higher education entirely had they been staunchly opposed to integration or integrated academic settings. Rather, the assimilationist casting of blackness as a "handicap," a problem that whites needed to overlook and blacks needed to surmount, lay at the root of escalating demands for recognition of the legitimacy and acceptability of African Americans in higher education. Advocates of integration believed that exposure to predominantly white institutions would allow young African Americans to "overcome" their racial handicap and become productive members of the American mainstream. Recruiters expected that black students would meld into the existing culture of campus life. Furthermore, they hoped, white students would learn racial tolerance and, perhaps, a color-blind acceptance of persons visibly different but, by virtue of their shared college experience, the same under the skin.

These expectations failed to take into account a developing black student resistance to the assimilationist assumptions embedded in integrationist recruitment efforts. Earl Armstrong, a student at Cornell, mused,

> We've always questioned why we were brought here, [to the university]. . . . I think they want to get us into this "mainstream" thing. They figure that after four years up here in this isolated world, you'll go back and fall into your $20,000–a-year job and never think twice . . . [b]ecause they'd rather have us like that than like Malcolm X.[3]

The expectations also underestimated an ensuing white backlash against the assertions of blackness contained in the confrontational rhetoric employed by critical masses of African American students between 1965 and 1968. James Perkins, president of Cornell University at the height of black student activism, conceded as much in hindsight. When creating its minority recruitment programs, Perkins observed, Cornell failed to anticipate the problems that have arisen out of the great drive for Negro identity, out of black separatism and out of growing militancy. . . . As soon as black students were numerous enough here, they no longer felt themselves a lost people. They did not wish to lose themselves in the largely white student body so they decided to combine.[4]

As black student activism became more verbally and physically confrontational, the public and political mainstreams increasingly insisted that college administrators toughen their stance against individuals and groups who disrupted the institutional status quo.

"An Opportunity to Exist"

Collective black student activism usually evolved out of smaller struggles to carve out space to be oneself, free from perceived and actual pressures to conform to "white" cultural and social modalities. A Cornell student, Ernest Dunbar, recounted an incident that illustrated black students' sense of themselves as culturally "under siege" at the university. According to Dunbar, a white female student complained to campus officials about a "pungent" odor coming from the room of a black woman student living on the same dormitory floor. The white student reported that she smelled marijuana fumes, but further investigation found that the odor emanated from the hot comb the black woman used to press (straighten) her hair.[5]

Also at Cornell, the impending expulsion of one black woman, named Alicia, mobilized other black students to act collectively on her behalf. According to former student Irene Smalls, Alicia

had fights in classes with white women. She was having fights with her roommate. They said Alicia played her music too loud, they didn't like the kind of music she played. Half the time, I didn't particularly like Alicia but I felt they [the administrators] weren't taking into account any of *her* rights.

Smalls's group first agitated to provide for women like Alicia "an opportunity to exist in her environment." Her expulsion was rescinded. The yearlong effort also resulted in the acquisition of Wari House, a dormlike residence for twenty undergraduate black women. The black students involved in getting Wari House founded the Cornell Afro-American Society. Once black students "began to deal with issues like 'We're entitled to our lifestyle, to our music, to our clothing, to whatever,'" Smalls recalled, "then the movement began to grow. We began to say, 'What about black history? What about black faculty? What about black counselors? Let's give us a full menu of options.' It developed into an entire black student movement."[6]

What is important to note here is the expanding scope of black student concerns during the mid-1960s: from comparatively marginal social and lifestyle issues to a broader focus on curriculum and faculty, individual and community empowerment, and institutional recognition. Those who joined black student unions struggled to reconcile their racial identity, their education, and their desire to serve as agents of change within and outside of the academy. "Right while they were in college," former student Ed Whitfield recalled, "their friends at home were struggling in a fairly concerted effort to change the way things were in those communities and give more power to the black communities there. So I think the natural response on the campus was, 'What can we do like what's going on at home?'"[7] Nascent black student associations at colleges and universities around the country wrestled with similar concerns regarding expressions of black identity and empowerment on campus.

Outside of the academy, black consciousness emerged during a mid-to-late 1960s transition in racial discourse from assimilationist integration to various forms of black nationalism. Each new incarnation embraced blackness, rejected the term *Negro*, and dismissed the concept of white superiority. Distinctions between *black* and *Negro* contained political ascribed characteristics similar, but not limited, to those Malcolm X outlined in a 1963 speech at the University of Pennsylvania: "This integrationist Negro is the one who doesn't want to be black—he is ashamed to be black—and he knows that he can't be white. So he calls himself a Negro. . . . But there is another type of Negro on the scene. This type doesn't call himself a Negro. He calls himself a black man. He doesn't make any apology for his black skin."[8] Not just a racial category or a skin color, "blackness" was also seen as a state of mind, an indeterminate identity around which black students organized to combat their cultural isolation and invisibility within predominantly white campus communities. Raymond S. Nunn, a member of Yale University's class of 1969, recaptured the sense of whiteness and alienation he felt during an interview for *Yale Alumni Magazine*:

> Yale is the epitome of white, Anglo-Saxon, high Protestantism. I don't think it's possible, ever, for a black student to have a total positive identification with Yale. . . . I could never walk around the Old Campus and consider myself 'a Yale man'—in my freshman year or five, even 20 years after I graduate from here—because I know what a Yale man is, and his position is one which is definitely counter to mine. Where he is in the establishment is certain to be the place

where I'm not. At best for me personally, all I can see is a momentary and reluctant participation in a social setting which is not my own.[9]

On predominantly white campuses with a critical mass of African American undergraduates, black student unions provided a haven for individual students to express their concerns as well as a collective voice for articulating group issues and negotiating resolutions with college and university administrators.

By the 1967–68 academic year, some black student unions were more aggressive than others in rejecting assimilationist integration and adopting a confrontational pose in both their rhetoric and their style of self-presentation in and beyond the campus community. Not all black students were members of collective organizations, nor did all black student associations necessarily espouse the same ideological or strategic approaches to issues of race and identity. Not all black students supported the tactics employed by the black student groups on their individual campus. Nonetheless, the verbal and physical methods of confrontation used by a few black student associations influenced the direction and the perception of black student groups nationally.

The Black Student Union at San Francisco State College was particularly effective in making its presence felt and its voice heard. Its role in campus activism became a paradigm for other groups, and thus its story is a particularly instructive lens through which to view the emergence of black student demonstrations in the late 1960s. San Francisco State's Black Student Union was not the first of its kind on a college campus, but its involvement in several widely publicized incidents during the 1967–68 academic year brought the group public notoriety well beyond the confines of the campus and the state of California.[10] BSU leaders adopted increasingly provocative stances, reflected in the language, the protest strategies, and the insistence on black-only organizational membership that alienated private citizens more comfortable with the idea of assimilationist integration. Furthermore, the presence and notoriety of the Black Panthers in the Bay Area gave the BSU more leverage with college administrators than most white student protest groups prior to 1968.[11] Several BSU members were also Black Panthers. As private citizens and public officials increasingly pressured college administrators to contain student dissidents, administrators could not easily ignore black student concerns because they feared the BSU's threats of campus disruption. Caught in the middle, administrators risked termination if they failed to maintain campus order. They faced the same risk if perceived to be conceding to "terrorist tactics."

At San Francisco State, the possibility of compromise evaporated in November 1968 with the BSU's threat to close down the school unless and until ten

"nonnegotiable" demands were met. Four of the demands concerned imple-
mentation of an "autonomous" black studies department. By "autonomous,"
the BSU leadership meant a program run by, for, and in the interests of blacks
without external interference. Black students at other institutions had also raised
the issue of including the "study of blacks" in their campus curricula. San Francisco State's Black Student Union, however, was arguably the first to make autonomy a mandatory component of its black studies demands. The specifics of the
strike, which began on November 6 and ended approximately four months later,
are beyond the scope of this essay.[12] The road to the strike, however, began during the summer of 1967 with H. E. Vandever's campaign against the graphic
sexual content of a San Francisco State student-run publication.

H. E. Vandever, the father of a white San Francisco State undergraduate,
wrote a letter in 1967 protesting that freedom of expression had gone too far.
He demanded that San Francisco State stop publication of the *Open Process*,
an alternative student newspaper, because he found the periodical's content
offensive and vulgar. Vandever mailed the letter, along with selected clippings
from *Open Process*, to several thousand private citizens, politicians, and media
outlets statewide in addition to San Francisco State's administrators. Sample
items included "a photograph of a reclining nude woman exposing her private
parts" and articles titled "Free Love," "The New Bisexuality," and "Masturba-
tors, Arise!" In the accompanying letter, Vandever asked recipients to "write
the governor, your state senator and assemblyman and ask them to investigate
this situation at SF State and find out who is responsible."[13]

The Vandever packet also contained a separate letter, signed by two members of the school's undergraduate government, critical of the Black Student
Union. The vice president and the speaker of the Associated Students of San Francisco State characterized the BSU as "a militant student black power organization subsidized by both student body revenues and federal anti-poverty funds"
used in a manner that California's taxpaying citizens might find "inappropriate
if not illegal." The student legislators alleged that members of the undergraduate government had "been threatened by Black Students members 'lobbying' for
funds for their 'projects.'" They claimed that in an effort to avoid "incidents,"
San Francisco State's administration "has countenanced these tactics of the Black
Students Union and has refused to take any action." Vandever and the legislators hoped that the combination of letters and clippings would incite a public
outcry and force university administrators to take disciplinary action against the
editors of *Open Process* and to investigate the charges against the BSU.

Vandever's complaints about the newspaper generated enough off-campus
extramural controversy and institutional embarrassment to prompt recently

inaugurated San Francisco State President John Summerskill to suspend publication of *Open Process* through the beginning of the fall 1967 term. Summerskill lifted the sanction in November after the new editors promised that the paper's future "tone and content would be appropriate to an academic institution." After publication resumed, however, the November 22, 1967 edition carried the photograph of a student writer—nude except for a strategically placed cluster of grapes—whose earlier sexual musings had contributed to the paper's previous difficulties. The accompanying caption read: "Just to be inconsistent, I guess I'll break my pledge against writing about sex. The following essay on sadomasochism is dedicated to [a senior faculty member and director of the school's health education program]."[14] Once again Summerskill shut down the paper, but this time he suspended both the student editor and the author of the offending essay. The president soon lifted these suspensions after being advised of an American Civil Liberties Union threat to file suit on the students' behalf.

While the *Open Process* controversy might seem an irrelevant and inconsequential part of the emerging racial conflict at the school, for members of the BSU, it became the standard by which the group gauged San Francisco State's response to complaints and incidents involving black students. The accusations unveiled in the student legislators' letter—physical intimidation of white students and fiscal mismanagement by the BSU—generated a spate of regional newspaper editorials and articles demanding investigations of the activities, funding, and off-campus affiliations of the Black Student Union. Furthermore, journalists sought to interview leaders of the union about the alleged misdeeds.

The images conveyed through newspaper coverage exposed the seemingly irreconcilable differences between black nationalism and assimilationist integration. James Garrett and other outspoken leaders of the student union used intentionally provocative rhetoric, designed to demonstrate to interviewers and the mainstream reading public that the organization's members were not "Negroes," but blacks prepared to "use the words they want to use—not just the words whites want to hear."[15] The consciously abrasive rhetoric provided ample fodder for subsequent articles and editorials that questioned whether programs and funds intended to bring the races together were being used, instead, to generate separatist, antiwhite, "anti-American," revolutionary activism.

Nowhere was the hostility between interviewer and subject more apparent than in a series of articles about the BSU written by columnist Marilyn Baker for the San Leandro *Morning News* and based in part on interviews with Garrett. In her articles, Baker contemplated whether Garrett, a senior English major and tutor for a high school outreach program sponsored by the BSU, should continue to accept a salary and receive programmatic support from the Office of Economic Opportunity given his political views and his alleged involvement in raising money to "free the gun-toting Black Panthers from jail" and in teaching "young Negroes . . . how to evade the draft and military service." She raised the specter of fiscal impropriety, citing Garrett's flight to a SNCC conference in Atlanta "on wings of money from the pockets of every student at SF State through the Associated Students." The columnist also suggested a subversive link between the BSU, the Student Nonviolent Coordinating Committee (SNCC),[16] and two members of SNCC who were "either in Cuba, consorting with communist Castro—or under indictment for inciting racial riots." Baker implied that individual BSU members and affiliated groups hypocritically accepted funding for community projects from the same federal government they denounced as racist. When Garrett characterized Vietnam as "a black war," Baker interjected that her son, "a white boy, was a marine in Viet Nam." Garrett replied, reportedly, "So, he was stupid." In a later installment of this series, Baker cites Garrett's answer to a question about the Vietnam War as, "Man—that's a black man's war, any white man over there fighting is just plain stupid!" Garrett's responses, as quoted in the Baker article, did little to endear him to the columnist or the mainstream public.

Throughout her series of articles, Baker's interview with Garrett and her use of public statements allegedly made by other BSU members reveal an interplay between reporter and subject designed to provoke and inflame. The stylized nationalist pose adopted by leaders of the BSU seemed intentionally jarring and controversial. To serve the larger political goal of differentiating between themselves and "Negroes," BSU spokesmen projected a disdain for explaining themselves or their motivations to white inquisitors. To respond publicly and sympathetically to "white" questions or anxieties would undermine the effect of public statements like, "It is possible that violence is the only way we can get our way." Unapologetically harsh, the words had greater impact because of their similarity to sentiments attributed to off-campus black nationalist organizations like the Black Panthers.

Marilyn Baker deliberately juxtaposed the students' nationalist rhetoric against the nonviolent, color-blind, assimilationist discourse of integration in order to stimulate public concern about "the problems of San Francisco State." She exacerbated the perception of the student union as a dangerous and subversive campus element by using provocative terms that likened the group to "segregationists," "Ku Klux Klan," "communists," and "ultra-militancy." In one instance, Baker began an article with the assertion that

> If you put white sheets over them, some members of the Black Student Union
> could well pose in the ranks of the Ku Klux Klan. They are militant, base their
> thinking and opinions strictly along color lines, brook no friendship between
> the races and don't hesitate to state that violence may be the only way to achieve
> their goals. Yet this B.S.U. is supported by money out of the SF State Associated
> Student Fund, money collected from a $10 per semester charge levied against
> all students, black and white, attending S.F. State.

For readers already skeptical of minority opportunity programs, the allusions
and inferences exacerbated their suspicions. For readers who believed that integration and minority admissions programs were laudable undertakings, the
Baker series gave reason for pause. How, for instance, could one reconcile support for racial equality and inclusion with the racial separation seemingly
advocated by black student unions? For readers concerned about the apparent
decline of civility and authority on campus, the series provided little reassur-
ance that the San Francisco State situation would improve. Nor did university
president John Summerskill's efforts at damage control.

Summerskill's editorial responses to criticism of the news coverage appeared to lend credibility to his detractors. Rather than take the BSU or the
Open Process editors to task—an approach that might have won him greater
public and political support—Summerskill denounced the Vandever/student
mail campaign as a "vicious, organized campaign of a few right wing individuals on and off campus." Others, like California state senator John Harmer,
saw the controversies differently. The senator doubted Summerskill's ability
to calm the "dangerously brewing storm" at San Francisco State. He blamed
the president's inexperience (he had less than a year as the chief administrator) and his reluctance "to assert his own position as President of the University and to define what standards he expected the students and faculty to
adhere to." Harmer's misgivings, which he stated in September 1967, proved
prophetic six weeks later.

Two related incidents—a melee in the offices of the school's official student paper and a subsequent demonstration protesting the penalties imposed
on the black students involved in the fight—elevated and shaped the Black
Student Union's public image while eroding John Summerskill's college presidency. On November 6, 1967, approximately fifteen Black Student Union members allegedly attacked *Daily Gater* editor Jim Vazko and several staff members.
Vazko suffered minimal injuries and spent a night in the hospital for observation. He pressed criminal assault charges against nine black students positively
identified by eyewitnesses and through pictures taken during the fight. John
Summerskill suspended the same nine students.

Speculation as to motive centered on resentment by BSU of Vazko's editorial reference to the group as a "club" rather than an "organization," and his characterization of boxer Muhammad Ali (whom Vazko called by his given name Cassius Clay) as "a clown . . . hysterian . . . and front man for a hate group as vicious as any Ku Klux Klan ever was." Another scenario offered for consideration cast the attack as a political tactic. A white student, claiming close ties to the Black Student Union, wrote an editorial addressed to Vazko that maintained:

> If they wanted to get just you, they would have gotten you alone. But they wanted publicity. And they thought an incident such as this would turn whitey against all Negroes, and that the moderates in the BSU should be polarized to the extremist fringe simply from white pressure on all Negroes on campus.[17]

Summerskill offered another viewpoint about the *Gater* incident in his presidential memoir. He described the fight as less an attack on Vazko than on

> the student newspaper—more accurately, what the student newspaper stood for. Baker [pseudonym for a BSU member] called it "the cutting edge," the cutting edge of white values, white feelings, white prejudices which shaped life at San Francisco State. Without even trying the *Gater* stood for everything white students took for granted—and everything that black students resented.[18]

The BSU offered no public justification.

Regardless of why the incident really happened, the official explanations failed to defuse public outrage throughout California. Pictures of the fight visually underscored the rhetorically militant public statements conveyed in the Marilyn Baker articles and alleged in the undergraduate legislators' letter. Most California newspapers published on November 6 and 7, 1967 carried UPI or AP wire service copy and photographs of the *Gater* episode, but each created its own headlines, some more inflammatory than others: "College Negro Militants Beat S.F. Campus Editor," San Diego *Evening Tribune* (AP); "Action Vowed Against Negroes Who Invaded College Newsroom," Whittier California *News* (UPI); "SF State Editor, Reporters Beaten by Afro-Americans," Berkeley *Daily Californian*; "Negroes Invade Papers, Beat Staff," Long Beach *Press-Telegram* (AP).

Editorial and opinion pages blamed both the BSU and Summerskill for contributing to an institutional climate where fundamental rights were either under assault or unprotected. Alumni, civic leaders, politicians, and others urged the president to exercise greater control over the campus community. David Schutz, *Gater* alumnus editor (1938) and president of the Associated Press Managing Editors Association, described the assault as "an obvious attempt to induce bodily harm and to substitute brute force for democratic action." Schutz warned that the school and local police would "share the guilt with those who actually did the slugging and kicking" if they failed to vigorously pursue the perpetrators. Another editorial, published in a paper for which Vazko had worked previously, likened the BSU to "the Gestapo, the NKVD [Soviet Secret Police before the KGB], the Ku Klux Klan, and the Mafia." Jerrold Werthimer, a journalism professor at San Francisco State, claimed to sympathize with the black students'concerns, but he lamented the group's failure to issue "a responsible statement" which might "clarify the attack on the security of a person, social order, peaceable assembly, freedom of speech, academic freedom, and freedom of the press." Max Rafferty, the conservative state superintendent of public instruction, rallied his colleagues on the California State College Board of Trustees to "do our job and change this campus from a gladiatorial arena back to what it ought to be—a place for sober, serious study by peaceful people." The *Gater* incident symbolized militancy's threats to the physical safety of white students, to the college's educational mission, to the U.S. Constitution, and to the right to dissent from dissent. From these perspectives, Summerskill failed to use his discretionary power to prevent campus tensions from escalating and potentially endangering the reputation of the California state college system.

Summerskill tried to demonstrate administrative "toughness" by suspending the nine alleged attackers. Unlike the way in which he dealt with the *Open Process* students, Summerskill refused to delay the *Gater* suspensions until after a hearing by the campus Board of Appeals and Review. With criminal charges pending against the *Gater* nine, Summerskill felt obligated and empowered to undertake unilateral disciplinary measures "when there was a threat to public safety or welfare."[19] While the *Open Process* incident did not meet this standard, Summerskill concluded, the *Gater* assault did.

The union maintained that its suspended members should be reinstated until completion of the appeal process. Unswayed by Summerskill's differentiation between the two incidents, the organization declared that the procedural distinction was racial. The *Open Process* students were white and had ACLU backing, and Summerskill rescinded their suspensions pending the review board's recommendations. Furthermore, at a campus antiwar rally, Summerskill apologized to the white *Open Process* students for making a "precipitous" decision, conceding, "I was mad and impatient and I acted improperly."[20] When it came to the suspended black students, however, he gave no ground. After the Board of Appeals and Review recommended more lenient disciplinary measures for the *Gater* nine, Summerskill amended the original sanctions to reflect the varying degrees of culpability brought out during the appeal process. Two students were suspended for one year, two for a semester, and the remaining five put on probation with "letters of warning" placed in their files.

Despite the reduced penalties received by the majority of the accused, the BSU remained convinced that the four suspended black students were victims of racism. Consequently, the group issued Summerskill an ultimatum: he could either overturn the suspensions within one week or prepare for a demonstration on December 6, 1967 during which the BSU and its community supporters "might even move to close down the campus!"[21] Moreover, a loose coalition of mostly white student activists called MAPS (Movement Against Political Suspensions) announced its intention to participate in the demonstration if MAPS's issues—getting local police off campus, ending recruitment of students by the military and war-related industries, and gaining student control of student-related campus publications—were not addressed.[22]

A MAPS demonstration could prove a nuisance, but Summerskill's greater fear was that the BSU's threat to rally five thousand supporters to join its campus protest might result in turbulence equal to "the vicious racial riots that had taken place in Los Angeles and other cities."[23] Though Summerskill "held tough" publicly, his private efforts to prevent BSU participation in the demonstration failed. Neither the president nor the BSU could back down without doing serious damage to their own credibility and reputation: Summerskill as an executive in control, and the BSU as willing to follow up its rhetoric with aggressive activism.

Classes began in their normal fashion on Wednesday, December 6. By the early afternoon, San Francisco State became the first California state college campus forced to close because of student unrest. White antiwar protesters denounced the Vietnam War and on-campus military recruitment, ending their protest with a march on the administration building. Summerskill watched these proceedings from the administration building-cum-command post along with other campus officials and a tactical squad of police advisors. From that vantage point, Summerskill later recalled, his perspective on the MAPS demonstration differed substantially from televised news footage: "It is one thing to look at a building with a broken window and another to have the glass exploding right in your face in your own living room."[24] No one was killed, and property damage was minimal.

What Summerskill did not see, however, were the "roving bands of Negroes" described by reporters as engaged in random acts of unrestrained vandalism and intimidation. Photographers' equipment was sabotaged so that their pictures could not be used to identify demonstrators engaged in looting, arson, and other forms of property damage during the two-hour rampage. Eyewitness reports chronicled in periodicals statewide recounted unprovoked attacks on white students. A white female graduate student eating lunch in the cafeteria, for instance, told a reporter that she had "been watching the demonstration outside the Administration Building, but nobody had announced any threats against US [sic], the students." The trouble began, according to this anonymous source, when black students entered the cafeteria:

> Then they went into the food area. They removed all the food. They threw it on the floor, some of them. They didn't pay. A white student—an ordinary sort of boy with a dark jacket—was trying to pay the cashier for his tray of food. He was surrounded by black students who urged him not to pay, to help in their "demonstration." A busboy tried to come to his aid, and he was also attacked. Neither of them hit back, as far as I could see, while they were under attack.

Although initially sympathetic to the BSU's issues, the informant reversed her opinion after witnessing the cafeteria display.

Most officers of the San Francisco State student legislature declared their opposition to the demonstration in general—and to the black component of the protest in particular—in a published statement issued the day after the disturbance. Signed by all of the officers except the student body president, the statement demanded that the BSU "give indication that the activities of Wednesday [December 6] are disavowed and that their activities are legitimate educational activities rather than destruction and looting of property." The student legislators threatened to "demand the expulsion of the BSU and of the leaders responsible for yesterday's activities" if the Black Student Union failed to comply.

Rather than "disavow" the demonstration, the BSU allegedly declared it a "victory." The group's confrontational tactics appeared to yield more substantive gains than traditionally nonviolent approaches. In the interim between the December 6 demonstration and the end of the spring 1968 term, the criminal court case against the *Gater* nine ended with the accused receiving fines and probation rather than jail time. With BSU encouragement, John Summerskill hired former Howard University professor Nathan Hare to coordinate development of a black studies curriculum, a set of courses centered upon the study of black African-descended peoples.[25] The college also approved a special admissions program through which to enroll an additional four hundred minority students for the 1968–69 academic year. In light of these gains, BSU directed its energies toward planning for the fall 1968 term rather than participating in the antiwar demonstrations that took place at the school between January and May 1968.

For John Summerskill, on the other hand, the December 6 protest accelerated external pressure for his removal from the presidency of San Francisco State. While his supporters publicly praised his decision not to use the police to end the demonstration, the greater proportion of editorial and political commentary perceived the president's "restraint" as weakness. Summerskill promised during a televised emergency meeting of the California State College Board of Trustees held three days after the demonstration to take stronger steps to ensure student safety in the future. By televising the proceedings, the trustees—led by Governor Ronald Reagan —had expected to show California's taxpaying citizens the board's commitment to protecting their investment in higher education from the forces of campus disorder, even if it meant removing a college president. Once San Francisco Police Chief Thomas Cahill endorsed Summerskill's decision making, however, the board backed down and expressed confidence in Summerskill's leadership.

Less than three months later, Summerskill gave notice that he would leave office at the end of the spring 1968 term. Caught in the grip of persistent antiwar protests, a polarized faculty, and an unsupportive board of trustees, he concluded that he "had neither the backing nor the material resources to make San Francisco State a better college."[26] California State College Chancellor Glen Dumke asked Summerskill to remain president until September in order to facilitate the search for his replacement and allow for a smooth transition. Instead, the California State College Board of Trustees "relieved" Summerskill of his duties in late May during an antiwar sit-in at San Francisco State.[27]

Summerskill's successor, Robert Smith, was drawn from San Francisco State's faculty. Smith, the school's third president in one year, assumed office immediately. Three months into Smith's presidency, a Black Student Union member, George Mason Murray, became the catalyst for renewed racial controversy at San Francisco State. Murray was a graduate student hired by the English department to teach in the experimental program for the new minority special admissions students expected in fall 1968. He was also the minister of education for the Bay Area Black Panthers. Furthermore, he was one of the *Gater* nine fined and placed on probation. The English department knew about Murray's previous entanglements and his high-profile affiliation with the Panthers before hiring him. It found him competent and apolitical in the classroom.

In September 1968, a San Francisco *Examiner* article profiled Murray, his Black Panther and BSU associations, his participation in the *Gater* incident, his summer trip to Cuba, and his appointment as a part-time instructor at San Francisco State. After the article appeared, several California State College trustees demanded Murray's termination. His presence and instructor status contradicted the board of trustees' hard-line pronouncements after the December 6 demonstration: disruptive and potentially dangerous dissidents would be expelled from state-supported colleges, Furthermore, both the college chancellor and the state superintendent of public instruction had political aspirations that hinged on the results of the coming November general election. Rafferty hoped to win a U.S. Senate seat, and Dumke was under consideration for a cabinet post if Richard Nixon became president of the United States. With the November election only weeks away, neither wanted the Murray controversy to remain unresolved and to adversely affect his prospects.[28]

College president Robert Smith had supported Murray's retention initially. But just before the election, controversial statements attributed to Murray moved Smith to cite "unprofessional conduct" as sufficient grounds for termination. The *Daily Gater*, for instance, alleged that Murray announced the following at an off-campus event: "We don't need any more speechmakers. What we need is killers, political assassins. We've got to revolt and continue it until it becomes an armed revolution."[29] Though Smith never heard these statements firsthand, he felt that the alleged declarations left him no choice but to surrender to the pressure for Murray's dismissal. Smith's position shifted from uncertainty to a

> firm conviction that Murray[,] by his volatile and violent rhetoric urging violence, assassination, and revolution was, as a black leader, deliberately sanctioning and encouraging the type of violence [that another Bay Area college] had experienced the week before. Furthermore, he was advocating homicide on our own campus, already tension-ridden, and naming specific persons as objects of violence.[30]

For the Black Student Union, Murray's dismissal served as both a cautionary tale and a catalyst for renewed activism.

From the BSU's perspective, the firing revealed the vulnerability of the programmatic and curricular gains made after the December 6, 1967 protest. If Murray could be discharged for expressing his political views in an off-campus forum, then any individual, group, or program could be eliminated if objected to by trustees, institutional personnel, politicians, or the public at large. What would stop the college or the trustees from reneging on or "coopting" the new black studies curriculum and minority admissions program if either's existence became controversial? To avoid that eventuality, the union returned to the strategy it had used successfully almost a year earlier: It issued an ultimatum and threatened to strike should its concerns remain unresolved. This time, however, the issues involved were more consequential than the commutation of student suspensions.

The chosen strike date, November 6, 1968, commemorated the first anniversary of the *Gater* melee. BSU leaders drafted a list of "non-negotiable" demands and proclaimed that San Francisco State would "not function" until they were met. Half of the ten demands concerned George Murray's reinstatement, increasing black student enrollment, protection of black student organizations from dissolution by the board of trustees, and amnesty for university-affiliated participants in the event of a strike.

The remaining demands concerned establishing a black studies department at San Francisco State. Instead of the curriculum already in place, the students demanded an *autonomous* department for which the "chairman, faculty, and staff have the sole power to hire faculty and control and determine [its] destiny."[31] By demanding an autonomous department with its own faculty, the BSU made a fundamental distinction between the "study of blacks" and "black studies." It sought to position "black studies" as an independent space to develop and pursue an empowering black educational agenda within a predominantly white academic institution, but "without the interference of the administration and the chancellor."[32] What constituted a "black" educational agenda was unsettled, but the function of racial and community empowerment lay at its core, to be resolved once the department was in place.

The "study of blacks" had become an issue on other campuses by fall 1968. Most proposals were for individual courses, curricula, or programs dependent on existing faculty and courses housed in external, predominantly white departments. These proposals lacked the kind of autonomy insisted upon by the Black Student Union.

> At the present time, the so-called black studies courses are being taught from the established departments, which also control the function of the courses. We, the black students at San Francisco State College, feel that it is detrimental to us as black human beings to be controlled by racists, who have absolute power over determining what we should learn.[33]

Such reasoning significantly altered the concept of black studies as demands for autonomous units spread from San Francisco State to predominantly white campuses nationwide.

San Francisco State's BSU moved black student activism to a new, more confrontational stage by threatening to strike on November 6, 1968. The group also exacerbated the intensity of both support for and opposition to its list of demands. The politicians and trustees who boldly intoned their resolve to deal harshly with campus disturbances depended upon college executives and administrators to suppress the threatened strike without giving in to activists' demands. Groups like the Black Student Union, however, felt they had to strike in order to preserve their credibility and use their leverage within and outside the university community. Otherwise, institutions could ignore their issues without fear of serious consequences.

College administrators caught in the middle, particularly at tax-supported institutions like San Francisco State, faced the very real possibility of termination or forced resignation if perceived as insubordinate or "weak." They served as convenient scapegoats when on-campus turmoil became public controversy. Consequently, few were surprised at Robert Smith's resignation less than three weeks after the November 6, 1968 strike; Smith resigned approximately six months after succeeding John Summerskill. Smith's "slowness" in responding to the call to fire Murray eroded his support among the trustees. He later mused, "I ended up being cited as a prime *cause* of the unresolved problems, and a conspirator in fomenting new disorders."[34]

The downfall of Summerskill, and then Smith, served as an omen for administrators on other campuses, illustrating what might happen if student unrest broke out at their institutions. Smith's successor, Samuel I. Hayakawa, learned from his immediate predecessor's experiences and implemented the "get tough" philosophy advocated by trustees and public officials. Despite his Japanese American ancestry, the new president was unmoved by student demands for Asian American, black, Chicano, and Native American faculty and programs of study. By using the police to quell demonstrations and refusing to negotiate with strike participants, Hayakawa was credited for returning order to the San Francisco State campus by March 1969. The reputation Hayakawa acquired during the strike endeared him to conservative interests who supported his successful bid for political office.

Some academic institutions sought to forestall the outbreak of a "San Francisco State situation" by implementing change before conflict escalated into unrest. Among California public institutions, for instance, University of California Chancellor Roger Heyns asked that Berkeley's Afro-American Students Union avoid "the agonies of SF State" by calling off a campus strike planned for January 22, 1969.[35] At the Hayward branch of the California State College system, however, the administration "read the writing on the wall," established a black studies program, and recruited black faculty and staff in 1969 before tensions on campus escalated to the point of wholesale disruption.[36] At the University of California, Santa Barbara, the Black Student Union took over the institution's Computer Center, threatening to destroy it unless demands for black faculty and black studies were met. Between 1968 and 1972, more than five hundred black studies programs, departments, curricula, research centers, and libraries were established by colleges and universities across the nation. Most did not require the kinds of extremes that had occurred at San Francisco State precisely because there *was* a San Francisco State.

In 1952, historian Richard Hofstadter maintained that the significance of a college curriculum lay in its revelation of "the educated community's conception of what knowledge is most worth transmitting to the cream of its youth ... and its revelation of what kind of mind and character an education is supposed to produce."[37] As the autonomous black studies phase of the black student activism unfolded, the levels of conflict and backlash escalated on campus and off because the stakes were so much greater than integrated access to higher education, the community of interests involved so much broader than the university, and the question of the desirable educated mind and character so much in dispute. At a narrow level, power was the real issue being contested. The "non-negotiable" demands were like a line in the sand. At the extremes, one side threatened prolonged disruption unless its terms were met; the other insisted that San Francisco State make no further concessions to coercion, and aggressively use its power to restore order. The substance of the "black studies" challenge to higher education was lost in the scuffle.

In broader terms, however, the confrontational stage of organized black student activism treated concerns increasingly at odds with the concept of assimilationist integration that had influenced black recruitment efforts through the mid-1960s. For the critical mass of black students attending predominantly white academic institutions during the interval between recruitment and resistance to assimilationist integration, this 1965–68 period represented one of the first opportunities to explore where blacks fit both as subjects and as participants in the production of "knowledge worth transmitting."

NOTES

The epigraphs are taken from J. Harvie Wilkinson, *From Brown to Bakke: The Supreme Court and School Integration, 1854–1978* (New York: Oxford University Press, 1976), p. 46; and Glen E. deChabert, "On Being Black at Yale," *Yale Alumni Magazine* (May 1969), p. 30.

1. Richard McCormick, *The Black Student Protest Movement at Rutgers* (New Brunswick, N.J.: Rutgers University Press, 1990), p. 14.

2. Irene Smalls in Joan Morrison and Robert K. Morrison, *From Camelot to Kent State: The Sixties Experience in the Words of Those Who Lived It* (New York: Times Books, 1987), p. 263.

3. Earl Armstrong quoted in Ernest Dunbar, "The Black Studies Thing," *New York Times Magazine*, April 6, 1969, p. 60.

4. James Perkins quoted in Dunbar, "The Black Studies Thing," p. 60.

5. Ibid., p. 65.

6. Irene Smalls quoted in Morrison and Morrison, *From Camelot to Kent State*, pp. 263, 264.

7. Ed Whitfield quoted in Morrison and Morrison, *From Camelot to Kent State*, pp. 256–58.

8. Malcolm X, "The Old Negro and the New Negro," in *The End of White World Supremacy*, ed. Imam Benjamin Karim (New York: Arcade Publishing/Little, Brown, 1971), pp. 91, 93–94.

9. Raymond S. Nunn quoted in deChabert, "On Being Black at Yale," p. 28.

10. The Soul Students Advisory Council at Merritt College in Oakland, California, was founded in 1966, arguably the first black student union on a college campus. See Reginald Major, *A Panther Is a Black Cat* (New York: William Morrow, 1971).

11. The Black Panther Party, founded in 1966, began when a small group of young black men from Oakland and San Francisco, California, met to devise a plan to combat police brutality and other abuses of civil authority in black Bay Area communities. Initially, two groups emerged from the meeting: the Bay Area Black Panthers, composed mainly of San Francisco blacks, tended toward cultural nationalism or the belief in the power of knowledge to foment revolutionary change; the Black Panther Party for Self Defense, on the other hand, were revolutionary nationalists who believed that oppressed people needed the means to effect revolution. Their slogan, according to Reginald Major, was "guns, baby, guns." The second group emerged as the dominant group in the public mind, though it did eventually incorporate the philosophy of cultural nationalism as part of its strategy for empowerment.

12. For additional treatments of the 6 November 1968 Black Students Union/Third World Liberation Front Strike at San Francisco State, see Dikran Karazeugian, *Blow It Up: The Black Student Revolt at San Francisco State College and the Emergence of Dr. Hayakawa* (Boston: Gambit, 1971); and William H. Orrick, Jr., *Shut It Down! A College in Crisis: San Francisco State College, October 1968–April 1969* (Washington, D.C.: Government Printing Office, 1969). For overviews of black student unrest on other campuses during the same period, see Fact Finding Commission on Columbia Disturbances, *Crisis at Columbia* (New York: Vintage Books, 1968); W. J. Rorabaugh, *Berkeley at War: The 1960s* (New York: Oxford University Press, 1989); Werner Sollors, Caldwell Titcomb, and Thomas Underwood, eds., *Blacks at Harvard: A Documentary History of African-American Experience at Harvard and Radcliffe* (New York: New York University Press, 1993).

13. Unless otherwise cited, the material dealing with San Francisco State College is housed in the University Archives of the school's J. Paul Leonard Library. Its Third World Liberation Front Collection contains an extensive clippings file, photographs, and administrative records collected by library archivist Helene Whitson.

14. Cited in John Summerskill, *President Seven* (New York: World Publishing Co., 1971), p. 123.

15. Stokely Carmichael, "What We Want," *New York Review of Books*, 22 September

1966. Cited in *Chronicles of Black Protest,* ed. Bradford Chambers (New York: New American Library, 1969), p. 218.

16. The Student Nonviolent Coordinating Committee began in 1960 as an integrated, non-violent group dedicated to organizing grass-roots civil rights activists throughout the South. By 1967, however, SNCC had abandoned integration as both a membership and as a philosophical goal. For further information, see Clayborne Carson, *In Struggle: SNCC and the Black Awakening of the 1960s* (Cambridge: Harvard University Press, 1981).

17. Smith et al., *By Any Means Necessary: The Revolutionary Struggle at San Francisco State* (San Francisco: Jossey-Bass, 1970) pp. 22–23.

18. Summerskill, *President Seven,* p. 118.

19. Ibid., pp. 123–24.

20. Ibid., p. 124.

21. Cited in Summerskill, *President Seven,* p. 125.

22. Smith et al., *By Any Means Necessary,* pp. 27–28.

23. Summerskill, *President Seven,* p. 128.

24. Ibid., p. 143.

25. Ibid., pp. 204–205, 216. Nathan Hare taught at Howard University and the University of Chicago before coming to San Francisco State. Summerskill hired Hare during the "lame duck" phase of his presidency. This act rankled several faculty members. They felt that Summerskill's unilateral move usurped the faculty's role in making academic personnel decisions.

26. Ibid., p. 196.

27. Ibid., pp. 208–210, 212–19.

28. Major, *A Panther Is a Black Cat,* pp. 83, 84; Smith et al., *By Any Means Necessary,* pp. 122n, 130–40.

29. Murray statement in *Daily Gater* quoted in Smith et al., *By Any Means Necessary,* p. 117.

30. Smith et al., *By Any Means Necessary,* pp. 117, 121, 161. Smith was referring to the turmoil at the College of San Mateo that followed the firing of a black administrator who failed to keep a militant black student off campus.

31. Ibid.

32. Cited in Smith et al., *By Any Means Necessary,* p. 150.

33. Cited in Debby Woodroofe, "Fifteen Demands for Self-Determination," *Young Socialist,* February 1969, n.p.; see Smith et al., *By Any Means Necessary,* pp. 148–49 for a complete list of demands and the Black Student Union rationale and interpretation of the response to those demands prior to the November 1968 strike.

34. Ibid., p. 201.

35. Roger Heyns, "To Students, Staff, Faculty, and Friends of the University" (Berkeley: Chancellor's Record Office, University of California 1969), pp. 3–4.

36. Personal interview with Al Smith, California State University-Hayward, 1982.

37. Richard Hofstadter, *The Development and Scope of Higher Education in the United States* (New York: Columbia University Press, 1952), p. 11.

Everything Seemed Beautiful

A Life in the Counterculture

Barry Melton

I first started coming to the San Francisco Bay Area during the spring and summer of 1964. I was supposed to have graduated high school that summer, just before my seventeenth birthday. But a motorcycle accident in my junior year put me in a hospital bed for many months and caused me to fall a full semester behind, so my graduation was delayed. While laid up in bed that summer of 1963, I read Jack Kerouac's *On the Road* and Woody Guthrie's *Bound for Glory*. And, more important, I somehow managed to get my parents to feel so bad that I spent my sixteenth birthday in the hospital, they reluctantly agreed that I could spend the entire summer of 1964 on the road with my guitar.

I grew up in North Hollywood, California, where my parents had migrated in 1955 after Senator McCarthy, the FBI, and the House Un-American Activities Committee forced my father out of the National Maritime Union in New York. During the Spanish Civil War in the late 1930s, my father had been a coordinator of "troop migration" for the volunteer Lincoln and Washington Brigades, which American men joined to fight against fascism in Spain. But because the American Communist Party and the Soviet Union were part of that struggle, participation became suspect in the Cold War years after 1945. The FBI was doing its best to drive "communists" out of the labor unions. Dad was no longer able to ship out and make a living, so we came to the West Coast to start a new life. Dad thought his brother, who was a union official at the General Motors factory in Van Nuys, California, could get him a job there. Dad was wrong. "Communists" weren't welcome at the General Motors plant, either.

Over the next ten years, Dad bounced in and out of a long succession of short-term jobs as a welder, machinist, life insurance salesman, and vacuum cleaner salesman. And he worked installing everything from air conditioners to carpets. I even remember spending a summer, post-hole diggers in hand, helping him install chain link fencing throughout the San Fernando Valley. His jobs were often menial, and we didn't have a lot of money, but my Dad took great pride in whatever work he did and believed there was no greater station in life than that of a manual laborer. When the McCarthy era was over, Dad was finally able to settle down to steady work in building maintenance and teaching trade-technical subjects at a community college.

In the years since their passing, I've come to understand that my parents were idealistic dreamers in the finest sense. They believed in a better world, and they made an extraordinary number of sacrifices for their beliefs. I remember clearly, during my family's migration from New York to California in 1955, standing on the side of an East Texas highway with Dad, Mom, and my older brother. We had been ejected from our bus because my mom had yelled at the driver for

BARRY MELTON has been a criminal defense lawyer for the past eighteen years and is currently chief assistant public defender of Yolo County, California. As a young man, he was a full-time political activist and musician living in the San Francisco Bay Area. He co-founded, with "Country Joe" McDonald, the seminal 1960s band "Country Joe and the Fish." (The only continuous member of "The Fish," he continues to be known by that nickname.) The primary objective of Country Joe and the Fish, from its inception, was to call attention to U.S. involvement in Vietnam and raise money for antiwar causes. They also raised money for the civil rights movement and many other progressive causes. He still works as a musical performer when time permits, and remains politically active. He lives in Davis, California, with his wife and two sons.

ordering an older black woman to sit at the back of the bus. My parents taught me to hate injustice and to never be silent in its presence.

When I returned to school in the fall of 1963, after spending my sixteenth birthday and the summer of 1963 in the hospital, I began losing interest. I wanted to be a folksinger and play the guitar, so I began cutting classes and hanging out at the houses of musician friends during school days. On the weekends I would drive into Hollywood to hang out at nightclubs like the Ash Grove. In 1963 and 1964, the Ash Grove was at the center of folk music in Los Angeles and everything that folk music stood for, including the civil rights movement and the newly forming movement against the war in Vietnam. And a young guitarist like me could sit in McCabe's Guitar Shop, just adjacent to the Ash Grove, and play with the great musicians who were wandering through town like the Reverend Gary Davis, Mance Lipscomb, Doc Watson, and Bukka White.*

My political commitment led me to sit-in at local lunch counters, to work at the downtown CORE office in support of the Freedom Riders, and to stand on a picket line at a downtown Los Angeles hotel shouting at the Nhu family to stop their oppression of the Vietnamese people. But something else was going on, too. I began buying an occasional sugar-cube dose of a "new" drug, LSD, from a woman who had a house right next to the North Hollywood police station.

There really wasn't any great worry about buying LSD next to a police station, because it wasn't yet illegal. For me, and a host of people I grew up with, LSD quickly became more than a drug. It became the article of faith and rite of passage of a new movement, a movement even more secret and more subversive than the group of political dissidents who were protesting for equal rights in the South and for an end to hostilities in Southeast Asia. This new movement would go far beyond just another restructuring of existing human institutions; this was a movement that would reshape the very boundaries of human consciousness itself—or so we thought at the time.

By the time the summer of 1964 rolled around, I was ready to hit the road. I was already part of the newly emerging drug and folk music counterculture in the Hollywood area. And there was a fantastic group of young musicians who

---

*These men were icons of the folk music revival of the early 1960s. The Reverend Gary Davis was a blind street singer and brilliant guitarist. The elderly Mance Lipscomb, a pre-blues-era songster, was working as a sharecropper in Texas when discovered by young folklorists in the 1960s. The great blind guitarist Doc Watson of Deep Gap, North Carolina, is one of the founders of bluegrass music. And Bukka White, who recorded for the Victor label in 1930, was rediscovered by my dear friend ED Denson, in 1963, and was brought north to perform at folk festivals. ED later became the business manager of Country Joe and the Fish.

were there at the same time, beginning to forge new musical styles from the rich treasury of American folk music that we all tried to emulate. Each young guitarist was an individual stylist, like the old bluesmen who appeared at the folk music clubs and festivals and whose styles we all devoured. I can almost hear the singing and solo guitar music of the young Ry Cooder, David Crosby, Jim McGuinn, Steve Mann, Taj Mahal, Mike Wilhelm, and the many other fine young Hollywood folk musicians of the time.*

When I came to the Bay Area to start my cross-country trip in the early summer of 1964, I had a long list of potential places to play or stay that I'd culled from musician friends. I made a brief stop in San Jose to look for Steve Mann's friend, "Jerry" Kaukonen.† He was supposed to be playing at a San Jose club called Offstage, but I never found him. So, I headed up to San Francisco where I expected to link up with some friends at the Blue Unicorn, another drug/folk underground landmark. After missing my Blue Unicorn friends, I ended up in Berkeley and the house of my friends Jerry and "Triple," who were not only fine folk guitarists, but also had a house full of their own paintings and sculptures. There, with a pot full of peyote tea cooking on the stove, we'd sit and drink throughout the day as we played and sang into the night.

Something else happened to me in Berkeley that summer, which didn't seem all that important to me at the time. I played guitar somewhere on the University of California campus with a group of musicians that included the very wonderful folk musician Malvina Reynolds. Malvina was quite a celebrity at the time, since she was well known for writing the song "Little Boxes," which was about the proliferation of look-alike houses and think-alike people in suburban America. It turned out that one of the other musicians accompanying Malvina that day was a young Berkeley folk musician named Joe McDonald. Unknown to either Joe or myself that day, our destinies would become intertwined for the next several years.

---

*McGuinn and Crosby later went on to found The Byrds, with Crosby moving from that band to Crosby, Stills, and Nash. Both Crosby and McGuinn continue to write and perform to the present day. So does Ry Cooder, who has had a series of albums bridging musical genres. His most recent work has been the acclaimed "discovery" of Cuban musicians with the album and film *Buena Vista Social Club*. Taj Mahal has been a staple on the folk music scene for decades and has recently incorporated African music and musicians into his repertoire. Mike Wilhelm was a cofounder of The Charlatans, an early San Francisco rock band.
†Jorma Kaukonen later was a founding member of The Jefferson Airplane and went on to be a mainstay of the band Hot Tuna.

Determined to sing my way across the country that summer, I headed out of Berkeley with my thumb pointed eastward through Salt Lake City and Denver. My destination was Chicago to hear a young guitar legend named Mike Bloomfield. A musician from Chicago that I'd played with, Joe Sanchez, told me that I had to play with Bloomfield. Sanchez said Bloomfield was the best young blues guitarist in the country and could be found at a place called "Mother Blues" in Old Town, Chicago.

I hit Chicago and called up the telephone number that Sanchez had given me for Bloomfield, but it was disconnected. So I made my way into Old Town and found out where he was playing that night, which I don't believe was in Old Town at all. I had been hitchhiking in the heat of summer, hadn't had a bath in days, and was dressed kind of funky, carrying an old Navy sea bag and a guitar. So when I went and introduced myself to Bloomfield as a guitarist and friend of Joe Sanchez, he probably thought I stank and I'm quite sure, in retrospect, that I must have smelled a bit. Regardless, Michael was kind enough to get me in for free. I did hear him play, and he really was the best young blues guitarist of my generation. He went on to become the lead guitarist in the seminal Paul Butterfield Blues Band and later founded the Electric Flag band. He had a distinguished career as a soloist and studio musician. About a decade later, I had the privilege of having Michael produce an album that I recorded for Columbia Records. Michael was found dead of a drug overdose, in a parked car in San Francisco, in 1980. I think of him often as the years roll by.

From Chicago, I caught a Greyhound bus to New York, where I stayed on and off with my aging grandmother at her Brooklyn apartment. I went up to the Newport Folk Festival that summer and heard Joan Baez, Bob Dylan, and José Feliciano. Among my most treasured memories, I went to the World's Fair in New York with my cousin Heidi, famed folk singer Mike Seeger and his family, and the legendary Appalachian banjo player Dock Boggs.

I also started to hone my musical performance skills a bit that summer, as I began to work the "basket houses" in Greenwich Village. Young folksingers from far and wide came to climb on stage and ultimately pass a basket among the audience to collect their earnings. There were a number of fine young performers that I remember seeing in the Village that summer, but one stands out in my mind—a young folksinger named Peter Tork, who later became one of the Monkees.

Most memorable of all were the marvelous folk music jam sessions near the Washington Square Park fountain, where dozens of young performers came to display their skills. Young guitarists and singers abounded in Greenwich Village, like David Bromberg, Stefan Grossman, and Richie Havens,* who filled the Village air with some of the finest music of the time.

I made it back home to North Hollywood in the fall of 1964, just in time to start my last semester of high school. After my taste of life on the road I was in no condition to be a successful student. But I only had to attend school half days, since I was only a few units short of what I needed to graduate. My unexcused absences started to mount as I wandered the Hollywood folk music scene, and I began smoking marijuana. I have fond memories of my English teacher that semester, who was a folk music fan himself and saw me play in a couple of the local clubs. I fell asleep in one of his classes after playing all night, yet he was kind enough not to send me to the dreaded boy's vice principal who ordinarily dealt with such matters most severely. I even got busted for drugs that year with my guitarist friend, Steve Mann, as we were riding in my car to the Chambers Brothers' house in the Silver Lake district near Hollywood. They only charged Steve, because he was the "adult."

Finally, in late January 1965, I graduated from high school and moved to San Francisco, ostensibly to study semantics with S. I. Hayakawa at San Francisco State College. But what I really wanted to do was to involve myself in the musical and political counterculture beginning to grow in the Bay Area. I stayed in college just long enough to be given a chance to play at the San Francisco State College Folk Music Festival by the president of the folk music club, Peter Albin. Peter later started a commune at 1090 Page Street in San Francisco's Haight-Ashbury District, which has since been described as the birthplace of the Grateful Dead and the cradle of the San Francisco rock music scene. Peter went on to become the bass player with Big Brother and the Holding Company, whose lead singer was Janis Joplin. Peter and I have played music together in a number of different bands for more than thirty years.

Within a couple of months of coming to San Francisco, I moved to the East Bay and became a regular habitué of the frequent political demonstrations and small folk music nightclubs that dotted the Berkeley landscape. There was actually a range of causes to become aligned with in Berkeley during that period. While the antiwar movement, the civil rights movement, and the free speech

---

*Bromberg is probably best known for his work as a sideman for Bob Dylan and Jerry Jeff Walker, but his fine body of solo work is considerable. Stefan Grossman was a founder of the Even Dozen Jug Band and perhaps the definitive fingerpicking guitar stylist of the generation. In the late 1960s Grossman expatriated to Europe, where he continues to perform and produce music. Richie Havens continues to be one of America's leading folk performers and still maintains an extensive touring schedule.

movement each had its own focus, demonstrations, and leadership, there was a good deal of overlap. Each of the movements shared the same repertoire of folk songs and the singers to sing them. When you showed up at a demonstration in Berkeley, everybody knew the words to the songs and sang along—including the cops.

By late spring 1965, at the invitation of a high school friend and a fellow folksinger from North Hollywood, Bruce Barthol, I had moved into the upstairs flat of a house on Telegraph and Russell Streets in Berkeley, situated right next door to a folk music club called the Jabberwock. We shared the apartment with another folk musician, Paul Armstrong, and lived on a diet of powdered milk, white bread, and peanut butter, except for the days when one or all of us performed at the Jabberwock and could count on a free meal from owner Bill Ehlert.

A few days shy of my eighteenth birthday, I got a call from Joe McDonald, who also was playing at the Jabberwock. He asked if I'd play guitar on a record of protest songs he was making. Until that time, I had been an acoustic guitarist. But I rented an electric guitar for one of the tunes, titled "Superbird," because we thought that as it had contemporary subject matter (the song was about President Johnson), it needed a contemporary sound. As the summer progressed I was playing in an ad-hoc musical group for political demonstrations called the "Instant Action Jug Band" which included Joe, my roommates Bruce and Paul, and several other musicians who were Jabberwock regulars.

By the fall of 1965 a small extended-play (EP) 33 $\frac{1}{3}$-rpm vinyl record I made with Joe and others came out under the band name Country Joe and the Fish. We promoted it in conjunction with the first teach-in against the Vietnam War held at the University of California's Berkeley campus. My most vivid memory of the teach-in was hearing Norman Thomas, who had succeeded Eugene Victor Debs as the standard bearer of the American Socialist Party in the mid-1920s, speak. Thomas was a mesmerizing orator whose voice was honed in the premicrophone days of public speaking. Although he was more than eighty years old at the time of the Berkeley demonstration, Thomas held the crowd at rapt attention while his powerful voice belted out a cadence of progressive ideas distilled during his more than half-century in public life.

Country Joe and the Fish was by no means meant to be anything more than a one-time name for a record intended to make a few dollars at antiwar rallies. But the group began to have some name recognition as a result of the record's release. The popularity of the record, which contained a lengthy civil rights protest song by a local songwriter named Peter Krug on one side and two antiwar songs performed by Joe and me on the other side, was actually getting us a little bit of work. Soon, Joe and I, along with washtub bassist Richard Saunders, did our first engagement under the name Country Joe and the Fish at the Berkeley campus. We shared the bill with Allen Ginsberg and the Fugs. The most memorable moment was when Fugs' guitarist Steve Weber took a sixteen-foot head-first dive from stage to floor while vocalists Ed Sanders and Tuli Kupferberg continued as if nothing had happened. After what seemed like forever, but was probably only a minute or two, Weber leaped to his feet and began playing again.

In the late fall, Joe and I took off for our first tour as the duo Country Joe and the Fish. The tour, which was of northwestern colleges, was sponsored by the Students for a Democratic Society (SDS), which, I suppose, was moved by the "I-Feel-Like-I'm-Fixin-to-Die Rag" contained on our first extended-play record release. We played Lewis and Clark College and Reed College, in Oregon, and ended up at the University of Washington in Seattle, staying with various SDS members along the way. I'll not soon forget dropping acid with Joe at the Reed College campus in Portland and falling into a small stream, later returning to the house of the professor with whom we were staying. We arrived at the professor's house giggling and too stoned to speak. It was obvious that the people whom we were staying with had no idea of the cause of our odd behavior. We vainly tried to communicate with the professor and his family by using hand signals as we continued on our nonstop course of cosmic laughter. Using gestures, we excused ourselves to the guest room when we could not muster a single word between us.

Drugs were not necessarily a central part of my life in those days, but drugs were certainly an ever-present part of life. I took it for granted that, with the exception of a few of the more traditional old-line leftists, people in Berkeley who saw things the way I did smoked pot regularly, if not every day. Pot smoking had also been an integral part of my late high school year in North Hollywood, my summer in Greenwich Village, and my first few months in San Francisco. In fact, I made the first "big" connection among my high school friends by pooling our resources and buying a kilo of marijuana for $50 from some guy who hung out at Barney's Beanery in Hollywood. At that price, the net cost of the marijuana worked out to be less than a dollar per ounce, a price that even a group of four or five high school students could afford. And even though the price of marijuana had risen to $90 a kilo by the time I was living in Berkeley, a price of less than $2 per ounce was still low enough to be affordable to starving musicians and students alike.

In contrast to marijuana, LSD was often given away and cost nothing. It was not to be taken with great frequency because it lost potency with repetitive use. It was not illegal and was considered somewhat sacred by those who took it. And because of its special status as a sacrament, at least in the early days, most users would have felt that profiting from the distribution of LSD would undoubtedly have given rise to a kind of "bad karma" worth avoiding. When possession of LSD finally became illegal at the end of 1966, its newly declared status as contraband seemed to give value to what was thought to be beyond value, and what was once free of exploitation became exploitable.

Walking down Telegraph Avenue in Berkeley or down Haight Street in San Francisco was very special in those days. Many if not most faces were friendly and wore a smile; there was no hard edge to being on the street. There was an incredible sense of community among the few hundred "hippies" participating in this strange social experiment that would soon begin to spread around the world. Free love was not a marketing concept for purveyors of pornography, but a genuine attempt by a handful of young people to redefine much of what was taken for granted about the way human beings relate to one another. People were in love with life, and sex was easy, available, and natural for a generation of young people who, since the availability of contraceptives became commonplace, no longer had to worry about pregnancy. Social diseases were easily excised by antibiotics and a week of abstinence. This sense of community didn't last long, but for a brief time everything seemed beautiful.

After returning from our SDS tour in the Northwest, Joe and I began putting together a rock band. We'd gone to Pauley Ballroom, on the Berkeley campus, and seen the Paul Butterfield Blues Band play. We were loaded on acid and decided that we had to make Country Joe and the Fish into a rock 'n' roll band. Joe left his first wife and moved into the Russell Street flat with me, Paul, and Bruce, and the four of us began playing music together. Joe sang and played rhythm guitar, I played lead guitar, and Paul and Bruce alternated between bass, guitars, and tambourines. I persuaded a guy named David Cohen, who played guitar with me in another band, to join our band as the keyboard player. The lineup was rounded out by a local drummer named John Francis Gunning. With financial backing from Moe Moskowitz, who owned Moe's Books in Berkeley, we cut another small extended-play vinyl record with our new rock band, which came out in the spring of 1966, and things began to take off.

By late spring, Joe and I thought we really had something, so we decided to hitchhike to New York to find a manager for our band. We had heard of Albert Grossman and knew he had a hand in the management of both Bob Dylan and the Paul Butterfield Blues Band. We figured that when we got to New York we'd ask Albert to manage our band. When we arrived, we stayed at a Lower East Side tenement apartment occupied by our friend from Berkeley, ED Denson, who had played a pivotal role in getting our first two records recorded and released. Denson knew about the music business, as he co-owned a small record company with a folk guitarist named John Fahey, and was in New York as the road manager for an up-and-coming rock band called the Blues Project. We never did meet Albert Grossman on that trip, but we ended up riding back to California with ED in the Blues Project's Volkswagen van. Soon after we got back ED quit the Blues Project and became our business manager.

Nineteen sixty-six was a great year to be playing rock 'n' roll in the San Francisco Bay Area. There were comparatively few good bands, Bill Graham was just getting his Fillmore Auditorium shows under way, Chet Helms was just beginning to put on shows at the Avalon Ballroom, and a community of creative young musicians was beginning to form in an atmosphere of cooperation and sharing that would revolutionize the music industry. Together with Big Brother and the Holding Company, the Grateful Dead, Jefferson Airplane, Quicksilver Messenger Service, and a small group of other young musicians, we were participating in a vast countercultural, LSD-influenced experiment, furthered by a talented community of young light-show and poster artists and musical promoters who all shared idealistic vision of a limitless future. We played music together, shared information with each other, and planned events together to benefit the community. We were earnestly trying to make a better world.

By early August 1966 I had moved back across the bay to San Francisco and was marching up Market Street in protest against the war, and later that month Bill Graham gave us our first job at the Fillmore Auditorium, substituting for the 13th Floor Elevator, which was not able to make its engagement there. Later that year we were at the Fillmore opening for both the Yardbirds* and Otis Redding, and early the next year Graham had us headlining our own shows at the Fillmore.

I had a long talk with Bill Graham about the early years of the Fillmore Auditorium just before he died in 1991. Bill proudly showed me his license as a "dance hall keeper," which he was required to obtain from the San Francisco city government to open the doors to the Fillmore. He told me he hated the idea of being designated a dance hall keeper when the license was first issued, but in the intervening years he'd become proud of the title. Bill had long expressed to me, as he did that night, his distress that, because of the financial success he experienced as a rock promoter, people did not think of him as an "ordinary" member of the 1960s counterculture. "I cared about the music, I cared

---

*By the time the band played the Fillmore in 1966, original Yardbirds guitarist Eric Clapton had been replaced by guitarist Jeff Beck, and original bassist Paul Samwell-Smith had been replaced by Jimmy Page. Page ultimately became the band's lead guitarist and, a few years later, formed his own band, Led Zeppelin.

about people, and all I ever wanted to do," said Bill, "was provide the kids a safe place to be in a turbulent time."

The San Francisco counterculture brought in 1967 with a "Human Be-In" in mid-January. I went with the intention of playing music, but got so stoned I couldn't get on stage. In early spring we tied our band to a flatbed truck and gave a concert in the Panhandle of Golden Gate Park in preparation for an enormous peace march scheduled the next day. On that day, April 15, 1967, we rode on the flatbed down Market Street playing music for one hundred thousand people. We all ended up at the antiwar rally in old Kezar Stadium. Our first commercial record came out to popular acclaim just a few weeks later, and Country Joe and the Fish began to climb the ladder of commercial success.

The Monterey Pop Festival and the record industry put us on the map by mid-June 1967. But the idealism had begun to give way to commercialism. Light shows were being dimmed in favor of traditional stage lighting and spotlights, and poster artists whose psychedelic designs announced concerts were replaced by rapid-fire radio advertising that could sell out a show in lightning-quick fashion. This is not to say that anyone deliberately "sold out," or otherwise betrayed their values. What happened was a more insidious erosion akin to that experienced by Geronimo, Chief Joseph, and Sitting Bull when they toured with Buffalo Bill's Wild West Show at the turn of the century. It seemed that the "Summer of Love" had become more of a sales hook than an expression of countercultural values.

Sure, we continued to play benefits of all kinds. Success never diminished our opposition to the Vietnam War and our support of progressive causes. In some sense the success of Country Joe and the Fish, and that of our musical contemporaries, directly reflected the success of the antiwar movement. As opposition to the war in Vietnam became the cultural mainstream, so did our music. And the rest of the decade turned out to be one heck of a ride. I got a front seat to the show playing in one of the house bands of the antiwar movement.

Perhaps it is only fitting that the last great musical event of the 1960s, Woodstock, has become the most enduring social document of the era. The festival began as a complete financial disaster, bailed out only by a speculative film venture. Woodstock was a logistical disaster. The endless miles of unmoving traffic and the endless demands on hospital emergency rooms throughout a large geographical area signaled the end of the great unstructured musical events that occurred throughout the United States during the late 1960s and heralded the demise of the '60s counterculture movement.

Local governments became unwilling to host the kind of event that might prove an unmitigated financial disaster by unexpectedly taxing local services.

Rock promoters were thus forced to move concerts into large arenas and stadiums that were specifically designed to handle large crowds. The move to numbered seats, along neatly aisled rows, did more than end the casual social interaction that had put rock at the center of the counterculture movement. In an arena or stadium a crowd could be monitored and controlled, and large-scale consensual illegal activities were no longer possible. And it forever separated the performer from the audience. Rock music was transformed into the same kind of controlled amusement as baseball or football.

Watching the Woodstock film brings me a sense of ambivalence, a simultaneous experience of both exultation and loss. Woodstock is not only a highwater mark of the 1960s counterculture, it is also a sad testament to much of what went wrong with it. I listen to the music, including my own, and swell with pride at our collective artistic achievement. I see the momentary sense of community and I think of all that could have been. But I also see the tremendous talent of Jimi Hendrix, Janis Joplin, and Al Wilson* lost to drug overdoses, and I'm reminded that not one of them lived to be thirty years old. Sadly I see what began as unbridled idealism being swallowed up by an uncontrolled hedonism in just a few short years.

But for me, the 1960s I want to remember will always be that relatively small community of people in the San Francisco Bay Area who made and listened to the music at places like the Jabberwock, the Fillmore Auditorium, and the Avalon Ballroom—the dancers, light-show artists, poster artists, and a host of creative people content to live with a ton of commitment and without a whole lot of money. I want to remember my mixed feelings of fear and pride and the incredible sense of community I felt when singing "We Shall Overcome" locked arm-in-arm with others at a civil rights sit-in. And I want to remember riding down the middle of Market Street in San Francisco on a flatbed truck, rigged for sound, playing antiwar songs with my band and looking out over a sea of tens of thousands of people marching and singing for peace.

Sure, it turned out there was a downside. It turned out we were too damned open for our own good. The 1970s came, the drugs turned hard, people started dying of overdoses, and some started dying of AIDS. Our openness to people oftentimes led to exploitation and unhappy outcomes. And most of the world's problems remain unsolved. We didn't end discrimination, hunger, or war.

But we did some really good things, perhaps despite ourselves. Most of us stopped using harmful drugs and used our brief glimpse of heaven to usher in

---

*Al Wilson performed and sang with the band Canned Heat. His vocal on "Goin' Up the Country" is the opening theme of the Woodstock movie.

a whole new era in psychology and religion. We came to understand that there were adverse effects to all drugs—even marijuana and tobacco—and powerful drugs like LSD could awaken uncontrollable demons in some people. We became conscious of our bodies, left the cities, started organic farms, and helped give the rest of the country a good idea of what constitutes a healthy diet. Or we stayed in the cities, helped to revitalize the neighborhoods, and improved the quality of life. We had the patience and tolerance to accept alternative medicine and therapies. Our questioning of basic assumptions about sex and relationships helped pave the way for both the women's and gay rights movements. We helped bring the world a whole new consciousness of the environment, and we helped tear down the Berlin wall. And, most of all, we helped teach the world that one person can make a difference. I sure don't want to go back to the 1960s, but I'm glad I was there.

Politics as Art, Art as Politics

The Freedom Singers, the Living Theatre, and Public Performance

Bradford Martin

In June 1963, an audience of more than two thousand New Yorkers turned out to see a "Salute to Southern Freedom" benefit concert for the Student Nonviolent Coordinating Committee (SNCC) at Carnegie Hall, featuring the SNCC Freedom Singers and gospel singer Mahalia Jackson. The Freedom Singers was a quartet of young African American vocalists, organized by SNCC for fund-raising purposes, that had debuted in a concert with Pete Seeger the previous November. Robert Shelton's *New York Times* review of the concert hinted that the audience displayed an even greater interest in the Freedom Singers than the renowned Jackson, attributing this to the fact that the Freedom Singers' songs "echoed with the imme-diacy of today's headlines the integration battle in the South." The Freedom Singers conveyed to its audiences the texture of the civil rights movement's daily confronta-tions, Shelton noted, "in a stirring fashion, musically and morally."[1]

On September 27, 1968, the Living Theatre performed the American premiere of *Paradise Now* in New Haven, Connecticut. During the opening segment, "The Rite of Guerrilla Theatre," which criticized various repressions of capitalist society, cast members chanted phrases such as "I don't know how to stop the wars," "You can't live if you don't have money," "I'm not allowed to smoke marijuana," and finally "I'm not allowed to take my clothes off." To underline this last phrase, company members stripped to the legal limit, the men in loincloths, the women in bikinis, and much of the audience followed suit. The production was well received by students sympathetic to the Living Theatre's message, and several hundred audience members followed the cast into the streets at the end of the evening. Police alleged that several individuals were completely naked. Eight people—five audience members and three company members—were arrested and charged with indecent exposure. The New Haven chief of police remarked: "As far as we're concerned, art stops at the door of the theater, and then we apply community standards."[2]

At first glance, there seem few similarities between the Freedom Singers and the Living Theatre. The Freedom Singers was a handpicked group of African American singers, sponsored by SNCC, who toured and sang freedom songs to publicize the cause of the civil rights movement. The formal quartet of Freedom Singers served to spread the work of a larger group of singers in the South who used music as part of the struggle for civil rights on a daily basis. In a sense, then, anyone who sang songs as part of the civil rights movement was a "freedom singer." The freedom singers' primary purpose was to advance the movement's integrationist and egalitarian goals of helping African Americans attain the privileges of full citizenship and inclusion in mainstream American society. While freedom singers created a rich and unique array of songs, their artistic purpose remained secondary to their reality as activists in a mass democratic movement. The Living Theatre, on the other hand, was a predominantly white theater company arising out of the New York avant-garde artistic scene of the 1950s. Julian Beck and Judith Malina, founders of the experimental theater company, struggled arduously to integrate their personal political beliefs, including anarchism and pacifism, into their theatrical productions. By their 1968–69 U.S. tour with a repertory that included the controversial *Paradise Now*, the Living Theatre emerged as a theatrical voice of the counterculture, advocating numerous personal freedoms including liberated sexuality and recreational drug use. They envisioned *Paradise Now* as beginning the work of a nonviolent revolution that would radically transform American society.

Yet singers in the civil rights movement and the Living Theatre shared an important characteristic; both pursued an impulse to stage performances and actions in public spaces, increasingly eschewing concert halls, theaters, and other venues of high culture. This choice enabled their cultural expressions to reach wider audiences and advance their politics. Public performance encouraged a convergence of everyday life, politics, and artistic concerns for freedom singers and the Living Theatre in a way that expanded the boundaries of what was considered political. The freedom singers and the Living Theatre shared this new vision of personal politics with many larger 1960s movements for social change including the civil rights movement, the New Left, the counterculture, and the emerging women's liberation movement.

BRADFORD MARTIN recently completed a dissertation titled "'The Theater Is in the Street': Arts and Cultural Groups in the 1960s," at Boston University. Prior to his career in academic life, he performed with various theater groups including the Living Theatre, Theater for the New City, and Bread and Puppet Theater. He currently teaches at Bryant College in Rhode Island.

Although the freedom singers owed their existence to the civil rights movement, it was in no way inevitable that the movement would involve singing,
especially in public. Prior to the Montgomery bus boycott, African American
initiatives for social equality achieved varying degrees of success, but none used
singing as such an important part of movement strategy. The earliest sit-ins and
demonstrations occurred in silence. As the movement progressed, however,
activists deployed freedom songs in a wider array of venues. The image of civil
rights demonstrators soulfully clapping and singing "Everybody Sing Freedom"
or "This Little Light of Mine" as they marched through Southern streets is now
fixed in the popular history of the civil rights movement. The early silent,
polite, direct action protests sought to expose the hypocrisy of the southern
social order by contrasting black civility with unruly white mobs in what historian Kenneth Cmiel refers to as a "bourgeois festival of misrule." Evidence
suggests, however, that other factors may have influenced decisions to keep early
protests silent. For instance, the leaders of the sit-ins of February 1960 were "very
conscious of being charged with rowdiness or uncouth behavior."[3] Movement
leaders knew that public singing constituted behavior that might result in a
pretext for local authorities to interfere with civil rights demonstrators and make
arrests. It seems likely that at the outset of the 1960s, when institutional bodies like the House Un-American Activities Committee still existed to mitigate
against dissent, activists lacked the confidence to use freedom songs in public
settings.

Furthermore, singing songs from the tradition of black spirituals did not
necessarily come naturally to the middle-class black students in SNCC, the group
that became most responsible for making singing a central element in the
movement. These black college students were an upwardly mobile group who
often associated spirituals with slavery and social backwardness. Movement
activists ultimately decided to use traditional black music because they believed
singing could be a valuable means of attaining goals such as freedom, equality,
integration, and civil rights. Singing provided a means of reorienting black
cultural identity and affirming a positive link with African American cultural
heritage, including traditions of black protest. It also bridged a social gap between the middle-class college students and local populations of rural southern blacks. Ultimately, this served SNCC's goal of fostering indigenous leadership in the black communities of the rural South. Moreover, singing created a
sense of unity among different groups and individuals within the movement
and gave the movement the appearance of unity to the general public. As freedom songs were used in a greater variety of situations, such as direct action
protests, mass demonstrations, and in jails after mass arrests, activists came to

regard singing as an important device for overcoming fear and sustaining courage in the face of violence and hardship. To hostile authorities and to white Americans outside the South, singing represented an outward demonstration of the activists' resolve. Finally, it encouraged public opinion to sympathize with the movement. This was accomplished not only through the efforts of the formal quartet of Freedom Singers, but through the masses of grass-roots civil rights activists for whom singing the body of freedom songs came to accompany movement activities from meetings to mass demonstrations. With their use of singing as movement strategy, freedom singers forged new parameters of public performance that opened up cultural space for such groups as the Living Theatre.

Singing and Black Cultural Identity

Historians have stressed SNCC's critical role in refashioning black cultural identity during the 1960s, contending that prior to the civil rights movement, many African Americans suffered from a negative self-image, the lingering effect of their feelings of inferiority to whites stemming from slavery-era oppressions. A more contemporary factor was the inequality written into the legal system and public accommodations in the Jim Crow South. As early as 1962, students in the movement began to question assimilation, integration, and legal equality as the movement's ultimate goals. They argued that both an enhanced sense of black cultural identity and economic justice were necessary to create a racially egalitarian nation. Ultimately, these sentiments resulted in the ideas of black power, black pride, and black nationalism that came to dominate African American discourse by the late 1960s. These ideas transformed the civil rights movement itself from a struggle for integration into mainstream American society to a struggle for identity in a society that the activists sought to remake to accommodate pluralism. The freedom singers played a pivotal role in this transition.[4]

During the Montgomery bus boycott, Christian hymns such as "Onward Christian Soldiers," "Lord I Want to Be a Christian," and even "Battle Hymn of the Republic" were often sung. As late as the 1960 mass meetings in Nashville, Fisk University student Julius Lester commented that activists "sang 'Battle Hymn of the Republic' to death, as well as a number of hymns."[5] The February 1, 1960, sit-in by four black college students at a Greensboro, North Carolina, Woolworth's lunch counter marked a turning point in the civil rights movement in a number of ways. This demonstration initiated a more confrontational phase of the movement, in which students figured prominently, using tactics of nonviolent civil disobedience to protest segregation. The Greensboro sit-in inspired the formation of SNCC in April 1960, and numerous other sit-in demonstrations, most notably in Nashville. When students from Baptist Theological Seminary, Tennessee State University, and Fisk University commenced the Nashville sit-ins eight days after the Greensboro sit-in, singing began to take on its unique character in the movement. During the Nashville sit-ins, freedom singers started creating a body of songs based upon traditional black spirituals, making lyrical changes and adaptations as necessary to reflect the daily confrontations and ideological principles of the movement.

Young civil rights activists used music to forge a positive new cultural identity for blacks. In Nashville, the freedom singers adapted songs by changing lyrics in ways that reflected efforts to dispel notions of black inferiority. For instance, the song "You'd Better Leave Segregation Alone" reworked a rock 'n' roll song originally titled "You Better Leave My Little Kitten Alone," and included the lyrics "You'd better leave segregation alone/ Because they love segregation like a hound dog loves a bone."[6] With the admonition to "leave segregation alone" the freedom singers referred, ironically, to blacks who conformed to the Southern system of segregation and warned them of the depth of white zeal for the system. The phrase "like a hound dog loves a bone" cast southern whites as canines, thus implying that white segregationists were less civilized than blacks. Thus, the lyrics of "You'd Better Leave Segregation Alone" employ an important strategy of the larger civil rights movement by contrasting polite, civilized young black college students with unruly, brutal white segregationists.

While "You'd Better Leave Segregation Alone" was adapted from a rock 'n' roll song, many of the other songs from the Nashville sit-ins drew upon black spirituals as their source. "(Everybody Says) Freedom," was adapted from "Amen," a traditional black spiritual in which a one-word lyric, "amen" was chanted over and over again. Church song leaders would evoke each new series of chants of "Amen," by calling out phrases such as:

> Everybody says
> > Amen Amen Amen Amen Amen
> Let the Church say
> > Amen Amen Amen Amen Amen
> Let the Deacons say
> > Amen Amen Amen Amen Amen

"(Everybody Says) Freedom" made use of the call-and-response vocal technique from traditional African American music but substituted lyrics specific to the civil rights movement. During the Nashville sit-ins student activists sang:

>Everybody says
>>Freedom Freedom Freedom Freedom Freedom
>
>All across the South
>>Freedom Freedom Freedom Freedom Freedom
>
>In Mississippi
>>Freedom Freedom Freedom Freedom Freedom

In the context of confrontations with Nashville's white segregationist establishment, this song became a powerful statement of the movement's goal. In certain situations the refrain "civil rights" was substituted for "freedom" as a way of specifying the particular type of freedom activists sought. "(Everybody Says) Freedom" also signified racial pride by affirming activists' connection through the music sung by previous generations of African-Americans who struggled under slavery and Jim Crow. SNCC's John Lewis identified "(Everybody Says) Freedom" as "the heart of the Nashville movement," and commented that he felt "uplifted" by the song.[7] His choice of words suggests that black college students, through freedom songs, increasingly viewed traditional African American culture, and music specifically, as a means to promote positive self-identity rather than as an unsophisticated remnant of black life in the rural South they hoped to abandon.

The strategic choice of spirituals manifested black students' growing sense of positive cultural identity. The lyrics of "This Little Light of Mine" overtly reflect concern with promoting feelings of self-worth as the chorus affirms: "This little light of mine/I'm gonna let it shine." Later, in the version of the song that freedom singers sang most frequently, one of the verses began, "We've got the light of freedom/We're gonna let it shine," establishing the "light" as a metaphor for freedom. In the Jim Crow South, where white supremacy's hold was so powerful that resistance had to be carried out surreptitiously if at all, declaring an intention to let the light of freedom "shine" was a bold statement of positive identity that demonstrated willingness to confront Southern segregationists.

Bridging the Gap: Freedom Songs, SNCC, and the Black Masses

If the freedom songs succeeded in shaping a positive identity, their use in promoting a sense of common identity is equally remarkable considering the diverse backgrounds of the participants in the civil rights movement. SNCC viewed developing indigenous leadership in the southern black communities in which it organized as a critical aspect of its mission. Ella Baker, a movement veteran who convened SNCC's founding conference, believed SNCC ought to be a vehicle for "the development of people who are interested not in being leaders as much as in developing leadership among other people."[8] Singing was one of the chief means by which SNCC fostered grass-roots leadership. Freedom singer and historian Bernice Reagon identified the repertoire of freedom songs as one of the few resources available to SNCC fieldworkers when they entered communities. The organization placed a premium on fieldworkers' songleading abilities, since singing was a means by which the educated, middle-class black student activists could effectively communicate with poor rural black southerners. "After the song," Reagon recalled, "the differences among us would not be so great. Somehow, making a song required an expression of that which was common to us all."[9] Freedom songs united socioeconomically different groups of black southerners, and were essential to creating successful mass meetings in the movement. Songleader Julius Lester amplified this point, claiming that the freedom songs "serve to crumble the class barriers within the Negro community. . . . The professor and the plumber, the society matron and the cleaning woman, the young college student and the unlettered old man stand beside each other, united by a song and a dream. They march together and are jailed together."[10] Lester's observation illustrates the diversity of black southerners in the civil rights movement and the role singing played in promoting cohesion. Freedom singer and native Mississippian Hollis Watkins clarified how this worked, pointing out that the repertoire of freedom songs was simple and that anyone could "pick them up" quickly. Singers could invent verses and then "hear their verses coming back to them." This process of inventing verses created an equality of musical opportunity, which promoted feelings of affinity between the urban, middle-class students and economically disadvantaged rural blacks. Singing was "something that people in the South did," explained Watkins. "If you sang with people, then you could talk about voter registration."[11]

Yet singing's influence was not limited to helping unify meetings in rural black communities. The student activists also viewed it as a force to develop leadership, and they accomplished this by transferring songleading responsibilities from fieldworkers to local songleaders. Fieldworkers attempted to identify local individuals with the potential to be songleaders, usually designating those with previous singing experience, often in church or school choirs. Fannie Lou Hamer is the preeminent example of an uneducated black woman from the rural South who became a civil rights leader thanks in part to her work as a songleader. Hamer worked as a sharecropper for eighteen years before becoming involved with SNCC in 1962 as part of voter registration efforts in Mississippi. She served as a delegate in the Mississippi Freedom Democratic Party, which SNCC helped organize through the umbrella organization of Council of Federated Organizations. Hamer received national recognition at the 1964

Democratic Convention with her party's bid to unseat the all-white Mississippi regular Democratic delegation. Hamer delivered compelling testimony before the Democratic Party's Credentials Committee, saying at one point, "If the Freedom Democratic Party is not seated now, I question America." Her nationally televised testimony and provocative remarks prompted Lyndon Johnson to preempt coverage of her concluding remarks to save the Democratic Party further embarrassment.

Yet television coverage of the 1964 Democratic Convention also showed Hamer leading a powerful rendition of "This Little Light of Mine." Bob Cohen, director of the Mississippi Caravan of Music, a group of folksingers that toured Mississippi as part of the 1964 Freedom Summer, explained that: "When Mrs. Hamer finishes singing a few freedom songs one is aware that he has truly heard a fine political speech, stripped of the usual rhetoric and filled with the anger and determination of the civil rights movement. . . . On the other hand in her speeches there is the constant thunder and drive of the music."[12] Hamer's identity as a civil rights leader who rose quickly from a humble background intertwined with her gifts as a singer and songleader.

Hamer was forty-four years old when she first became aware of SNCC, but SNCC helped develop younger songleaders as well. In McComb, Mississippi, one of the most hostile locales in the South, Hollis Watkins, who was then a local high school student, emerged as a songleader. During the Montgomery bus boycott, a group of three elementary school girls were among the most prominent local songleaders at mass meetings. From the college students in SNCC emerged another group of young people whose songleading experience gave them confidence as activists. Bernice Reagon wrote of her songleading while in the Albany jail: "I found that although I was younger than many of the women in my section of the jail, I was asked to take on leadership roles. First as a song leader and then in most other matters concerning the group, especially in discussions, or when speaking with prison officials."[13] Reagon's account suggests that in the context of SNCC's attempt to function as a "leaderless" organization—and thereby embody within their organization the egalitarian principles they hoped to establish in the South—songleading fostered a kind of organic and tacit leadership necessary to conduct the day-to-day affairs of the movement. Reagon's testimony shows how songleading functioned as a *de facto* power from which other powers, such as speaking on behalf of the group to prison guards, naturally flowed. For this reason it is probably not coincidental that some of the most prominent individuals in the history of the civil rights movement, including Hamer, James Farmer, and Cordell Reagon, were also prominent songleaders.

"We Shall Overcome"

Perhaps the most recurring observation in freedom singers' accounts concerns the role of singing in achieving unity among different groups within the civil rights movement. In addition to singing's capacity to foment unity within the movement, activists valued singing because it conveyed the appearance of movement unity to outsiders. Most emblematic of the way freedom singers used music to attain unity is the ritual that came to attend the singing of "We Shall Overcome," which was recognized as the movement's theme song by 1963.

"We Shall Overcome" was originally a song sung in black churches titled "I'll Overcome Someday." During a 1945 strike, the predominantly black Charleston, South Carolina, Local of the Food, Tobacco, Agricultural, and Allied Workers Union adapted the song for use on picket lines. Significantly, the strikers not only added nonvocal modes of participation to the traditional church song, such as rhythmic clapping and stomping, but they also changed the song from the first-person singular to the first-person plural, changing the lines to "*We* will win our rights," "*We* will win this fight," and "*We* will overcome." This crucial lyrical change allowed the song to function as a statement of unity and perseverance.

The 1945 strike ended successfully, and some of the strikers brought the song to the Highlander Folk School, a progressive adult education school in Monteagle, Tennessee. At Highlander, two women from the Charleston Local taught the song to Zilphia Horton, the wife of Highlander's founder, Myles Horton. Zilphia Horton added several verses to the song and taught the song to Pete Seeger, who changed "We will overcome" to "We shall overcome," and added two more verses. In April 1960, Guy Carawan, a white songleader and musical director at Highlander, attended the founding conference of SNCC in Raleigh, North Carolina. At the conference, Carawan taught students "We Shall Overcome" among other songs. The members of SNCC quickly adopted the song into the repertoire of freedom songs, making melodic and rhythmic changes that moved the song closer to its gospel origins.[14]

From its introduction to SNCC members at the founding conference, "We Shall Overcome" demonstrated its ability to create unity. The Southern Christian Leadership Conference (SCLC), a group composed of black religious and community leaders who tended to be more moderate than SNNC's activists, sponsored the SNCC conference to harness the momentum generated by the student sit-in movement. Both groups sang "We Shall Overcome" together at the conference, pledging their commitment and unity.[15] "We Shall Overcome" quickly emerged as the theme song of the civil rights movement. By the summer of 1963 the singing of "We Shall Overcome" typically closed civil rights meetings and demonstrations of not just SNCC, but several other organizations as well. Activists also developed a set of rituals physicalizing the sentiment of unity expressed in the lyrics of "We Shall Overcome." Robert Shelton of the *New York Times* observed, "As its stately cadences are sung, the participants cross arms in front of themselves, link hands with the persons on each side and sway in rhythm to the music."[16] The image of civil rights activists with linked hands, swaying and singing "We Shall Overcome," served as a powerful demonstration of unity and remains a vivid popular icon of the 1960s.

When Cordell Reagon, a songleader and field secretary in the Nashville sit-in movement, arrived in Albany, Georgia, in the fall of 1961 to help organize a campaign to desegregate a broad spectrum of public accommodations and municipal jobs, he found that black students in Albany were already singing a version of "We Shall Overcome." These students remembered the song from television coverage of the sit-ins, but they sang the version they were more familiar with from their singing experiences in church, which included the use of the first-person singular "I'll overcome someday." Reagon quickly showed the Albany students the "proper way" to sing "We Shall Overcome," using the first-person plural "we," singing it at the end of meetings, and linking hands.[17] The ritual singing of "We Shall Overcome" had become a powerful tool for unity in the movement.

"We Are Not Afraid Today": Singing to Overcome Fear

Initially freedom songs were used solely in meetings rather than during actual demonstrations. This changed during the Albany movement in December 1961, as activists made the crucial transition to using freedom songs first in jails and then on the front lines of demonstrations themselves. Police Chief Laurie Pritchett instituted mass arrests in the Albany movement; 760 demonstrators were arrested in December 1961 alone. Once jailed, demonstrators sang to overcome fear, maintain unity and morale, and simply to pass the time. While the Albany protests failed in the sense that they did not generate the publicity and media attention needed to pressure local authorities to desegregate the city, they succeeded in legitimizing singing in the movement's public protests. Since students knew they would be arrested anyway, they believed they might as well sing. By the summer of 1962, freedom songs were sung in marches, during demonstrations, and in jails.[18] As the venues for singing broadened, freedom singing began to take on the vital role of quelling activists' fears in potentially dangerous situations.

Singing helped strengthen civil rights workers' resolve in two ways. First, the act of singing itself relieved the tension and pressure of potentially violent situations. Candie Anderson, a white demonstrator in the Nashville sit-ins of February 1960, commented that singing was "truly good for the spirit" and helped her overcome apprehension during her stay at the Nashville City Jail.[19] In Albany, Chief Pritchett used the tactic of mass jailings, without resorting to overt police violence, to harass the demonstrators and diffuse their momentum. Pritchett's strategy often entailed significant jail time for demonstrators, and they grew to recognize the "value of this singing in keeping the courage and morale of the students high." One student remarked that singing "helped to ease the knot in the pit of my stomach."[20] Clearly, singing comforted civil rights workers in situations where they faced the potential for violence and other hardships.

The second way freedom songs actively strengthened activists' resolve in the face of threats of violence involved adapting freedom songs lyrics' on the front lines of specific confrontations. This practice served to fortify civil rights workers' commitment to the struggle. Bob Zellner described a march on the mayor's office in Talladega, Alabama, to protest police brutality:

> The march was stopped about a block and a half from the campus by 40 city, county, and state policemen with tear gas grenades, billy sticks and a fire truck. When ordered to return to the campus or be beaten back, the students, confronted individually by the police, chose not to move and quietly began singing "We Shall Not Be Moved."[21]

With its affirmation that "like a tree, planted by the water" the singers would not be moved, this song's lyrics reinforced the activists' commitment to the protest. Likewise, "Ain't Gonna Let Nobody Turn Me Round" overtly declared the singers' intention to continue fighting for civil rights. Furthermore, "Ain't Gonna Let Nobody Turn Me Round" featured another device that freedom singers wielded effectively. In this song, the songleader introduced new verses naming specific oppressors in local civil rights campaigns. For instance, in Albany, the singers called out the names of Chief Pritchett and Mayor Asa Kelley, avowing their intention not to let these two men thwart their protest:

> Ain't gonna let Chief Pritchett turn me 'round, turn me 'round, turn me 'round
> Ain't gonna let Chief Pritchett turn me 'round,
> I'm gonna keep on a walkin', keep on a talkin'
> Marching up to freedom land.
>
> Ain't gonna let Mayor Kelley turn me 'round . . .

During the 1965 march for voting rights from Selma to Montgomery, singers adapted a verse that declared, "Ain't gonna let Governor Wallace turn me 'round ...," demonstrating their intention to persevere despite the resistance of the Alabama governor who only two years earlier had promised "segregation now, segregation tomorrow, segregation forever." According to Watkins, naming local oppressors in freedom songs was "a way of getting personal" and holding individuals in the Southern segregationist power structure accountable for their actions. Watkins claims that this tactic made a considerable impression on local officials, who "didn't know that you changed the names each time you came to a new town."[22]

Carrying the Story North: The SNCC Freedom Singers

The Albany movement received national media attention for its musical creations and innovations. This momentum sparked plans to form a group of traveling freedom singers and in the summer of 1962, Cordell Reagon organized the SNCC Freedom Singers. The initial group of Freedom Singers consisted of Reagon, Charles Neblett, Rutha Mae Harris, and Bernice Johnson (later Bernice Reagon). While the group's purpose was ostensibly fund raising, the Freedom Singers also performed the work of moral and ideological suasion. As Neblett remarked: "Our real purpose is to carry the story of the student movement to the North. Newspapers and UPI often won't give the real story."[23] The Student Nonviolent Coordinating Committee believed that it had to find another way to communicate this story to those outside the South, and that singing could be a powerful instrument with which to shape public perception.

Bernice Reagon elaborated on this point, explaining how the Freedom Singers mixed freedom songs with spoken narrative to illustrate the struggles of blacks in jails, marches, and rallies around the South. Reagon contends that in live performance the songs possessed a greater emotional power than the spoken words, and that the songs "became a major way of making people who were not on the scene feel the intensity of what was happening in the south."[24] The Freedom Singers, then, achieved a measure of success in establishing close communion with its audience, which was also a key concern of the Living Theatre. Both groups hoped to use this close relationship to influence the audience's political beliefs and actions.

While influencing public opinion was a key goal of the Freedom Singers, fund raising was important as well. In fact, singing was used in conjunction with fund raising at every level of the civil rights movement. For instance, one SNCC volunteer recalled, "We used to sing for our lunch," during the Mississippi Freedom

Summer of 1964.[25] The Freedom Singers' appearance at the Carnegie Hall concert reflected their fund-raising aspirations. Symbolizing northern elite high culture and society, Carnegie Hall represented the kind of venue that could attract the kind of affluent patronage that often sympathized with liberal causes and might offer financial support to the movement. Formal performances such as the one at Carnegie Hall functioned as an extension of movement activities in the South by spreading public awareness of these actions. This extension made both freedom songs and the "real story" of the civil rights movement available to a wider public outside the South. Northerners sometimes became sufficiently motivated to sponsor their own concerts on behalf of the movement, such as the SNCC benefit concert that New York Philharmonic conductor Leonard Bernstein organized with violinist Isaac Stern during the summer of 1964.[26]

Aside from fund raising and the suasion of public opinion, the Freedom Singers' work generated several other important consequences. First, they received considerable critical acclaim for their musical talents. Moreover, the sense of conviction in the Freedom Singers' *a cappella* vocals sparked the imaginations of the predominantly white folk singers of the "folk revival," who previously relied primarily on guitar and banjo accompaniment. The folk revival included performers such as Pete Seeger, Bob Dylan, Joan Baez, Phil Ochs, and Peter, Paul & Mary, and unlike the frivolous mainstream popular music of the early 1960s, it provided young people with music often infused with serious political content. Increasingly, the Freedom Singers shared venues with performers in the folk revival, such as the 1963 Newport Folk Festival. The Freedom Singers' influence pervaded this event, as nearly every white folk performer included an *a cappella* number and a freedom song in his or her repertoire. Civil rights movement themes became common in the lyrics of the topical songwriters of the folk revival. Dylan's "Oxford Town" dealt with James Meredith's attempt to become the first African American student to enter the University of Mississippi, "The Lonesome Death of Hattie Carroll" exposed the race and class biases of the southern legal system, and "Only a Pawn in Their Game" sought to extract meaning from the murder of Mississippi NAACP leader Medgar Evers. Dylan also produced a politically driven body of songs, such as "Blowin' in the Wind," "A Hard Rain's a-Gonna Fall," and "The Times They Are a-Changin'," which discussed on a more symbolic level themes such as civil rights, the threat of nuclear war, and generational politics. Another topical songwriter who addressed civil rights was African American folksinger Len Chandler, whose "The Time of the Tiger" called for an awakening spirit of black militancy, and whose pointed variation of the old labor song "Which Side Are You On?" exhorted the black middle class to commit to the movement with direct action and financial support. The subject matter of the folk revival's topical songwriters mirrored both the themes and the fund-raising imperative inherent in the mission of the Freedom Singers.[27]

In addition to spreading the story of the movement outside the South, the Freedom Singers also performed in the South. In July 1963, Seeger organized a folk festival in Greenwood, Mississippi, a town in the heart of the Mississippi Delta, where white resistance to integration was particularly severe, as part of SNCC's voter registration drive. The performers, including Seeger, Bob Dylan, and the Freedom Singers, were a racial mix, itself a provocation in the Deep South. The audience was predominantly black and estimated at between two hundred fifty and three hundred people, including about twenty young whites. Thus, this concert, with its racially mixed audience, can be viewed as a type of public direct action since it enacted the movement's vision of an integrated southern society. The Freedom Singers were well aware of the larger public exposure for this event, as the *New York Times* and a television camera crew from New York were on hand.[28]

While freedom songs contributed to the success of the movement, singing these songs also generated an important by-product. Media coverage of the public activity of singing freedom songs altered notions about the relationship between culture and politics. As Americans watched on television freedom songs used to support what most viewed as a righteous cause, this eroded the taboos and self-censorship against politically oriented cultural expressions that dominated the 1950s. This remarkable development reflected a logical outgrowth of the early civil rights movement's goals, since the segregated South's local custom of racial exclusion made public spaces the logical sites at which to contest the Jim Crow system. In the spirit of participatory democracy, so evident both in the New Left and the civil rights movement, individuals at the local level tried to liberate themselves from their own oppression. Singing became a galvanizing force in achieving unity and overcoming activists' fears about the violence they hoped to provoke to dramatize their cause. The freedom singers' use of the public space as a cultural forum broke down the McCarthy-era prohibition on mixing art and politics and wrought a profound influence on several other cultural groups with political goals.

The Living Theatre Begins: Poetic Drama and the Revolution of Form

> The theatre is in the street. The street belongs to the people. Free the theatre. Free the street. Begin.
>
> From the Living Theatre's
> *Paradise Now*[29]

The civil rights movement's entrance into the public space in the early 1960s signaled the end of the McCarthy-era stranglehold on political dissent. The central place of singing in the movement created "cultural space" in which other artistic and cultural groups with oppositional and alternative political agendas could emerge. Although the agendas of these groups often had little to do with civil rights, most endorsed the freedoms and equality for which civil rights activists fought. A case in point is the avant-garde countercultural theater troupe the Living Theatre, which toured the United States in 1968–69 with a spectacle called *Paradise Now*, which attracted national publicity. This production ended with the actors encouraging audiences to move from the theater to the street to begin the work of nonviolent revolution. While singing freedom songs in public spaces represented a strategy in the civil rights movement's struggle for integration, the Living Theatre's move to the streets resulted from the convergence of personal political beliefs and artistic concerns that dated back to the early 1950s.

Julian Beck and Judith Malina founded the Living Theatre in the early 1950s as a repudiation of both contemporary Broadway theater, which featured banal star vehicles and high ticket prices and the stylized realism of modern drama. As early as 1948, Malina wrote in her diary, "Broadway buries itself under a sugary realism."[30] She expressed a distaste for modern realistic drama with its naturalistic yet stylized acting and scenic elements. Beck and Malina sought a larger, more epic, non-naturalistic style without the "plush seats" and inflated admission prices of Broadway theaters.[31] They planned to create a theater emphasizing contemporary poetic drama performed in repertory for reduced prices. Their vision was shaped by Malina's work with German director Erwin Piscator, who was renowned for staging classical plays against the backgrounds of contemporary sociopolitical events. After emigrating from Germany, Piscator sought to use his Dramatic Workshop at the New School for Social Research to stimulate an avant-garde theater movement in New York. The Living Theatre emerged as the most significant product of Piscator's conviction that theater should not act as mere entertainment, but rather should convey a social message.[32]

At first the Living Theatre conveyed only messages about the form of the theatrical event itself. It produced poetic dramas such as William Carlos Williams's *Many Loves*, Paul Goodman's *The Young Disciple*, Gertrude Stein's *Doctor Faustus Lights the Lights*, and Jean Cocteau's *Orpheus*. Beck described the work of the Living Theatre's poetic dramas as trying to "revivify language" to prevent it from remaining "outmoded" and thus to "enlarge the limits of consciousness."[33] This effort to revitalize theatrical language centered on its effect on the audience. Beck and the Living Theatre wanted language to affect the audience not just in the sentimental way that modern realistic drama attempted to elicit tears or laughter, but rather to affect the audience on a spiritual, transcendental level.

These principles reflected the period's cultural and political milieu, a landscape dominated by the repression and paranoia perpetuated by the McCarthy hearings. The aesthetic principles evident in the Living Theatre's work during the 1950s had counterparts in the art and music worlds. The artistic revolutions that took place in the 1950s, from Jackson Pollack's splattered paintings to John Cage's atonal musical compositions, focused on expanding the boundaries of expression in art forms themselves rather than employing art as a vehicle for social and political expression. As Beck put it, "there was a peculiar kind of aesthetic law which dominated at least American art at that time . . . that you cannot mix art and political thought, that one despoils the other."[34] This ideology produced inherently conservative consequences. If the arts were not perceived as a legitimate place for social and political commentary, then a major forum for dissent was eliminated.

Although the Living Theatre confined its experiments during the 1950s to exploring the form of theater as opposed to its content, this did not mean that its founders, Beck and Malina, were devoid of politics. On the contrary, during the 1950s Beck and Malina began to form the political views that animated the company's future work. The two most salient political influences were the anarchism of writer and philosopher Paul Goodman and the pacifism of Dorothy Day, founder of the *Catholic Worker* newspaper and the benevolence movement by the same name. Beck and Malina enjoyed close personal relationships with Goodman and Day; they produced several of Goodman's plays and got arrested with Day for protesting civil defense drills. A 1957 protest resulted in prison terms for both Beck and Malina, and like civil rights activists, prison tended to radicalize their politics rather than to deter them.[35] Their civil defense protests constituted a kind of public performance that prefigured the Living Theatre's eventual movement toward street theater. After the air raid sirens sounded, the vast majority of citizens who complied with the drills went to shelters, while the protesters remained alone on the streets in the presence of news reporters and photographers. These acts made a public statement of their moral and political beliefs, which became a defining feature of their theatrical performances by the late 1960s.

The Connection and *The Brig*: Heightened Realism, Heightened Politics

The Living Theatre's production of Jack Gelber's *The Connection* (1959), which the Beat literary movement's relationship with improvisational jazz music helped inspire, represented a turning point in the company's ability to combine its experiments with theatrical form with its political and social vision. The play's title referred to heroin addicts' term for their dealer, and the main action of the play revolved around junkies' attempts to procure their next fix. The production combined scripted dialogue and improvisational action to depict the junkies' daily lives. The main characters in *The Connection* were either junkies or jazz musicians or both, and the production featured live jazz throughout the performance. Beck envisioned the project in humanistic terms which anticipated the New Left's concern with poverty and other urban ills during the 1960s: "We had to talk about heroin and addicts. It was important to show that these people who, in 1959, were considered the lowest of the low . . . were human . . . and that what the addicts had come to was not the result of an indigenous personality evil, but was symptomatic of the errors of the whole world."[36] For New York theater in the late 1950s, this was highly transgressive subject matter. Casual profanity and actors "shooting up" onstage were a calculated challenge to standards of mainstream theatrical propriety. Typical of the reaction of mainstream reviewers was *New York Times* critic Louis Calta's description of the production as "a farrago of dirt, small-time philosophy, empty talk and extended runs of cool music."[37] These critical reviews revealed an unwillingness to accept *The Connection* as a piece of theater designed for a social and political purpose rather than as mere entertainment.

A handful of reviewers, including Robert Brustein of *The New Republic* and Jerry Tallmer of the *Village Voice*, recognized the value of *The Connection's* rejection of stylized realism in favor of the "hyperrealism" typified by Julian Beck's comment that "There had to be real dirt, not simulations" on the play's set.[38] These encouraging reviews combined with word of mouth sustained *The Connection* for more than two years and seven hundred performances. The play garnered several Obie awards for off-Broadway theater and established the Living Theatre's reputation. The production also made the Living Theatre realize that fusing social, political, and moral beliefs with artistic expression hinged on increasing the audience's direct involvement in the theatrical event. The company began searching for a vehicle to further the improvisatory techniques with which *The Connection* attempted to bridge the gap between the performers and the audience. They found it in Kenneth Brown's *The Brig*.

The Brig took place in a United States Marine Corps penal facility, where prisoners were disciplined by harsh methods of depersonalization. They were called by numbers rather than names, expected to be silent except when spoken to by guards, and were required to ask permission to cross over the white lines that separated various areas of the brig. The play's action consisted of a day in the life of these prisoners, including reveille, washing, gymnastics, and cleanup, among other activities, all of which are carried out in strict observance of the rules. When a prisoner broke any of the rules, the guards punished him physically. The punishment was usually a punch to the solar plexus, staged realistically by having the actor continue the punching motion until his closed fist met the other actor's solar plexus, and then opening the fist so that at the last instant the punch became a slap. Guards also punished prisoners by psychological humiliation, such as having them scream their transgressions into a toilet. Theatrically, *The Brig* allowed greater possibilities for improvisation than *The Connection* because, although the dialogue was scripted, in those scenes in which a prisoner broke a rule, a guard could alter the course of the action by changing his orders, dealing out punishment for infractions, or ordering the prisoners to break down for frisks and shakedowns.

Thematically, *The Brig*, in its representation of military cruelty, marked the first significant infusion of Beck's and Malina's pacifist politics into the Living Theatre's artistic work. The writings of French director Antonin Artaud exerted a profound influence on the theatrical style of this production. Artaud called for a "Theatre of Cruelty" in which the actors would become "victims burnt at the stake, signaling through the flames."[39] Artaud advocated a kind of theater that renounced artifice, "talking heads," and the audience's intellectual experience, and instead made use of the actors' physicality and emotion to affect the audience on a visceral level. The Living Theatre began to apply Artaud's theatre of cruelty to *The Brig*. The theater's founders hoped that representing violent acts as graphically and "cruelly" as possible would physically purge spectators of the impulse to commit violent acts in their everyday lives. Malina commented: "When the first blow is delivered in the darkened brig . . . the prisoner winces and topples from his superbly rigid attention position, the contraction of his body is repeated inside the body of the spectator." *The Brig*'s improvisations enhanced the reality of violence for spectators. The Living Theatre believed that heightened realism held the key to rendering the audience unable to perform similarly violent acts in their daily lives.[40] Thus, *The Brig* merged the Living Theatre's pacifist political goals with their aesthetic goals of honesty and reality in the theater. Since *The Brig* the company's art and politics have been inseparable.

The Living Theatre's precarious financial situation at the time of *The Brig* precipitated an episode that ultimately helped articulate the company's aesthetic and political sensibilities. On October 18, 1963, Internal Revenue Service agents seized the troupe's theater, claiming the founders owed $28,435 in back taxes. The company responded by staging a sit-in reminiscent of the civil rights movement, stating they would not leave the building until the troupe's actors were given a chance to earn the wages of which the IRS's actions deprived them. As part of this public act of civil disobedience, the company staged renegade performances of *The Brig* inside the theater. This tactic managed to involve some forty audience members in the protest, since in order to view the performances, audiences were forced to climb over rooftops and through a fire door to enter the seized property. Twenty-five people were arrested on charges of "impeding a federal officer in the performance of his duties."[41] Beck and Malina used the ensuing trial as another opportunity to mix politics and art, turning the courtroom into a theatrical forum for airing their political views. Opting to conduct their own defense, Beck and Malina sought to portray themselves as "the standard-bearers of beleaguered beauty and art," while they portrayed the IRS agents as "the anonymous instruments of oppression of the military-industrial complex."[42] As to the charges of failure to pay back taxes, Beck and Malina virtually conceded the point, choosing instead to transform the trial into a public statement of anarchist politics. They defended their not paying taxes on the grounds that, had they paid taxes, they could not have paid their actors, and *The Brig* and *The Connection* would have closed prematurely. As Julian Beck wrote, "It was a matter of insisting on art before money."[43]

The psychic and legal fallout from the closing of their theater forced the Living Theatre to confront philosophical and practical issues concerning its relationship to money. To an extent, the Living Theatre had always attempted to find strategies to avoid having artistic endeavors dominated by financial considerations, building sets out of scavenged wood, creating costumes out of discarded rags, and sometimes playing for donations rather than charging admission. Ultimately, however, the company wanted to compensate its actors, and in order to do so it spent considerable time and effort financing the theater's productions. Beck remarked that the company spent as much as 85 percent of its time fund raising and soliciting prospective donors, including quintessential capitalist institutions such as the Ford and Rockefeller Foundations. They also raised ticket prices, which had the affect of appealing to exactly the same kind of "middle-income theatregoer" whose political sensibilities they were trying to shock.[44] For the Living Theatre, striving to produce politically challenging art while at the same time depending on middle-class audiences' ticket revenues, hoping for favorable reviews in establishment publications such as the *New York Times*, and courting funding from major foundations produced contradictions. In the summer of 1964, the company decided to go into voluntary European exile to rethink issues surrounding the relationship between art, commerce, and politics.

Making Art and Politics One: *Paradise Now* and the "Beautiful Nonviolent Anarchist Revolution"

From the summer of 1964 to the fall of 1968, the Living Theatre troupe toured extensively in Europe, living communally and creating several new productions. Perhaps the most significant development during this period was the emergence of a technique the troupe referred to as "collective creation." This technique encouraged rehearsing company members to offer their individual suggestions on how productions should be staged. Collective creation sought to eliminate or minimize "the authoritarian position of the director."[45] Thus, collective creation echoed the New Left's ethos of participatory democracy, giving decision-making power to individuals, as well as SNCC's attempts to function as a leaderless, grass-roots organization. These approaches shared a common impulse to enact a politics of equality in everyday life. For the Living Theatre specifically, collective creation constituted a practical experiment in the type of anarchist society the company envisioned politically. Most important, it led to the development of the Living Theatre's most famous work, *Paradise Now*.

The Living Theatre created *Paradise Now* in Cefalu, Sicily, during the winter and spring of 1968. The production combined the troupe's anarchist/pacifist politics with theatrical spectacle and made the audience an indispensable part of the event. The Living Theatre viewed *Paradise Now* as a direct action aimed at fomenting a nonviolent anarchist revolution and providing a blueprint for an alternative society.[46] The company sought to build on the revolutionary spirit of the late 1960s, which company members experienced firsthand as participants in the May 1968 student riots in Paris. *Paradise Now* premiered at the Avignon Festival in France that July. The city's mayor banned the play, worried about the presence of more than two hundred spectators and company members in the streets, chanting for revolution at the performance's conclusion. Rather than substitute another play, the Living Theatre chose to leave the festival, citing an unwillingness to compromise the company's commitment to freedom amid an atmosphere of censorship. In August, the Living Theatre performed *Paradise Now* in Geneva, before embarking on a United States tour in September 1968.[47]

Paradise Now's structure consisted of a map of steps, or "rungs," on a ladder leading toward paradise, culminating with the performers leading the audience into the street to begin what the Living Theatre referred to as the "Beautiful Nonviolent Anarchist Revolution." The eight rungs of the ladder each contained a "Rite," a "Vision," and an "Action," which focused on a specific aspect of the revolution. The Rites were "physical/spiritual rituals/ceremonies" performed by the actors. The Visions, also performed by the actors, were "intellectual images, symbols, dreams." The Actions of *Paradise Now*, which were "enactments of political conditions," demanded active audience participation. These conditions were geographically specific to the venue and designed to "lead to revolutionary action in the here and now."[48] For instance, in the Action of the First Rung, the actors urged the audience to participate by calling out phrases including the following:

> New York City. How The Rite of Guerrilla Theatre and The Vision of the Death and Resurrection of the American Indian lead to The Revolution of Cultures. Free theatre. The theatre is yours. Act. Speak. Do whatever you want. Free theatre. Feel free. You, the public, can choose your role and act it out. New York City. Eight million people are living in a state of emergency and don't know it. Manhattan island is shaped like a foot. At the foot of New York is Wall Street. Free theatre. In which the actors and the public can do anything they like. Free theatre. Do whatever you want with the capitalist culture of New York. . . . Act. . . . Be the police. Be a foot. . . . Show the violence. Show the anti-violence. Be the Statue of Liberty. . . . Be the forces of repression. Be the students at Columbia. Undo the culture. . . . Enact the culture of New York. Change it.[49]

It is significant that the Living Theatre used the phrase "free theatre" to describe its work. Since audience members paid admission on the 1968–69 tour, the company obviously did not intend the word "free" to imply that no pecuniary charge was involved. Rather, the Living Theatre associated the concept with an array of concerns about personal freedom which figured centrally in the larger counterculture. For instance, in the "Rite of Universal Intercourse" section of *Paradise Now*, the company, already stripped to the legal limit (men in G-strings, women in bikinis) assembled into a pile and began touching and caressing each other and welcomed the audience to join them. Audience members accepted this invitation frequently, and often in complete nudity, since they were not bound by the same statute as the performers.

Paradise Now tried to use audience participation to radicalize the audience to "a state of being in which nonviolent revolutionary action is possible."[50] Thus, *Paradise Now* joined the Living Theatre's foremost theatrical concern, audience involvement, with its primary political goal, nonviolent anarchist revolution. In *Paradise Now*'s final Action, after a performance that lasted as long as four and a half hours, the company led the audience out of the theater to begin the revolution, imploring, "The theatre is in the street."[51] Audience members frequently emerged naked and cast members virtually naked, so that, irrespective of politics, the procession into the streets tended to provoke local authorities. In Philadelphia, police arrested members of the company for indecent exposure and inciting a riot, and the administrations of the Massachusetts Institute of Technology and the University of Southern California banned performances of *Paradise Now* after seeing the negative press that preceded the Living Theatre's scheduled visits. Malina lamented:

> Poor *Paradise!* It has been busted for so many different reasons:
>> for making noise in the streets
>>
>> for indecent exposure
>>
>> for breach of the peace
>>
>> for too many people outside
>>
>> for too many people inside
>
> None of the officials will say they don't want a play that advocates anarchism. Or perhaps they are saying they don't want a play that demonstrates the conditions of anarchism.[52]

Malina, and the Living Theatre Company, believed that *Paradise Now* met with repression because it threatened to undermine the fabric of established society. Indeed, during the U.S. tour, *Paradise Now* benefited from a climate of campus activism in which students were primed for the play's revolutionary exhortations, and local authorities often tried to pre-empt any burgeoning rebellions they thought the production might arouse.

While the Living Theatre encountered abundant and expected hostility from the Establishment, some elements of the radical Left also criticized the troupe's politics. In New Haven, members of the company got involved in a verbal dispute about the issue of revolutionary violence with members of a black militant group called the Hill Parents Association. While the Living Theatre staunchly defended pacifist principles, the spokesman for the Hill Parents group argued that nonviolent revolution was no longer possible in the United States: "That nonviolent shit died when King was shot. . . . We ain't talking nonviolence anymore. . . . You cats better get your shit together and find out what's happening here. . . . You lay that shit down in Brooklyn (the next stop on the tour) and some of those Bedford-Stuyvesant cats'll bust your head open."[53] This confrontation exposed one of the main problems the Living Theatre experienced while touring with *Paradise Now*: the production contradicted the prevailing spirit of revolutionary fervor in the United States at that particular moment. Because the company had created *Paradise Now* in Europe, and witnessed and participated in the student protests in Paris, the troupe was enthusiastic about the possibility of nonviolent revolution. When the company returned to the United States, it encountered the radicals' disillusionment with nonviolence in the wake of the assassinations of Martin Luther King, Jr., and Robert Kennedy, and the violence surrounding the 1968 Democratic National Convention in Chicago. In her diary of this period, *The Enormous Despair*, Judith Malina indicated her disappointment with a revolutionary impulse increasingly dominated by radicals who defended the use of violence.[54]

In addition to its critics within the radical Left, the Living Theatre incurred the wrath of the critical establishment. Many establishment critics opposed *Paradise Now* on political rather than artistic grounds. Under particular fire were the company's methods for engaging the audience, which many critics condemned as aggressive and hostile. For instance, at one performance actor Steven Ben Israel screamed at an audience member: "If you think violence is good for anything, I think you are an asshole." *New York Times* critic Eric Bentley believed that such belligerent behavior contradicted the Living Theatre's pacifist politics: "The comedy here is black . . . and suggests just what is hateful in The Living Theatre's arch enemy, the Establishment, the habit of praising nonviolence while bringing more and more violence into being." Company members themselves may have been uneasy with the tension between the Living Theatre's political commitment to pacifism and its confrontational theatrical style. Judith Malina commented: "We ask the audience to say whatever they want, but we don't warn them they are going to be beleaguered for what they say." Moreover, the *Oakland Tribune*'s John Rockwell charged that *Paradise Now*'s form lacked the flexibility to address audiences that were already radicalized, such as the one in Berkeley.[55] In an example of the striving for consistency between political beliefs and artistic expression that was characteristic of the Living Theatre, the company reflected on these criticisms and sought strategies to "adapt our theatre to be better able to facilitate revolutionary change."[56] This soul-searching culminated in the Living Theatre's January 1970 decision to divide the company into four groups, or "cells," each of which planned to address a different aspect of revolutionary change.

The most prominent and enduring of these Living Theatre "cells," which included Beck and Malina, focused on making political street theater. In February 1970 the company devised a brief scene for the Paris Métro protesting rate increases, but police intervention prevented its performance. Undaunted by this aborted attempt, the company relocated to Brazil, mounting an ambitious series of street plays in Brazilian *favelas* (ghettoes), which protested exploitative labor practices and aimed to bring theater to the poorest of the poor. In 1974–75 the Living Theatre established residency in Pittsburgh, creating street productions that dramatized conditions produced by the slumping steel industry and offered the workers a radical perspective on their struggles.[57] Julian Beck explained the Living Theatre's evolution to street performance:

[E]verything we learned from the *Paradise Now* trip brought us to this moment. In *Paradise Now* had we not brought the audience to the doors of the theatre and said, "The Theatre Is In The Street!"? And, did we not stand there, at the doors face to face with the police? The police who do not want life to reach and surpass the privileged position occupied by art, who do not want the streets to be free. It was there at the doors of The Theatres, that we knew the street was where we had to go.[58]

Thus, street theater emerged as the logical next phase of development for an avant-garde company, which for twenty years sought ways of engaging audiences in order to transform them politically. The transition to street theater allowed the Living Theatre to reach individuals for whom traditional theater presented economic and cultural barriers. By its nature, street theater encouraged audience participation, a hallmark of the Living Theatre's work. The company also benefited from street theater's capacity to address political themes broadly and directly by claiming the public space as a forum for dissenting views. Sadly, however, street theater did not produce enough revenue to sustain the Living Theatre, whose membership constantly shifted, but usually consisted of at least two dozen actors, designers, and technicians.

Although economic circumstances forced the Living Theatre back into formal theaters late in 1975, street theater has survived as a vital part of the Living Theatre's work even through the politically conservative Reagan/Bush years. The troupe's 1989 production of *Body of God* dramatized the plight of New York City's homeless population and questioned the right to the public space itself, employing both company members and homeless people previously unaffiliated with the company. *Waste*, an environmentally minded street theater piece, investigated the cultural tendency to waste natural resources and suggested possible alternatives.[59] Finally, several company members performed street theater actions protesting the Persian Gulf War, and their production of *Rules of Civility* (1991) ended with a nightly procession to the streets in a candlelight vigil for peace.

The Continuing Value of Public Performance

The histories of the freedom singers and Living Theatre suggest that performance in public spaces emerged as an important and influential tool in direct action politics during the 1960s. Singing freedom songs effectively opened public spaces to numerous cultural expressions that social and political forces restricted in the 1950s. It paved the way for The Living Theatre's spontaneous civil disobedience "play-ins" in resistance to the IRS, *Paradise Now*'s conclusion that "The theater is in the street," and the company's emphasis on street theater in the 1970s. The tendency to use the public space as a forum for combining performance and politics emerged as the artistic sensibility of the 1960s era, adopted by myriad groups. The San Francisco Mime Troupe, a multiracial "artist and propaganda group," performed political street theater in the style of *commedia dell'arte* in the San Francisco parks. El Teatro Campesino, a theater group concerned with Chicano cultural identity, performed its *actos* using striking migrant farm workers on the United Farm Workers Association picket lines of the mid-1960s California grape strikes. The Diggers, a community group in San Francisco's Haight-Ashbury section, performed street theater puppet shows such as the "Death of Money Parade," and distributed free food in Golden Gate Park. Bread and Puppet Theater led processions featuring giant puppets through New York City to protest the Vietnam War. And the Art Workers Coalition, a coalition of visual artists, as part of a "Mass Antiwar Mail-In," paraded mailable antiwar artworks to New York's Canal Street Post Office, including a papier-mâché "bomb," and mailed them to the "Joint Chiefs of War" in Washington. These groups represent only a sampling of the collectives that emerged in the late 1960s that infused their political statements with a theatrical sensibility and derived their power from public performance.

Developments in the 1990s suggest the continuing relevance of this approach. In late January 1991, as the United States military intensified its prosecution of the Persian Gulf War, there were some significant domestic protests despite the overwhelmingly prowar public opinion. The alternative media collective Paper Tiger Television sponsored one of the most effective protests in New York City, which specifically criticized media coverage of the war. This demonstration featured protesters dressed as cheerleaders with the acronyms of the three major television networks (CBS, NBC, ABC) printed on their sweaters. The cheerleaders vividly illustrated the point that in an age when, for instance, General Electric, a leading military contractor, possesses a controlling interest in NBC, journalistic objectivity might be another of the war's casualties. The demonstrators concluded their march at the ABC headquarters where they projected visual images onto the building's facade, including juxtapositions of President Bush and Adolf Hitler. This spectacle blurred the lines between art, theater, and political protest to make a powerful (if somewhat complex) statement against media coverage of the war.

The Paper Tiger demonstration deftly used the public space to rally against media coverage of the war, and it expressed its objections in a highly imaginative, theatrical style. In deploying public performance as a vehicle for political views, Paper Tiger owed much to the legacy of political art, music, and theater of the 1960s. Attempts to use live performance as a catalyst for political change are especially important in the current cultural climate, an era in which government has sought once again to exert control over political artists, as demonstrated by the National Endowment for the Arts controversies during the Bush administration, and in which information is increasingly disseminated by electronic media whose control is consolidated among an ever smaller number of large corporations. In the NEA affair, artists' grants were revoked for failing to conform to "general standards of decency." Four of the artists sued, charging the NEA for making its decision on political rather than artistic grounds, since the cases deemed "indecent" all dealt with issues of concern to the gay community. The NEA controversy suggests how seriously people take the political impact of art; if political art didn't matter, would it be deemed such a threat?

Public performance maximizes art's potential for social impact since it minimizes mediating factors between performers and audience, such as dependence on granting agencies, high ticket prices, and cultural inhibitions to entering theaters, concert halls, museums. Furthermore, live street performance resists the common tendency to turn "alternative" forms of artistic expression into just another commercial product of mainstream culture—the way the underground spirit of grunge rock or rap, for example, is vulnerable to co-optation as a fashion statement and as a high-profit media commodity. At its core, performance in the streets joins performers and audience on an immediate level, with minimal governmental, corporate, and electronic filtering. There is always the possibility for communion and transformation. In an era of declining voter turnout and general post-Watergate, post–Iran-Contra, post–presidential sex scandal political cynicism, live performance of the sort offered by the freedom singers and the Living Theatre constitutes an exercise in participatory democracy which reminds spectators of the streets' importance as a forum for free speech and public discourse. As the Living Theatre's Judith Malina phrased it, "We are the test of liberty."

NOTES

1. Robert Shelton, "Negro Songs Here Aid Rights Drive," *New York Times*, 22 June 1963, p. 15.

2. Judith Malina, *The Enormous Despair* (New York: Random House, 1972), p. 42; Judith Malina and Julian Beck, *Paradise Now: Collective Creation of The Living Theatre* (New York: Random House, 1971), pp. 15–17; William Borders, "Indecent Exposure Charged to Becks," *New York Times*, 28 September 1968, p. 27.

3. Bernice Johnson Reagon, *Songs of the Civil Rights Movement, 1955–1965: A Study in Culture History* (Howard University Ph.D. diss., 1975), p. 101.

4. See, for instance, Clayborne Carson, *In Struggle: SNCC and the Black Awakening of the 1960s* (Cambridge: Harvard University Press, 1981), and Kerran Sanger, *"When the Spirit Says Sing!": The Role of Freedom Songs in the Civil Rights Movement* (New York: Garland, 1995).

5. Josh Dunson, *Freedom in the Air: Song Movements of the Sixties* (New York: International Publishers, 1965), p. 35.

6. Reagon, *Songs of the Civil Rights Movement*, p. 104.

7. Ibid., pp. 102–103; Pete Seeger and Bob Reiser, eds., *Everybody Says Freedom* (New York: W.W. Norton & Company, 1989), pp. 32–33.

8. Ella Baker quoted in Carson, *In Struggle*, p. 20.

9. Bernice Reagon, "In Our Hands: Thoughts on Black Music," *Sing Out!*, November 1975, pp. 1–2.

10. Julius Lester, "Freedom Songs in the South," *Broadside*, 7 February 1964, unnumbered.

11. Interview with Hollis Watkins, 14 March 1998.

12. Bob Cohen, "Mississippi Caravan of Music," *Broadside*, October 1964, unnumbered; Reagon, *Songs of the Civil Rights Movement*, p. 152.

13. Reagon, "In Our Hands," p. 2.

14. "Moment of History," *New Yorker* 27 March 1965, pp. 37–38; Reagon, *Songs of the Civil Rights Movement*, pp. 64–89.

15. Reagon, *Songs of the Civil Rights Movement*, p. 82; Carson, *In Struggle*, p. 19.

16. Robert Shelton, "Rights Song Has Its Own History of Integration," *New York Times*, 23 July 1963, p. 21; "Battle Hymn of the Integrationists," *U.S. News & World Report*, 5 August 1963, p. 8.

17. Reagon, *Songs of the Civil Rights Movement*, pp. 131–32.

18. Henry Hampton and Steve Fayer, eds., *Voices of Freedom* (New York: Bantam, 1990), pp. 97–114; Guy and Candie Carawan and the Student Nonviolent Coordinating Committee, *We Shall Overcome!: Sons of the Southern Freedom Movement* (New York: Oak Publications, 1963), pp. 57–76; Reagon, *Songs of the Civil Rights Movement*, pp. 128–39.

19. Anderson quoted in Carawan et al., *We Shall Overcome*, p. 16.

20. Carawan et al., *We Shall Overcome!*, p. 62.

21. Zellner quoted in Carawan et al., *We Shall Overcome!*, p. 21.

22. Interview with Hollis Watkins, 14 March 1998.

23. Reagon, *Songs of the Civil Rights Movement*, pp. 128–39; Neblett quoted in Reagon, *Songs of the Civil Rights Movement*, p. 140.

24. Reagon, "In Our Hands," p. 2; Reagon, *Songs of the Civil Rights Movement*, p. 140.

25. Interview with Hollis Watkins, 14 March 1998. Quote is from interview with Reebee Garofalo, 14 March 1998.

26. Howard Klein, "Bernstein Joins Stern in Concert," *New York Times*, 31 August 1964.

27. "Northern Folk Singers Help Out at Negro Festival in Mississippi," *New York Times*, 7 July 1963, p. 43; "'Without These Songs . . . ,'" *Newsweek*, 31 August 1964, p. 74; Reagon, *Songs of the Civil Rights Movement*, pp. 141–46.

28. "Northern Folk Singers Help Out," p. 43

29. Malina and Beck, *Paradise Now*, p. 140.

30. Judith Malina, *The Diaries of Judith Malina, 1947–1957* (New York: Grove Press, 1984), p. 50.

31. Pierre Biner, *The Living Theatre* (New York: Horizon Press, 1972), p. 24.

32. Maria Ley Piscator, *The Piscator Experiment* (New York: J.H. Heineman, 1967), p. 103.

33. Julian Beck, "Storming the Barricades," in Kenneth Brown, *The Brig* (New York: Hill and Wang, 1965), p. 7.

34. Julian Beck interview in *Yale/theatre* 2, 1 (spring 1969): 21.

35. John Tytell, *The Living Theatre: Art, Exile, and Outrage* (New York: Grove Press, 1995), pp. 133–37.

36. Beck, "Storming the Barricades," pp. 26–27.

37. Louis Calta, "*The Connection*: A Play about Junkies," *New York Times*, 16 July 1959, p. 30.

38. Robert Brustein, "Junkies and Jazz," *New Republic*, 28 September 1959, p. 29; Jerry Tallmer, "Theatre: *The Connection*," *Village Voice*, 22 July 1959, p. 90; Beck, "Storming the Barricades," p. 26.

39. Antonin Artaud, *The Theater and Its Double* (New York: Grove Press, 1958), p. 13.

40. Judith Malina, "Directing *The Brig*," in Brown, *The Brig*, p. 98.

41. Julian Beck, "How to Close a Theatre," *Tulane Drama Review* (Spring 1964): 189–90; Elmore Lester, "The Living Theatre Presents: Revolution! Joy! Protest! Shock! Etc.!," *New York Times Magazine*, 13 October 1968, p. 94.

42. Lester, "The Living Theatre Presents," p. 94.

43. Beck, "How to Close a Theatre," p. 186.

44. Ibid., p. 183.

45. Julian Beck, *The Life of the Theatre* (New York: Proscenium Publishers, 1972), p. 5.

46. Beck interview in *Yale/theatre*, p. 16.

47. Tytell, *The Living Theatre*, pp. 235–36; Charles Marowitz, "You Can Go Home Again?," *New York Times*, 8 September 1968, Sect. 2, pp. 1–5.

48. All quotes in this section are from the "Preparation" section of Malina and Beck, *Paradise Now*, p. 5.

49. Malina and Beck, *Paradise Now*, pp. 23–25.

50. Ibid. p. 6.

51. On the length of performances, see, for instance, Clive Barnes, "Stage: Living Theatre's 'Paradise Now,' a Collective Creation," *New York Times*, 15 October 1968. p. 39. The quote is from Malina and Beck, *Paradise Now*, p. 140.

52. Renfreu Neff, *The Living Theatre, U.S.A.* (New York: Bobbs-Merrill Company, 1970), p. 117; Malina, *Enormous Despair*, p. 117.

53. Quoted in Neff, *The Living Theatre, U.S.A.*, p. 44.

54. Malina, *Enormous Despair*, pp. 180–81.

55. Eric Bentley, "I Reject the Living Theatre," *New York Times*, 20 October 1968, p. 35; Malina, *Enormous Despair*, pp. 169–70; John Rockwell in *Oakland Tribune*, 22 February 1969, quoted in Aldo Rostagno, *We, the Living Theatre* (New York: Ballantine Books, 1970), p. 170.

56. Beck, *The Life of the Theatre*, p. 221.

57. Interview with Tom Walker, 24 August, 1998; Beck, *The Life of the Theatre*, pp. 38–41; Tytell, *The Living Theatre*, pp. 275–82.

58. Beck, *The Life of the Theatre*, p. 221.

59. Tytell, *The Living Theatre*, p. 345.

Sources of the Second Wave

The Rebirth of Feminism

Sara M. Evans

When our group started . . . it was a wonderful time to be in the women's movement. It may have been a unique moment. It felt then almost as though whatever stood in our way would be swept away overnight, with the power of our ideas, our simplicity, our unanswerable truth.

Bread and Roses

All of the social movements of the 1960s—civil rights, student New Left, antiwar, counterculture—emphasized the personal nature of political action. They expressed the existential yearning for authenticity and meaning of a generation raised in postwar affluence, and idealistic rage at the betrayals of the American dream: hunger in the midst of plenty, racism in a democracy, and imperialism by the leader of the "free" world. The women's liberation movement burst on the scene in the late 1960s to take this yet one step further by declaring that "the personal is political." With this critical insight, women challenged the ways power and sexism shaped relationships from the bedroom to the boardroom, and they demanded that American society redefine the meanings of masculinity and femininity.

The 1960s were the launching pad for a massive feminist movement that matched in size and fervor the suffrage movement half a century earlier. To understand the energy feminism unleashed in the 1970s, we need to understand how the turbulence of the 1960s stirred up deep contradictions in women's lives, while at the same time providing a free space in which women could challenge both cultural and legal expectations and develop the skills to build a movement for change.

The Setting

Throughout the 1950s U.S. popular culture was suffused with images of—and paeans to—domesticity. The housewife, with her suburban, technology-filled kitchen, became a symbol of U.S. superiority in the Cold War when Vice President Nixon and Soviet Premier Nikita Khrushchev debated in the kitchen of a mock American home in 1959. "Would it not be better to compete in the relative merits of washing machines than in the strength of rockets?" Nixon argued as he and Khrushchev lingered over a model kitchen at the American National Exhibition in Moscow. Gesturing to a built-in, panel-controlled washing machine, Nixon boasted, "In America these are designed to make things easier for our women."[1] These were the legendary "happy days" mythologized in the 1970s sitcom, when Mom was in her kitchen and all was right with the

SARA EVANS is Distinguished McKnight University Professor of History at the University of Minnesota, where she has taught women's history since 1976. She is the author of several books including *Personal Politics: The Roots of Women's Liberation in the Civil Rights Movement and the New Left* (1979) and *Born for Liberty: A History of Women in America* (2nd edition, 1997). Born in a Methodist parsonage in South Carolina, she was a student activist in the civil rights and antiwar movements in North Carolina and has been an active feminist since 1967.

world. By 1960, Americans who wanted a bit more zing and glamour in their feminine ideals were happy to shift their allegiance from the grandmotherly Mamie Eisenhower to the beautiful and stylish Jacqueline Kennedy.

The assumption that women's proper place was in the home undergirded the legal reality that women had few protections in public. Employment want ads routinely listed jobs separately for men and women. The labor force was extremely segregated, with women crowded into a small number of lower-paid occupations primarily in the service sector. When they did do the same work, women could be paid less than men, as many employers had separate pay scales. Professional schools in law and medicine set restrictive quotas to limit the proportion of female students to as low as 5 percent. In many states married women could not even obtain credit in their own names or without their husband's signature.

In this case, domestic ideology, later called "feminine mystique" by author Betty Friedan, served to obscure and temporarily contain dramatic changes. Since the Second World War, during which women had broken through many of the traditional barriers to work outside the home, American women's entry into the labor force accelerated dramatically as did their access to higher education. Within racial minority groups, women had of necessity traditionally worked outside the home, and they took leading roles in the upsurge against discrimination and segregation. Yet, such changes remained obscured and denied by a popular culture of family sitcoms such as *Father Knows Best* and *Leave It to Beaver*, which portrayed a placid, all-white, suburban, middle-class world.[2]

The rumblings of the civil rights movement signaled new—but still unrecognized—possibilities. For example, in 1955, Rosa Parks, secretary of the Montgomery, Alabama, NAACP, was arrested for refusing to move to the back of a segregated city bus. Black women in Montgomery had been organizing and planning behind the scenes for some time, and they seized on Parks's arrest as the moment to initiate a boycott of the city bus system. The story of the Montgomery bus boycott has entered American mythology in a way that obscures the work of the Montgomery Women's Political Council. The boycott, called by the local NAACP chapter, was effective because the Women's Political Council—an organization of middle-class African American women, parallel to the League of Women Voters in the white community—was able, overnight, to print and distribute literally thousands of fliers at every bus stop in the black community. Most of the riders were women who used buses to get to their jobs as domestics in white neighborhoods. The buses remained empty for months, as women walked and carpooled to work and gathered with others in community churches to hear the inspiring rhetoric of Dr. Martin Luther King, Jr., and other civil rights leaders.[3]

The sit-in movement, which began in Greensboro, North Carolina, in 1960, also produced a number of courageous young women leaders, including Diane Nash in Nashville and Ruby Doris Smith in South Carolina, who chose the strategy of "jail—not bail." Later, the towering figure of Fannie Lou Hamer of Sunflower County, Mississippi, rocked the country with her story of the brutal beating and the loss of home and livelihood she endured for daring to register to vote.

Another early sign of renewed activism was the emergence of a peace movement that challenged the nuclear arms race in the name of motherhood. Five women who had been active in the Committee for a SANE Nuclear Policy started Women Strike for Peace in 1960 to raise "mothers' issues" like the dangers of nuclear testing to children through the radioactive contamination of milk. They called for a one-day "strike" on November 1, 1961, as a radioactive cloud from a Russian test floated across the United States. Using female networks in PTAs, the League of Women Voters, peace organizations, and personal contacts, leaders of Women Strike for Peace spread the word. Fifty thousand turned out to lobby government officials to "End the Arms Race—Not the Human Race." Women Strike for Peace activists (61 percent of whom were housewives) were intellectuals and civic-minded women who were increasingly concerned about the dangers of nuclear war. Inspired by the courageous examples of civil rights activists in the South, and drawing on their own histories of involvement during the war years of the 1940s, they insisted that their point of view as mothers deserved recognition. Leader Dagmar Wilson, conscious that "the housewife was a downgraded person," set out to show "that this was an important role and that it was time we were heard."[4]

As housewives began to mobilize, professional women were subjected to blatant discrimination and openly accused of failing to be proper wives and mothers. The silence domestic ideology imposed was a source of pain and confusion, especially for educated women who simply could not resolve the contradictory messages in their own lives. Professional women in the 1950s faced a lonely struggle. Maria Iandolo New, chief of pediatrics at Cornell University Medical College, still remembers the chastising words of a medical school dean in 1950 in response to her plea that her application be judged on its merits and not dismissed because she had married: "You are an impertinent young lady, and I am more sure than ever that we do not want you in our medical school."[5] Major law firms routinely rejected female applicants like Ellen Peters, first in her class at Yale Law School in 1954, and Ruth Bader Ginsburg, top of her Columbia Law School class in 1959, who went on to become the second woman appointed to the Supreme Court. In 1957, Madeline Kunin, a student at Columbia University Graduate School of Journalism, applied for a newsroom job at the *New York Times*; she was offered a job in the cafeteria. She later became governor of Vermont. Many women dropped out of higher education, overwhelmed by academic pressures and the unsupportive professors who openly believed that "women don't belong in graduate school." Those who persevered paid careful attention to dress and demeanor and hid their pregnancies. In professional settings, male colleagues routinely assumed that the white women they encountered were secretaries and the black women domestics.[6] While most professional women pursued their careers in relative isolation, networks in the Women's Bureau of the Department of Labor, the United Auto Workers Women's Department, religious groups, the YWCA, and other organizations continued to raise issues of women's roles and rights that would prove critical to the revival of feminism.

A new generation raised in postwar affluence flooded colleges and universities in the 1960s. They believed they could "have it all," but had no models for what that might mean. Many recall bitterly how they had no idea what their work should be or how to imagine themselves as adults. They knew they were supposed to marry, have children, age gracefully, and enjoy grandchildren, but their actual life choices included college, graduate school, and professional expectations. "In my generation," as Sara Ruddick put it, "women's work histories were so buried in our love histories as to be barely visible." Unable to write her dissertation while her husband pursued his first academic job, she wrestled with an indescribable "pain of worklessness." "I had learned to think of life as a matter of personal relations, to think about myself as a daughter, wife, friend, and lover. I knew more about myself as a mother, more about babies even before I ever had children, than I knew about myself as a worker." For such women there was "an invisible, almost amorphous weight of guilt and apology for interests and ambitions that should have been a source of pride," a sense of an invalidated life.[7]

While women with graduate degrees were still a small minority, broad changes in behavior began to occur as millions of women—and men—made choices that were different from those of their parents. They married older (or not at all) and rejected their parents' pronatalism, which emphasized early childbearing and large families. As a result, the baby boom vanished precipitously. Married women and women with children entered the labor force in massive numbers. Those who dropped out to bear and raise children devoted fewer and fewer years to child care as an exclusive occupation. A rising tide of older women returned to school to continue and complete educations suspended in the 1950s. Millions, then, knew that something was amiss, that their ideological relegation to private life was increasingly intolerable, but they had no name for the phenomenon that linked their individual experiences or a forum to express their collective grievances.

These were the women who in later years talked about the moment when everything "clicked," after which the world looked and sounded and felt different—crystal clear and infuriating.[8] As feminism rekindled, these women found their ways into consciousness-raising groups, where they felt immediately "at home," and set out, in a thousand different ways, to *do something* to reshape the landscapes of U.S. daily life.

Mobilization

The mobilization of professional women was the first tremor in the quake that set off the second wave of women's rights activism in the twentieth century. Its beginnings can be traced to the President's Commission on the Status of Women, established in 1961. Esther Peterson, Kennedy's appointee to head the Women's Bureau, formulated the idea for the commission, chaired by Eleanor Roosevelt, that would reexamine women's place in the economy, the family, and the legal system. The commission, its staff, and seven technical committees were drawn from labor unions, women's organizations, and governmental agencies.

Lawyers, government officials, union organizers, academics, commission members, and their staff documented in great detail the ongoing realities of employment discrimination, unequal pay, legal inequities, and lack of child care and other social services. They were stunned by their findings. Individually they had all experienced the problems, but the pervasiveness of discrimination and the hardships that accompanied women's "double burden" of household and labor force responsibilities validated that experience. The study allowed them to develop a set of shared goals and gave them a sense of mission.[9]

The President's Commission on the Status of Women put women's issues back on the national political agenda, and the publication of the commission's report in 1963 resulted in two immediate policy changes. The president issued an order requiring the federal civil service to hire for career positions "solely on the basis of ability to meet the requirements of the position, and without regard to sex." Congress then passed the 1963 Equal Pay Act, making it illegal to set different rates of pay for women and men for equal (i.e., the same) work.[10] The pressure for change broadened as governors in virtually every state appointed commissions on the status of women to conduct similar state-level investigations.

Nineteen sixty-three was also the year that Betty Friedan published *The Feminine Mystique*. In a brilliant and thoroughly researched polemic, Friedan gave a name to the malaise of housewives and the dilemma of those who did not fit the mold. Popular culture, psychologists, and educators, she argued, defined women in a way that excluded them from public life (and paid work) and coerced them into a passive and childlike domesticity. Thousands of letters flooded Friedan's mailbox, as women poured out the stories they had thought no one would ever understand. "My undiluted wrath," wrote one, "is expended on those of us who were educated and therefore privileged, who put on our black organza nightgowns and went willingly, joyfully, without so much as a backward look at the hard-won freedoms handed down to us by the feminists (men and women)."[11] Others turned their anger inward, resulting in depression and despair.

Despite the ripples from the commission report and publication of *The Feminine Mystique*, Congress was surprised when, during the debate on the 1964 Civil Rights Act, Representative Howard Smith of Virginia suggested that the Title VII prohibition against employment discrimination on the basis of race, creed, and national origin should also include "sex." As an ardent segregationist, his primary motive may have been to kill the bill. Ironically, as a longtime supporter of the Equal Rights Amendment (ERA), he was also quite serious about the amendment itself.[12] His efforts drew a chuckle from his male colleagues, but Senator Margaret Chase Smith of Maine was not amused. She and Congresswoman Martha Griffiths of Michigan set to work to ensure that the amendment passed. When their bipartisan effort (Chase was a Republican; Griffiths, a Democrat) succeeded, women suddenly had a potentially powerful and far-reaching legal tool.

Title VII provided an outlet for the thousands of women who knew that they faced discrimination but previously had no place to file their grievances. The Equal Employment Opportunity Commission (EEOC) received a flood of complaints against employers (and also against unions). But the bureaucrats were slow to take them seriously. Most, including those at the EEOC, still considered the inclusion of sex a bit of a joke. The *New York Times* referred to it as the "bunny law," on the theory that a Playboy Club might be sued for refusing to hire a male applicant as a bunny/waitress.[13]

The rumbles were beginning to be audible, but women still had no organized force to demand the enforcement of laws like Title VII. At a 1966 conference of State Commissions on the Status of Women, several women gathered in Betty Friedan's hotel room to discuss the situation. They submitted a resolution to the conference but were told that action of any kind was not permitted. They decided on the spot that they had to form a new organization. On the last day, Betty Friedan recalled, they "cornered a large table at the luncheon, so that we could start organizing before we had to rush for planes. We all chipped in $5.00, began to discuss names. I dreamed up NOW on the spur of the moment." The National Organization for Women was born with a clear statement of purpose: "To take action to bring women into full participation in the mainstream of American society now, assuming all the privileges and responsibilities thereof in truly equal partnership with men."[14]

The organization challenged the assumptions of the feminine mystique head-on and demanded full and equal access for women to education, work, and political participation. "It is no longer either necessary or possible," NOW's organizers argued in their founding statement, "for women to devote the greater part of their lives to child-rearing."[15] Using the United Auto Workers Women's Department as its headquarters, NOW sparked pickets and demonstrations across the country against sex-segregated want ads and "men only" clubs. They pressured the government to enforce antidiscrimination laws, especially Title VII. By 1968, the membership insisted on an endorsement of the ERA, which forced UAW women to withdraw from NOW until their union changed its position. The adoption by NOW of a strong position in support of legalizing abortion precipitated another split. A number of lawyers who wanted to focus on legal and economic issues felt that abortion was too controversial and would hamper their efforts. They broke away from NOW to found the Women's Equity Action League (WEAL).

Women's Liberation

While professional women's networks began to mobilize—building organizations and legal challenges to inequality—the foundation for an even more explosive challenge to women's place in American culture was being laid among the younger activists in the civil rights, student, and antiwar movements.

First in the civil rights movement and then in the student New Left, young women encountered a set of radically egalitarian ideas. Visions of the "beloved community" and of "participatory democracy" were not distant images but rather were understood to be the realities of life in the movement. Members acted on an idealized vision of what the world should be. In the civil rights movement, that meant a belief that every individual regardless of race should be treated with dignity and equality, and that every person should be admitted to full citizenship and have access to the American dream. When participants sang—and lived—the dream of "black and white together" they *were* the beloved community, and they showed the world that it was possible.

Similarly, in New Left organizations like Students for a Democratic Society (SDS), the ideal of participatory democracy asserted that everyone should participate in "the decisions that affect their lives." They adopted and adapted the consensus model of decision making that had developed in SNCC (Student Nonviolent Coordinating Committee) in which groups would debate all night if necessary before reaching a conclusion. If that is what it took to live out these ideals, then so be it.

Finally, young, usually middle-class women, both black and white, found inspiring models of courageous womanhood in the lives of local black women in the civil rights movement such as Fannie Lou Hamer, Ella Baker, Septima Clarke, and Rosa Parks. On a local level there were "the Mamas," the backbones of their communities, who took young civil rights workers into their homes at the risk of their own lives and livelihoods, who urged and cajoled and shamed their neighbors into registering to vote, and who defied the worst violence southern whites could bring down on their communities. From them, younger women in the movement learned that being female and being a leader were not antithetical. From their lives young women saw examples of nurturing, courage, power, and indomitable self-respect. If they needed new models of womanhood to replace the feminine mystique, they had them close at hand.[16]

For women, it seems in retrospect a short step—ideologically—from "freedom now" to "women's liberation." But that was actually not an easy step to take. On the one hand, young women in the civil rights movement and the student New Left generally believed that they were already liberated. Their participation required them to break many of the social rules with which they had been raised. They risked their lives, sometimes in defiance of their frightened parents. They developed powerful organizational skills when they taught in freedom schools and organized in poor northern communities. When the movement was small and human scale, they felt visible and valued, and joyfully joined in the personal and erotic intensity of building this new community and new movement. Sexual liberation was another of the boundary breaking aspects of this generation, and women certainly participated.

Yet, both women and men in the civil rights movement had also been deeply socialized to think in terms of traditional sex roles, and even as they broke many traditional rules they also bumped up against expectations which put them back "in their place." Ironically, when people returned from jail, women found that they were still expected to clean up the "freedom house," do most of the cooking and laundry, and, of course, the typing. Both men and women generally expected that visible leadership would be male. Men overwhelmingly dominated the heated ideological debates (which were frequently also contests over leadership) excluding all but a few women in tone and style. Even when women spoke up, they frequently were not taken seriously.

The sexual revolution also had its dark side. In the absence of any critique of traditional sex roles, sexual "liberation" was quickly defined in terms of cultural images of male sexuality. Women, in many instances, lost the right to say "no," accused instead of being "uptight." They shared the New Left conviction that it was essential to embed their ideals in their daily lives, but found that when it came to relationships between women and men, egalitarian ideals were difficult to put into practice.

Such contradictions finally produced an explosion of youthful feminist activism that quickly named itself the women's liberation movement. Young women used the skills they developed to apply the ideals of the movement to themselves. When they did so, they met with extreme hostility from many men. Accused of dividing the movement and told that their concerns were unimportant, they broke away to meet separately to explore and redefine what it meant to be female in America.

The women's liberation movement emerged from several years of conversation and debate within the civil rights and New Left movements. In the fall of 1967, following a rebuff on women's issues at the National Conference for New Politics, small groups of women gathered in Chicago, New York, and Seattle. It was a turbulent and utopian moment. The civil rights movement and the New Left emphasized participation and intense personal engagement. Around these movements, an emerging youthful counterculture challenged the values of commercialism, work, and competitive success. The black power movement, against a backdrop of growing urban violence in black ghettoes, argued forcefully that oppressed groups needed to organize and affirm themselves and so to develop collective strength. The antiwar movement contested the righteousness of U.S. military goals in Vietnam and the association of manliness with militarism. Everything, it seemed, was up for grabs. Even revolution was possible.

Women's liberationists engaged in "consciousness-raising," using the prism of their own experiences to rethink everything they had been told. It was a brilliant tool that released thousands of women from isolation through the discovery that others shared their experiences and the empowering strength of sisterhood. At first they simply did what New Left groups had been doing for years: talk—for hours and hours—to come to some agreement on what the issues were and what to do about them. The talking itself, however, turned out to be more powerful than anyone imagined. Some shared what it felt like *as women* in the movement—speaking without being heard, being relegated to clerical and housekeeping tasks, women's status being linked to their relationships with leading men, sexuality being exploited. Others discussed their desire for meaningful work, the social pressures they felt not to pursue those dreams, or the overt discrimination they faced in school and on the job. Still others talked about childhood—what it was like to grow up as a girl, what expectations they experienced, what their brothers could do that they could not, about menstruation, sex, housework and who does it, motherhood, and their own assumptions that women on the whole were silly, trivial, and boring. Seeking common ground as women, they suddenly found that their individual pains were not unique. They were not isolated; there were patterns, and those patterns provided the basis for a new way of seeing the world. As a New York group, Redstockings, put it:

> We regard our personal experience, and our feelings about that experience, as the basis for an analysis of our common situation. We cannot rely on existing ideologies, as they are all products of male supremacist culture. We question every generalization and accept none that are not confirmed by our experience.
>
> Our chief task at present is to develop female class-consciousness through sharing experience and publicly exposing the sexist foundation of all our institutions.[17]

Consciousness-raising was an intense form of collective self-education. For the founders of Bread and Roses, a Boston women's liberation group, "It seems impossible that adults have ever learned so much so fast as we did then. We taught each other sexual politics, emotional politics, the politics of the family, the politics of the SDS meeting."[18] Bread and Roses member Jane Mansbridge described consciousness-raising as "the feeling that we were, like Columbus, sailing at the edge of the world. Everything was new and intense."[19]

Through 1968 and 1969, the women's liberation movement grew at an accelerated rate. No one was keeping a list—and many groups existed without knowledge of others nearby—but the experience in city after city was that groups would form and multiply almost effortlessly. In some places, like New York City, where the movement tended to be highly ideological, this multiplication often looked like sectarian hairsplitting in search of "true" feminism. Yet the energy of the groups' ideas found expression in dozens of mimeographed articles, manifestos, newsletters, and, by 1969, journals that included *Notes from the First Year* (New York), *Up from Under* (New York), *No More Fun and Games* (Boston), and *Women: A Journal of Liberation* (Baltimore).

The immense creativity unleashed by the women's movement between 1967 and 1975 owed much to the practices of both NOW and the women's liberationists that encouraged local initiatives and allowed issues and ideas to flow from grass-roots experiences. Women's liberation, with its antistructure, anti-leadership, and "do your own thing" ethos, spawned thousands of projects and institutions, as consciousness-raising groups put their words into action. NOW's structure encouraged the creation of "task forces" at the local and national levels on virtually any topic. The task forces, in turn, issued a string of reports—on sexism in education, legal discrimination, and violence against women—with recommendations for action. Eleanor Smeal recalled the early 1970s in Pittsburgh:

> We were not real philosophical in those days. . . . We became instant experts on everything. On child care. Started our own nursery school. We worked on employment cases. . . . First we started organizing local NOW chapters. Then we organized the state. I went to every village and town, organizing; if you have just one or two people, you can get a chapter going. I organized housewives. Because that's where I was. You have to do what you know. It never occurred to me that we weren't going to get housewives, and we did.[20]

Making the Personal Political

The contagiousness of feminism lay in its ability to touch women at a deeply personal level, giving political voice to issues that had gone unchallenged and bringing new opportunities for action. When *Newsweek* published a cover story on the women's movement, it hired a freelance writer, having rejected versions by one of the few females in its ranks of reporters and editors. The day the cover story reached the newsstands, however, a group of women on the staff called a press conference to announce that they had filed a sex-discrimination complaint with the EEOC. At that time all but one of *Newsweek*'s research staff were women, and all but one of its fifty-two writers were men.[21]

Women responded to the movement's ideals even though the media's presentation of this new movement was decidedly hostile. For example, the epithet "bra burners" was a media fabrication. No bras were actually burned at the Miss America Pageant demonstration in August 1968, though one of the organizers suggested ahead of time to a journalist that they might be. Instead, participants tossed "objects of female torture"—girdles, bras, curlers, issues of the *Ladies Home Journal*—into a "freedom trash can," auctioned off an effigy of Miss America ("Gentlemen, I offer you the 1969 model. She's better in every way. She walks. She talks. AND she does housework"), and crowned a live sheep.[22]

In general, media coverage sensationalized and mocked women's liberation with nicknames like "women's lib" and "libbers."[23] One editor was known to have instructed a journalist to "get the bra-burning and karate up front."[24] It did not matter. For a few years, positive or negative publicity served to bring women out in droves.

When NOW called for a "women's strike" on August 26, 1970 in commemoration of the fiftieth anniversary of the passage of the Nineteenth Amendment to the Constitution, which granted women the right to vote, the national scope of this new movement became visible to activists and observers alike. Its insistence on the politics of personal life was likewise on display as women took action under the slogan "Don't iron while the strike is hot." *Life* magazine reported that

> in Rochester, NY, women shattered teacups. In Syracuse they dumped 50 children in the city hall. In New York City, Boston, and Washington thousands marched and rallied and hundreds more held teach-ins and speech-ins in dozens of other cities. Women's liberation is the liveliest conversational topic in the land, and last week, all across it, the new feminists took their argument for sexual equality into the streets.[25]

In New York City, between twenty thousand and fifty thousand women staged the largest women's rights rally since the suffrage movement, completely blocking Fifth Avenue during rush hour. Branches of a movement springing from different roots intertwined in theatrical and humorous actions: guerrilla theater in Indianapolis portrayed the middle-class female life cycle, from "sugar and spice" to "Queen for a Day"; Boston women chained themselves to a huge typewriter; women in Berkeley marched with pots and pans on their backs; New Orleans reporters ran engagement announcements under photos of future grooms; flight attendants carried posters challenging discriminatory airlines rules: "Storks Fly—Why Can't Mothers?"[26]

Coverage of the women's strike gave the nation a glimpse of the surge of creative energy (driven by a powerful combination of anger and high expectations) that flowed into the movement. Consciousness-raising groups were seedbeds for what grew into diverse movements around issues ranging from women's health, child care, violence, and pornography to spirituality and music. The groups formed child-care centers, bookstores, coffeehouses, shelters for battered women, and rape crisis hot lines—new institutions they could wholly own. At the same time, other feminists built enclaves within mainstream institutions—unions, churches and synagogues, and professional associations.

Consciousness-raising meant, from the outset, that feminist deliberation would center on the most intimate aspects of personal life. As groups analyzed childhood experiences for clues to the origins of women's oppression in relations with men, marriage, motherhood, and sex, discussion led to action, and action on one topic led to another. For example, in an early meeting of New York Radical Women, several women described their experiences with illegal abortions. For most it was the first time they had told anyone beyond a close friend or two. The power of this revelation, however, contrasted sharply with the current debates surrounding proposed liberalization of the abortion law in New York, which were conducted with clinical detachment. A group of women—subsequent founders of Redstockings—decided to disrupt a legislative hearing scheduled to hear testimony from fourteen men and one woman (a nun). Women who had undergone abortions were the "real experts," the feminists argued, and they went to Albany to tell their stories. When the committee declined to hear them, they held a public "speak-out" on March 21, 1969, drawing an audience of three hundred. Thousands of women, hearing about such speak-outs, experienced a release from lonely silence. Journalist Gloria Steinem recalled, "For the first time, I understood that the abortion I had kept so shamefully quiet about for years was an experience I had probably shared with at least one out of four American women of every race and group."[27]

With this and numerous other actions and demonstrations women's liberation groups made themselves the "shock troops" of abortion rights, joining an already active abortion law reform movement. For the most part, they sought to intervene directly, offering services, public education, and assistance to women rather than lobbying for reform. In Chicago, a group within the Chicago Women's Liberation Union called "Jane," which began doing counseling and referrals in the late 1960s, shifted in 1971 to performing the abortions themselves. Between 1971 and 1973, Jane performed eleven thousand illegal abortions with a safety record that matched that of doctor-performed legal abortions.[28] Sarah Weddington, an unemployed law school graduate who belonged to a consciousness-raising group in Austin, Texas, investigated the legal risks of providing an underground abortion referral service. Her research revealed the possibility of a legal challenge to laws against abortion based on the right to privacy. Thus began the process that ended in the landmark Supreme Court case *Roe v. Wade*, in which Sarah Weddington argued her very first case at the age of twenty-six.[29]

Similar processes led to the creation of the first shelters for battered women, rape crisis hot lines, and women's health clinics. As women focused on personal issues and the body, they forced new issues on the political agenda and set out to provide immediate responses to women in need. A Boston group offered a course on women's health and wrote *OurBodies/OurSelves*, thereby inventing a new form of self-help literature designed to empower women to take charge of their own health. Twenty-five years and many editions later, it is still in print.

Within the women's liberation movement the issue of lesbianism erupted as yet another form of personal politics. The gay rights movement, born after the Stonewall Riots in 1969, began a dramatic shift from the closet to public action. Lesbians in the gay rights movement wanted to organize consciousness-raising groups and to challenge the male domination of their movement. At the same time, lesbians in the women's movement responded to the focus on personal issues and sexual autonomy by raising their own concerns, only to be met by anxiety, hostility, and resistance from their heterosexual "sisters." They challenged the movement's prejudices by asserting, in papers such as "the Woman-Identified Woman," that lesbianism was the purest form of feminism, the only way to live a life completely independent of men. Throughout the country the intense experiences of consciousness-raising groups evoked sexual tensions. The intimacy of such groups, the emotions they unleashed, felt to many like a kind of falling in love. At the same time, homophobia was one of the chief weapons wielded by antifeminists in the media. In December 1970 *Time* magazine exposed feminist writer Kate Millett's bisexuality with the comment that "her disclosure is bound to discredit her as a spokeswoman for her cause, cast further doubt on her theories and reinforce the views of those skeptics who routinely dismiss all liberationists as lesbians."[30] Through the 1970s, lesbian feminism emerged as a creative focal point for many aspects of the movement, and, while the tensions never disappeared completely, most activists recognized not only the vast common ground between women's liberation and gay liberation but also the necessity for solidarity in the face of public attack.

In contrast to the rapid emergence of lesbian feminism and the intense internal struggles it raised, the realities of women's racial diversity remained only partially visible in the earliest years. The civil rights movement had inspired both branches of the new feminist movement, and liberal groups had strong minority leadership from the outset. Women's groups that sprang from the New Left, however, tended to be overwhelmingly white, for several reasons. Politically, their model was black separatism, and the African American women with whom they wished to ally were activists in separatist groups like the Black Panther Party. But the black movement, in its most separatist phases, was extremely hostile to feminism, which threatened to rupture racial solidarity. Black women, acutely aware that black separatism emphasized the reclamation of black manhood at their expense, began their own feminist conversations among themselves. Still, they were deeply suspicious of white women whose privileges made claims of oppression seem ludicrous. While white women sought access to work outside the home, many black women in low-paid and demeaning jobs yearned for the choice to devote themselves primarily to family and private domesticity.

In the liberal branches of the women's movement, NOW and the National Women's Political Caucus, minority women were involved from the outset because it was clear to them that they had a stake in the struggle for legal equality and antidiscrimination laws. Within a few years, they began to organize their own groups, such as the National Black Feminist Organization, MANA (Chicanas), and the National Association of Puerto Rican Women, in order to speak about their specific situation. By the mid-1970s many compelling feminist literary voices were those of women of color, such as novelists and poets like Alice Walker, Maxine Hong Kingston, Toni Morrison, Audre Lorde, and Gloria Anzaldua. Within a decade of its founding, second-wave feminists placed the problem of racial and class differences at the center of their theoretical analyses.

The Golden Years: Women as a Political Force

From the late 1960s through the mid-1970s, lawmakers rushed to appease a newly aroused constituency that potentially represented more than half of the voting public.[31] Hearings, votes, and legislative victories came with breathtaking speed, and Congress passed more laws on behalf of women's rights than it had considered seriously for decades. These victories represented the combined efforts of diverse groups of women, including policy-oriented feminist activists, feminists in key administrative posts and other Washington "insider" positions, and working women who initiated EEOC complaints and court actions against discriminatory employers and unions. The actions of these women took place amid the roar of the cultural debate on "women's place" in kitchens, bedrooms, and offices.

With the passage of the Equal Pay Act in 1963 and Title VII of the Civil Rights Act in 1964, working women had new legal tools, which they proceeded to employ with vigor. In the EEOC's first year, more than a third of the complaints submitted concerned sex discrimination. Though these complaints, which numbered in the hundreds, were independent from the organized women's movement, they came in response to the same social pressures and expectations and led commissioners like Aileen Hernandez and Richard Graham to articulate the need for an "NAACP for women." Even progressive unions like the United Auto Workers and the International Union of Electrical Workers, whose leaders had been involved in the President's Commission on the Status of Women and had a history of attention to women's issues, found their members restless and willing to use governmental remedies when local leaders did not take them seriously. Unions and corporations alike argued that they were required by state protective laws to deny women access to overtime or higher paying jobs.[32] In turn, courts, prodded by feminist lawyers, began to rule that protective laws were discriminatory and thereby in violation of Title VII of the Civil Rights Act.

The landmark employment sex discrimination case began when Lorena Weeks sued Southern Bell Telephone Company for refusing to promote her to a job she had handled many times as a substitute and instead hiring a man with less seniority. When Weeks lost her case in 1967, Marguerite Rawalt of the NOW legal committee offered assistance on appeal. Attorney Sylvia Roberts of Baton Rouge prepared the case with Rawalt and argued it before the Appeals Court. Standing only five feet tall, Roberts marched around the courtroom carrying the equipment required for the job in one hand, while arguing that the weight-lifting restrictions the company placed on women's jobs did not constitute a "bona fide occupational qualification."[33] The decision handed down in March 1969, in *Weeks v. Southern Bell*, denied the validity of the exemption for Bell's weight-lifting restrictions and set a new standard of proof. No longer would a demonstration that many, or even most, women could not perform a specific job requirement justify such a restriction. Instead, employers (and states) would have to show that all or "substantially all" women could not perform the required task. The choice of whether to accept a particularly difficult job would rest with the woman, as it already did with men.[34]

The idea of an Equal Rights Amendment (ERA), which would provide simple constitutional equality on the basis of sex, had long been opposed by supporters of protective laws for women. The *Weeks* decision and similar cases, executive orders forbidding discrimination, and the many EEOC complaints under Title VII began in the 1960s to convince key union leaders and other former opponents of the ERA that the protective laws unfairly prevented women from access to higher paying jobs.[35] By 1970, the ranks of ERA supporters included the League of Women Voters, Business and Professional Women, the YWCA, the American Association of University Women, Common Cause, and the United Auto Workers. Together they formed a coalition that succeeded in mounting a massive two-year campaign that generated more mail on Capitol Hill than the Vietnam War.

In 1970 the ERA received its first committee hearing in decades. The hearing was the result of a NOW demonstration in February during which twenty women from the Pittsburgh chapter, led by Wilma Scott Heide, disrupted a hearing on the eighteen-year-old voting age to demand immediate action on the ERA. By July 20, a constant flow of letters and telegrams to reluctant congressmen had helped Representative Martha Griffiths collect the 218 signatures needed to bring the ERA to the House floor. On August 10 (after a debate in which Emanuel Celler of New York argued that there was "as much difference between a male and a female as between a horse chestnut and a chestnut horse"), it passed the House 350 to 15.[36] By March 22, 1972, both houses of Congress finally had approved the ERA. By the end of the year, twenty-two of the needed thirty-five states had ratified it.

Through the 1970s ERA became the symbolic focal point for social debates over women's rights and the place of women in American society, the rallying point for antifeminists. Ratification stalled in the face of enormous social anxieties about the transformations in gender roles and expectations that the women's movement had wrought. After 1975, antifeminist forces mobilized with great effect, finally defeating the ERA in 1982. Yet by that time, most discriminatory laws had already been changed legislatively or declared unconstitutional. Underlying structural changes—in labor force participation, in family composition, in sexual norms, in access to education—could not be rolled back.

It is a sign of continued ambivalence about female equality that the United States has yet to grant it in our founding document, but the forces unleashed by the eruption of women's liberation in the late 1960s continue to transform life in this country, and neither politics nor personal life will ever be quite the same again. Feminism erupted onto the landscape of American life during a time that was already turbulent with social movements: conflict over the Vietnam War, racial strife, and a national crisis over the meaning and inclusiveness of democracy. It challenged Americans to rethink the most fundamental aspects of personal as well as political life, indeed of human identity. As it did so, it mobilized a new kind of political power that could be felt in the bedroom as well as in the courtroom, the boardroom, and the halls of Congress.

NOTES

The epigraph is quoted in Ann Hunter Popkin, "Bread and Roses: An Early Moment in the Development of a Socialist-Feminism," Ph.D. dissertation, Brandeis University, 1978, p. 59.

1. "The Two Worlds: A Day-Long Debate," *New York Times*, 25 July 1959, 1:4.

2. On the family in the 1950s, see Elaine Tyler May, *Homeward Bound: American Families in the Cold War Era* (New York: Basic Books, 1988).

3. Jo Ann Gibson Robinson, *The Montgomery Bus Boycott and the Women Who Started It: The Memoir of Jo Ann Gibson Robinson*, edited with a foreword by David G. Garrow (Knoxville: University of Tennessee Press, 1987).

4. Amy Swerdlow, "Ladies Day at the Capitol: Women Strike for Peace versus HUAC," *Feminist Studies* 8 (fall 1983): 510.

5. Susan Chira, "Ginsberg's Spirit Is Echoed by Other Pioneers," *New York Times*, 2 August 1993, p. A1.

6. Ibid.; Sara Ruddick and Pamela Daniels, eds., *Working It Out: 23 Women Writers, Artists, Scientists, and Scholars Talk about Their Lives and Work* (New York: Pantheon, 1977).

7. Sara Ruddick, "A Work of One's Own," in Ruddick and Daniels, eds., *Working It Out*, pp. 129, 145.

8. Jane O'Reilly, "The Housewife's Moment of Truth," *Ms.*, premiere issue (spring 1972), pp. 54–59.

9. See Jo Freeman, *The Politics of Women's Liberation: A Case Study of an Emerging Social Movement and Its Relation to the Policy Process* (New York: McKay, 1975).

10. Cynthia E. Harrison, "A 'New Frontier' for Women: The Public Policy of the Kennedy Administration," *Journal of American History* 67 (December 1980): 630–35.

11. Betty Friedan, *The Feminine Mystique* (New York: W.W. Norton, 1963). Letter quoted in May, *Homeward Bound*, p. 210.

12. Leila Rupp and Verta Taylor, *Survival in the Doldrums: The American Women's Rights Movement, 1945 to the 1960s* (New York: Oxford University Press, 1987).

13. "Desexing the Job Market," *New York Times*, 21 August 1965, p. A20.

14. Judith Hole and Ellen Levine, *Rebirth of Feminism* (New York: Quadrangle Books, 1971), p. 84.

15. Freeman, *Politics of Women's Liberation*, p. 74.

16. Sara M. Evans, *Personal Politics: The Roots of Women's Liberation in the Civil Rights Movement and the New Left* (New York: Knopf, 1979).

17. "Redstockings Manifesto," *Notes from the Second Year* (1970): 113.

18. Popkin, "Bread and Roses," p. 98.

19. Quoted in Flora Davis, *Moving the Mountain: The Women's Movement in America Since 1960* (New York: Simon & Schuster, 1991), p. 143.

20. Quoted in Suzanne Levine and Harriet Lyons with Joanne Edgar, Ellen Sweet, and Mary Thom, *The Decade of Women: A Ms. History of the Seventies in Words and Pictures* (New York: Paragon, 1980), p. 188.

21. Freeman, *Politics of Women's Liberation*; Sandie North, "Reporting the Movement," *Atlantic*, March 1970, pp. 105–106.

22. See Evans, *Personal Politics*, chapter 8; Alice Echols, *Daring to Be Bad: Radical Feminism in America, 1967–1975*. (Minneapolis: Univ. of Minnesota Press, 1989), pp. 92–96.

23. *The Reader's Guide to Periodical Literature* first listed "women's liberation" as a subtopic under "women" in Volume 29, March 1969–February 1970, with three entries. The next year there were more than 75 entries under "Women's liberation."

24. Susan Brownmiller, *Against Our Will: Men, Women and Rape* (New York: Simon and Schuster, 1975), p. 27.

25. "Women Arise," *Life* 69, 4 September 1970, B16.

26. See Davis, *Moving the Mountain*, pp. 114–16; Georgia Painter Nielsen, *From Sky Girl to Flight Attendant* (New York: ILR Press, 1982).

27. Levine and Lyons, *The Decade of Women*, p. 9.

28. Laura Kaplan, *The Story of Jane: The Legendary Underground Feminist Abortion Service* (New York: Pantheon Books, 1996).

29. See Sarah Weddington, *A Question of Choice* (New York: G. P. Putnam's Sons, 1992); see also David J. Garrow, *Liberty and Sexuality: The Right to Privacy and the Making of Roe v. Wade* (New York: Macmillan Publishing Co., 1994).

30. *Time* 14 December 1970, p. 50.

31. In the 1968 presidential election women voted, for the first time, in equal numbers to men. By the 1980s they were, in fact, a majority of voters.

32. Susan M. Hartmann, "Allies of the Women's Movement: Origins and Strategies of Feminist Activists in Male Dominated Organizations in the 1970s: The Case of the International Union of Electrical Workers," Paper presented at the 1993 Berkshire Conference on the History of Women, Vassar College, Poughkeepsie, N.Y., June 1993. This material was subsequently published in Susan Hartmann, *The Other Feminists: Activists in the Liberal Establishment* (New Haven, Ct.: Yale University Press, 1998).

33. Since the Georgia legislature had repealed its weight-limitations law, the company's only defense lay in the Title VII exemption for "bona fide occupational qualification."

34. See Davis, *Moving the Mountain*; Hole and Levine, *Rebirth of Feminism; Weeks v. Southern Tel. & Tel. Co.* (CA-5, 3-4-69) 408 F. 2d rev. & rem. S.D. Ga 277 F. Supp. 117.

35. Interviews with Olga Madar, Detroit, 10 December 1982; Dorothy Haener, Detroit, 21 January 1983; and Millie Jeffry, Detroit, 11 December1982.

36. Davis, *Moving the Mountain*, pp. 121–27; Hole and Levine, *Rebirth of Feminism*; Marguerite Rawalt, "The Equal Rights Amendment" in *Women in Washington: Advocates for Public Policy*, ed. Irene Tinker (Beverly Hills, Calif.: Sage Publications, 1983), pp. 49–78.

Placing Gay in the Sixties

John D'Emilio

I was born in New York City in the opening years of the Cold War. My Italian-American family shared the conservative social, political, and cultural outlook of many Catholics during the crusade against communism. My parents loved Joe McCarthy, Richard Nixon, Robert Taft, and Barry Goldwater, and, as a child and an adolescent, I did, too. In high school speech and debate tournaments, I delivered trophy-winning orations about the wisdom of U.S. policy in South Vietnam and the need for the government to prevent labor strikes through a system of compulsory arbitration.

Arriving at Columbia's Morningside Heights campus as a freshman in the fall of 1966, I seemed to be immediately drawn into an unceasing effort to shed every vestige of my upbringing. In no time at all I was attending ecumenical services at which the renegade Catholic priests Daniel and Philip Berrigan gave antiwar sermons; I was dodging eggs thrown at me as I marched around campus protesting the administration's cooperation with the Selective Service system; I was running through the streets of midtown Manhattan as police on horseback dispersed the crowds who had come to protest an appearance by Dean Rusk, the secretary of state; and I was picketing in front of the residences of New York City draft board members in the hope that, through their neighbors, we could shame them into resigning from what, to me, seemed a murderous occupation.

The "sixties" are the era that shaped me. I think of them with great nostalgia. I remember those times as thrilling, exhilarating, hopeful, exuberant. The universe cracked open and revealed to me endless possibilities. True, some of what it exposed seemed to be the face of evil itself: heartless politicians who ordered the bombing of peasant villages, National Guardsmen who shot to kill in urban ghettoes, and police who beat students who were standing up for truth and justice. But it also displayed the irrepressible human spirit, the determination of ordinary people to speak truth to power, and the capacity of a generation to reimagine the world.

The trouble with this picture is that, if you press me to talk about "the sixties," almost every one of the stories that would spontaneously erupt from my memory are about events that occurred in the 1970s and are associated in one way or another with the gay liberation movement. At first glance this might seem odd, a glaring fault in the workings of my historian's mind that should be very attuned to time and chronology. But I prefer to use it as the jumping off point for a useful observation about historical eras: the "sixties" are less a time period bound by the start and the end of a decade than they are about an era organically bound together by events, outlook, and mood. My guess is that for many gay men and lesbians, the "sixties" happened in the 1970s.

Gay liberation or, more broadly, homosexuality, is largely absent from historical accounts of the 1960s. It is the forgotten—perhaps, even, the unwanted—stepchild of the era. On the surface, this exclusion seems completely plausible; there is even a certain irrefutable logic to it. History as it is written, after all, is rarely the story of everything that happens but, instead, a narrative of what is salient, what marks a period in some special way. Since the power of homophobia in the post–World War II United States was so strong, it necessarily forced things gay into the background. When the gay liberation movement was finally born in response to the 1969 riots that occurred in Greenwich Village after New York City police raided the Stonewall Inn, a gay bar, the 1960s were just about over. Thus a new era dawned for gay people just as the previous one was ending for everyone else.

But keeping gay out of the "sixties" also has an insidious, even if unintended, effect. It helps to shape a certain kind of interpretation of the 1960s, and a certain kind of interpretation of homosexuality and its place in American life. The view of the 1960s to which I refer has had a long shelf life. One can find it expressed in some of the first historical accounts of the decade, written in the early 1970s, and in some of the most recent assessments, published in

---

JOHN D'EMILIO was an undergraduate at Columbia University from 1966 to 1970. Student protests against racial injustice, the war in Vietnam, and the university's role in both of these seemed a daily part of life in those years. In the 1970s he went on to play an active role in the gay liberation movement; he has pioneered in the research and writing of gay history. His books include *Sexual Politics, Sexual Communities: The Making of a Homosexual Minority in the United States* (1983); *Making Trouble: Essays on Gay History, Politics, and the University*; and, with Estelle Freedman, *Intimate Matters: A History of Sexuality in America* (1988). He was the founding director of the Policy Institute of the National Gay and Lesbian Task Force, and currently teaches in the gender and women's studies program at the University of Illinois at Chicago.

the mid-1990s.[1] It is an interpretation framed by the idea of declension, a dizzying rise and just as dizzying a fall of social forces and political movements that initially promised a new era of peace and justice in America. This version of the 1960s begins with the inspiration of black student sit-ins in the South and the idealistic rhetoric of the Kennedy presidency. It continues through the uplifting civil rights march on Washington and the historic civil rights legislation of mid-decade, and rises to the crescendo of reform embodied in Lyndon Johnson's Great Society. It ends with ghettoes burning, troops occupying urban black neighborhoods, campuses in turmoil, rioting everywhere, and a presidential administration spying on its citizens and subverting the Constitution.

For historians writing sympathetically about the great popular movements of the 1960s, this outline embodies tragedy. What started hopefully ends despairingly; what began as unifying political impulses degenerated into harsh divisiveness. The inspiration of a militant but determinedly nonviolent civil rights movement and the vision of an early student New Left that imagined a world of peace and justice for everyone dissolved into movements whose rhetoric was polarizing and often filled with hatred, and whose concept of revolution involved picking up a gun. In other words, there is a "good" '60s and a "bad" '60s.

Now stop for a moment, think about this intepretive trajectory of rise and fall, and consider what the exclusion of gay from the 1960s inevitably does. By relegating it to the end of the story, to a brief mention of the Stonewall riots as the country is spinning out of control, historians inevitably imprison homosexuality and gay liberation in a narrative of decline. While millions of gay men and lesbians around the world look to 1969 as the dawn of a bright new age, everyone else reads it as part of the "bad" '60s and all that follows. And what is it that follows? Not the dawning of the age of Aquarius, as the young singers in the musical *Hair* proclaimed. Not the arrival of racial justice, world peace, and an equitable international economic order. Instead, the bad '60s ushers in a generation-long conservative ascendancy—the triumph of market principles, the dismantling of the welfare state, the decline of the public sector, increasing racial and ethnic polarization, a politics of greed, hatred, and resentment. This is where everything gay belongs. Thus, without exactly saying as much, gay becomes associated with reaction, backlash, and social decay. We might as well be reading Edward Gibbon's *The History of the Decline and Fall of the Roman Empire*, the classic eighteenth-century work that tied Rome's collapse to sexual immorality.

I would like to suggest some ways in which gay can be put back into the 1960s. At the very least, my goal is to correct an exclusion. But I also think this exercise can lead toward more creative ways of placing the 1960s in the stream of recent American history and of understanding what they were about–for those who lived through the era and for Americans today.

Gay as Echo

One of the most invidious forms that homosexual oppression took in the United States during the Cold War was the psychology of separation and marginalization it enforced. Throughout this era, society found endless ways of repeating the message that there was something deeply wrong with being gay: homosexuality was sick, sinful, criminal, depraved, menacing. That message was enacted through police harassment and arrest, firings by employers, physical beatings by thugs, institutionalization by families. For most gay men and lesbians, the result was an abiding sense of difference, reinforced and magnified by the felt need to keep one's identity hidden, secret, and invisible. During these decades, mainstream America and its gay minority engaged in a quiet conspiracy to make it seem that nothing could be more removed from the trends and currents that characterized the nation's life than the experience or aspirations of its homosexual citizens.

Yet if we look closely at one significant expression of gay experience—and of the nation's—in the 1960s, we find not difference, not a huge gaping separation, but surprising parallels. In the realm of collective political action, the gay movement seemed to echo developments in the society around it.

The African American students who initiated the southern sit-in movement in February 1960 launched a kind of political activism that was new to the era. To be sure, the civil rights movement of the 1940s and 1950s had been vigorous and assertive. But its approach to change had come largely through the lobbying and litigation efforts of an organization like the National Association for the Advancement of Colored People. There had been important exceptions to the NAACP's legalistic approach—A. Philip Randolph's march on Washington movement during World War II; the targeted direct action campaigns of Congress of Racial Equality (CORE) in northern cities; the mass rallies in Washington organized by Bayard Rustin in the late 1950s; and, of course, the Montgomery bus boycott. But none of these activities seemed to provoke waves of imitators in the way that the action at a Woolworth's lunch counter did. After the Greensboro sit-in, citizen action took on a decidedly different flavor. Imbued with a conviction that justice was on their side, activists conducted themselves as if they were authorized to make change, as if their judgment about right and wrong deserved precedence over the laws and customary procedures of the society in which they lived.

At the time of the sit-ins, a fragmentary gay and lesbian movement existed in the United States. The Mattachine Society and the Daughters of Bilitis, the two primary organizations, had formed in the 1950s, published magazines, and were setting up chapters in a few major cities. But they were also caught within the constraints of the McCarthy era in which dissent and nonconformity carried a price. Gay was so far beyond the norm that these first spokespeople for homosexual equality felt obliged to rely, as one of them phrased it, on "pillars of the community" to make their case for them.[2] The early gay movement, in other words, doubted its ability—and authority—to speak on its own behalf. Instead, it depended on the goodwill of enlightened lawyers, doctors, and ministers to win a hearing from society.

By the early 1960s, with the model of the civil rights movement before them, new voices emerged among gay activists. Frank Kameny, an astronomer who had been fired from his government job for being gay and who, since most work in his field required a security clearance, was virtually unemployable, led and typified the more militant approach. He peppered his writings and speeches from these years with references to the struggle for civil rights. The Negro, he wrote in 1964, "tried for 90 years to achieve his purposes by a program of information and education. His achievements in those 90 years, while by no means nil, were nothing compared to those of the past ten years, when he tried a vigorous civil liberties, social action approach." Holding up as an example the self-confidence exhibited by nonviolent demonstrators in the South, he told a gay audience, "We cannot ask for our rights from a position of inferiority, or from a position, shall I say, as less than WHOLE human beings."[3]

Kameny amplified his confident assertion of self, which soon won him a bevy of allies in gay and lesbian organizations in the Northeast, in two forms of activist expression central to the spirit of the 1960s. One was a rebellion against authority. Whether it was southern sheriffs enforcing segregation statutes, or university administrators cooperating with the draft during the Vietnam War, or city governments ignoring the needs of the poor, or psychoanalysts describing woman's allegedly passive nature, authority found itself challenged on every front in the 1960s. Increasingly, the targets of institutional power insisted on the right to define their own experience and claim fully the power to shape their lives. In the case of homosexuality, the church and the medical profession were the twin pillars of cultural power, stigmatizing gay men and lesbians by rendering their sexual desires immoral or pathological. Kameny roundly rejected the external authority of church and science. "I take the stand," he declared, "that not only is homosexuality . . . not immoral, but that homosexual acts engaged in by consenting adults are moral, in a positive and real sense, and are right, good, and desirable, both for the individual participants and for the society in which they live." As to the theorizing of medical scientists, Kameny's organization, the Mattachine Society of Washington, D.C., bluntly announced that "homosexuality is not a sickness, disturbance or pathology in any sense, but is merely a preference, orientation, or propensity, on par with, and not different in kind from, heterosexuality."[4]

The other activist form that Kameny appropriated was public protest. The civil rights movement and the antinuclear movement of the early 1960s had incorporated various forms of direct action into their repertoire of tactics. In doing so they won publicity, attracted new recruits, pressured the targets of their protests into making change or, by the resistance they provoked, aroused the supportive anger of their fellow citizens. But public protest by gay men and lesbians was no easy matter since it meant relinquishing the invisibility—the ability to pass—which protected individuals from sanctions. By the mid-1960s, protest had become so widespread in the United States—mostly around issues of racism, but increasingly about issues of war and peace as well—that some gay men and lesbians were willing to absorb the risk. In Washington, Kameny and others mounted picket lines outside the headquarters of the Civil Service Commission, the Pentagon, and the Department of State, all agencies implicated in the harassment and persecution of homosexuals. As the 1960s wore on, the impulse toward protest expanded, as did the targets of gay protesters, which included the police in Los Angeles, where several hundred gays rallied in the streets after a particularly violent police attack on a gay bar, and doctors known for their hostile views about gay life, when they spoke at a New York City medical school forum on homosexuality. In a number of cities, gay activists found themselves taking up the cry that African Americans had raised against police brutality, and calling for civilian review boards and other forms of citizen control over police behavior.

Before the end of the decade, gay activists were also following the lead of other social movements of the Left in the effort to create "alternative institutions" to replace what were seen as the corrupt oppressive institutions of liberal capitalism. In San Francisco and Los Angeles, the first gay newspapers were established. Designed to cover the news that the mainstream media ignored and to provide a different viewpoint on the stories that did appear, they especially exposed the police harassment which was endemic to gay life in that generation and pushed an ethic of gay pride. In 1968 Troy Perry convened the first meeting of what became the Metropolitan Community Church, a nonsectarian Christian congregation founded to allow lesbians and gay men to worship without censure. In New York City, Craig Rodwell opened the Oscar Wilde Memorial Bookshop, stocking his shelves with gay titles that most bookstores eschewed and that many gay men and lesbians would have been too scared to buy in a mainstream retail establishment; soon it became more than a bookstore, serving as an informal community center for the exchange of news and information about gay politics and the gay community.

The gay echo could be heard not only in the arenas of collective protest and community organizing, phenomena quintessentially associated with the 1960s, but elsewhere as well. From the late 1950s through the mid-1960s the Supreme Court issued a series of decisions on the matter of censorship that dramatically expanded the range of expression protected by the First Amendment. In the course of the decade, writers and artists—and pornographers, too—expanded the boundaries within which creators of literature, art, photography, theater, and film worked. The formal power of Victorian sensibilities, surviving even several decades into the spread of a modernist outlook in the arts, was finally toppled. In its place, Americans found themselves possessors of a much more substantial freedom, as creators and consumers of cultural products, than had previously been the case.

Manifestations of gay experience can be found coursing through the mid-century cultural revolution that we identify with the "sixties": in the San Francisco censorship trial of *Howl*, Allen Ginsberg's controversial collection of poems, and the boost it gave to Beat cultural dissent; in the ability of a writer like James Baldwin to put sexual issues front and center in his fictional depiction of the ravages of racial conflict in contemporary America; in the shifting content of the Broadway theater, as expressed in a hit musical like *Cabaret*, which was based on the stories of Christopher Isherwood, a gay writer, and which portrayed a range of sexualities; in the explosive growth of the paperback pulp novel, sold in drugstores across the United States, which offered romance and sexual adventure for a broad spectrum of erotic sensibilities. It can also be found in the writings of a new breed of social scientists who, in the 1960s, were breaking with the detached pose that had characterized much intellectual work during the Cold War. Sociologists like Howard Becker, Erving Goffman, Edwin Schur, and Martin Hoffman frequently drew on the example of gay life and gay oppression to illustrate a theoretical perspective preoccupied with enlarging the sphere of human freedom. Martin Hoffman used the historical example of religious freedom and the Constitution to urge "radical tolerance for homosexual object-choice" as a solution to the "problem" of homosexuality. Writing in the one-hundredth anniversary issue of *The Nation*, in 1965, Becker used the courage of lesbian activists to make the point that sex ought to be "the politics of the sixties" and that sexual expression ought to be one of the "inalienable" rights guaranteed to Americans.[5]

Rather than identify the Stonewall riots of June 1969 as the *birth* of gay liberation at the *end* of the 1960s, perhaps we would do better to see them for what they were: as symbolic of a shift that had been in the making for a number of years. Rather than containing homosexuality within a narrative structure of "rise and fall," perhaps we can use the eruption of a full-fledged gay freedom movement for a different interpretive purpose: as a sign of just how deeply the changes wrought by the 1960s reached into the structures and assumptions of American life. As Charles Kaiser wrote of the 1960s in *The Gay Metropolis*, a history of gay male life since World War II: "Because everything was being questioned, for a moment anything could be imagined—even a world in which homosexuals would finally win a measure of equality."[6] By noticing the many forms that the "gay echo" took in the 1960s, by including it in our historical repertoire of what the era provoked, we can interpret the '60s not as an era that failed, not as a story of declension, but as a watershed decade out of which nothing in American life emerged unchanged.

Gay as Sensibility

I cringe a little when I look at that heading. The notion of a sensibility skirts the boundary of stereotyping. When applied to a social group, it smacks of the suggestion that there are some inherent characteristics that all members of a group share other than their oppression. In a gay context, the notion of sensibility also conjures up certain images and associations widely held in American culture—of camp and gender bending, of the aesthete and the dandy; of the sensitive young man of artistic bent. But I mean gay sensibility in another way, and am ascribing to it a content very different from what it usually has.

When I think about the 1960s, especially about what from the era has retained value and meaning for me across the decades, certain figures come into mind: James Baldwin, Allen Ginsberg, Bayard Rustin, Paul Goodman. None of them are the "top tier" names that we associate with the decade—Kennedy, King, Malcolm X, the Beatles, Dylan. Two of them, Rustin and Goodman, functioned far enough below the radar screen of history that one needs to be an afficionado of the 1960s even to know who they were. Yet, as one scans the decade, it is remarkable how they, and their influence, keep surfacing.

In many ways, these men were dramatically different from one another. Ginsberg was a poet of the cultural fringe, an artistic rebel whose verse ran along the edges of madness and who incorporated into his literary output a mystical spirituality that crisscrossed the boundaries of religious traditions. Without attachment to institutions or organizations, he wandered the globe in the 1950s and 1960s, somehow managing to make appearances at what proved to be key moments in the unfolding of the '60s. By contrast, Baldwin won mainstream success and plaudits, even as he often cultivated in his writing the stance of outsider. Where Ginsberg employed the frenzy of insanity in his verse, Baldwin's prose, whether in his fiction or in the essays that reached a mass audience in the decade, had a razor-sharp realism, a lucidity that left little room for confusion or ambiguity. Moving back and forth in the 1960s between the United States and Europe, he served almost as a roving conscience of the nation's racial crisis.

While Ginsberg and Baldwin moved primarily in the arena of literature (though heavily doused with social commentary), Rustin and Goodman operated, respectively, in the spheres of political activism and social criticism. In some ways, Rustin can be considered the "invisible hand" of 1960s activism. A Gandhian radical who came of age in the 1930s, he was a stalwart of the post–World War II peace and civil rights movement. Rustin was especially known for his command of the tactics and strategy of protest and social change. He was a close adviser of Martin Luther King, Jr., in the early stages of King's public career and played an important role in creating for King a national profile; he trained a large number of the key younger activists of the 1960s; and he was the mastermind behind the historic 1963 March on Washington. A practical, hardnosed realist, he was always looking for the ways that progressive change, whether in the realm of international affairs or America's racial order, might be institutionalized and made permanent. While Goodman cared about progressive social policy, he was more the utopian, imagining ideal systems. When he did address himself to what he called "practical proposals," he devoted little energy to detailing the political strategy of making them achievable. A philosopher by training, Goodman wrote prolifically, and his books and essays critiquing American education and examining the role of youth in modern society won him a wide appreciative audience among the students who constituted the New Left of the 1960s.

To me, the differences among the four are of the formal variety, the kind that surface when one is pigeonholing an individual with a short tag line: poet; political organizer; philosopher. What they had in common ran much deeper.

One area of experience they shared was homosexual attraction and, to varying degrees, a public profile as gay or bisexual. In the late 1990s, this may not seem to be much to share, or even especially significant. So many men have come out of the closet, and gay life is so visible, that we are more easily aware of the differences—of class, race, ethnicity, and political viewpoint. How much, after all, do a gay Republican and a queer nationalist, a gay union activist and a gay corporate executive, a gay rock star and a gay waiter, have in common? But in the 1950s and 1960s, secrecy and invisibility were core features of the gay experience and, though there was a well-developed public discourse about homosexuality, most of it was condemnatory and written from the outside. A generation ago, then, gay was an even more powerful marker of identity than it is now, and few chose to have themselves marked in this way. To be public implied either great trouble or great integrity, or both.

Ginsberg embraced homosexual passion openly. For those in attendance, his 1955 public reading in San Francisco of "Howl," a poem that described gay sexuality as joyous and holy, seemed to crystallize the literary and cultural movement known as Beat, itself a portent of the sixties. The censorship trial in 1957 gave the slim book of poetry a wide audience, and as the media began to spotlight the Beat rebellion, Ginsberg became perhaps the most visible homosexual in America. Baldwin, too, could be considered openly gay by virtue of what he chose to write, though the codes of discretion observed in the 1950s and 1960s meant that one was generally not labeled gay unless one committed a misdeed or made a public declaration of identity. Nevertheless, the fact that Baldwin published a gay novel, *Giovanni's Room*, and peopled his bestseller of the early 1960s, *Another Country*, with gay characters, marked him in the eyes of the knowledgeable as queer.

Rustin's case was different from either Ginsberg's or Baldwin's in that he never chose to have his homosexuality be a matter of public record. Within his circle of friends and political associates, Rustin was quietly open about his sexual and emotional leanings as early as the 1940s, an unusual choice for a gay man to make in those years. But his sexuality also became a matter of public controversy on several occasions because of the trouble it brought his way. While imprisoned as a conscientious objector during World War II, he was confronted with charges of sexual misconduct on the eve of an inmate strike that he was organizing against racial segregation. In 1953, while on a speaking tour in southern California, he was arrested and convicted for homosexual activity. Then, in 1963, shortly before the march on Washington that Rustin was coordinating, he had the dubious distinction of being labeled, in a Senate speech by Strom Thurmond of South Carolina, a sexual pervert.

Goodman's situation was more complex, since he married twice and was the father of three children. A political and philosophical anarchist, he seemed to delight in injecting matters of sex into situations not typically defined as sexual. It was a propensity that, in more than one case, cost him a job, including a position at the experimental Black Mountain College in North Carolina. But Goodman was also bold enough to write openly about homosexuality. The subject appeared in *Growing Up Absurd*, his commentary about youth and education, which was extremely influential among radical college students in the 1960s. It also surfaced in his poetry and fiction, which was heavily autobiographical.

As I suggested above, gay identity may not seem such an overriding commonality at the turn of the new millennium, all the hoopla about "Ellen" coming out notwithstanding. But a generation ago, it was a big deal. Whether it happened by choice or imposition, assuming a public profile as a sexual *deviant*, as someone heavily stigmatized by the overwhelming weight of cultural opinion, meant taking on a characteristic of which one was always aware. It branded one's consciousness with a marker of difference, even if one had the independence of character to resist the negative definition that American society attached to it. It necessarily made one perpetually aware of separation, of division in the body of humanity, of marginalization and ostracism. Admittedly, Rustin and Baldwin as African Americans and Ginsberg and Goodman as Jews living in the wake of the Holocaust had other reasons to experience exclusion. Yet Jews and African Americans also had access to strong traditions of community that homosexuals in America did not.

As I think about these four men and try to make sense out of what they offered the United States in the 1960s, the abiding perception of estrangement that America's sexual order forced upon them leads me to highlight a second commonality among them. Each in his own way functioned as an apostle of hope. Each held out the conviction that the bitter conflicts and the cruel inequalities that caused deep rifts in American society could be overcome. Each believed in an ideal of community expansive enough to include everyone.

In the case of Bayard Rustin, this claim is easy to make. A Quaker by upbringing, in the early 1940s he abjured his involvement with the communist movement in the United States in part because he rejected the unscrupulousness of its methods–the willingness to rationalize any tactic or strategy if it seemed to advance the final conflict in the international war of the classes. Instead, he chose allegiance to a Gandhian philosophy of *satyagraha*—"truth-force" or "love-force"—with its commitment to active but nonviolent resistance to injustice. Throughout the 1940s and 1950s, in his pacifist activities and in his work to challenge American racism, Rustin faced personal danger again and again without deviating from his attachment to a respectful nonviolence designed to win over his opponent. In his many speeches in these decades, he reiterated his belief that the evil at the heart of war and racism was the sundering of human community, the shattering of a natural impulse toward love and fellowship.

For Rustin, whose sexuality and political radicalism together placed him at the fringe of American life in the Cold War decades, the March on Washington in August 1963 was a revelatory moment. It was not simply that the event's spirit and tone seemed to capture perfectly the sense of unity and community toward which he was always striving in his work. The support that the march won seemed to promise the mainstreaming of a social vision; the power that the march embodied suggested the political ability to implement the vision as well. And so Rustin, who had lived and worked on the margin for his entire adult life, devoted himself in the middle years of the 1960s—before the spirit of the decade had shifted from the "good '60s" to the "bad '60s"—to arguing for a shift "from protest to politics." He believed that the progressive forces in the United States had to find allies, work in coalition, and shift from a rigid outsider mentality as protesters to a more flexible ability to engage the political and economic system from the inside. He believed that the civil rights movement, the emerging white student movement, and the expanding peace movement could forge ties with the churches, organized labor, intellectuals, and the most socially conscious of American liberals. Together they could build a broad progressive alliance capable of becoming the working majority of the Democratic Party and of transforming the American political economy.

We can never know, of course, whether such a strategy, if initiated and pursued by the democratic Left in the United States, might have worked in those years. We do know that it was embraced by very few. Major segments of the black freedom movement instead chose a more militant politics that polarized, that created lines of division, that despaired of winning over white America, and particularly white liberals, to their side. Major segments of the white student movement came to see liberalism as intrinsically compromised through its connection to a U.S. capitalist world order. Major segments of the peace movement placed their opposition to U.S. policy in Southeast Asia above their commitment to peace and reconciliation, and built an antiwar movement that was at least as anti-American as it was antimilitarist, and that supported uncritically the militarism of the other side.

All of these developments, central to how the 1960s unfolded, signified in important ways a politics that intertwined rage and despair. And, to many of the actors in these dramas, Rustin's perspective seemed to be a politics of compromise and betrayal. But I wonder if it is not more accurate to see Rustin's efforts as a continuing commitment, under the changed conditions of the 1960s, to reach for unity by building a movement meant to embrace an ever larger part of the American nation. Rustin, in other words, was offering not crass compromise but wild hope, the hope that the vivid exposure of injustice and evil, combined with practical politics, might lead to renewal, to the restoration of community.

One could make a comparable claim for Baldwin in these years. Like many African American cultural figures in the twentieth century, Baldwin chose the existence of an expatriate in France as a way of escaping the grueling, insistent cruelties of white America's racism. But as the civil rights movement became the most dynamic social and political force in the United States, Baldwin spent more time on this side of the Atlantic. He rallied other black artists, met with members of the Kennedy administration, and appeared at major public forums with political activists like Rustin. And, always, he wrote—both the fiction which was at the heart of his creativity as an artist but also substantial essays in which he commented on the state of the United States.

At first glance it might seem strange to label Baldwin a voice of hope in the 1960s. To be white, as I am, and to read either *The Fire Next Time* or *Another Country*, his two widely read books of the first half of the 1960s, is inevitably to squirm. Whether as novelist or essayist, Baldwin was unflinching in his description of racism and its impact on African Americans, and merciless in his indictment of whites. "This is the crime," he wrote in *The Fire Next Time*, "of which I accuse my country and my countrymen, and for which neither I nor time nor history will ever forgive them, that they have destroyed and are destroying hundreds of thousands of lives and do not know it and do not want to know it."[7] In *Another Country* he depicts various sexual couplings of blacks and whites mangling each other with the sharp edges of their society's racial history. He dressed down Robert Kennedy, the attorney general, for the inadequacies of the Justice department's initiatives on race; he exploded with fury after the Birmingham church bombing that killed four young black girls.

But Baldwin, like Rustin, believed that redemption could only come if one looked injustice squarely in the face and named it. His critique was meant as pathway to another place. "We can make America what America must become," he wrote.[8] Choosing to close *Another Country* on a note of hope, he uses his gay characters to deliver the message. He ends with a young French gay man arriving in New York, embracing his new country and his American lover.

As with Baldwin, one can find in both Ginsberg and Goodman this dual perspective: the naming of all that is wrong with modern America yet, still, a message of hope. Whether it be Ginsberg leading a gathering of hippies in a

Buddhist chant in San Francisco's Golden Gate Park or Goodman determinedly producing one of his utopian essays, the two of them projected some measure of optimism about the ability of right-thinking Americans to chart a saner course for a nation that by the late 1960s did seem to be spinning out of control. Like Baldwin, too, their note of hope oftentimes seemed attached to their experience of gay sexuality. In an essay Goodman published late in 1969, he explicitly addressed his gay identity and the politics of homosexuality. "In my observation and experience," he argued, "queer life has some remarkable political values. It can be profoundly democratizing, throwing together every class and group more than heterosexuality does. Its promiscuity can be a beautiful thing."[9] Frank in his criticism about the things that were not right with gay male life, he nonetheless saw it as a counter to the coldness and fragmentation that characterized contemporary America.

Now let me be clear, at least, about what I am *not* saying. I am not trying to claim that there is something about male homosexuality and gay life that inherently points gay men in the direction of community and makes them messengers of hope in a fractious society. I am not saying that this is even true of gay men as a group in this particular era of history. But imagine, for a minute, other groupings of key male activists or engaged cultural workers associated with the 1960s. If I had chosen Stokely Carmichael, Norman Mailer, Malcolm X, and Jerry Rubin, would the themes of hope and community so readily emerge?

I am trying to point our attention to an opening, an unobserved window onto an understanding of the 1960s. When we look at the careers of the four men I have highlighted, at the animating vision behind their work, we find something that stands outside an interpretation that emphasizes failure. Not, mind you, because they succeeded, or because their dreams of a new world were realized, but because they felt impelled to hold them out steadfastly to the rest of us, and to hold on to them for themselves in the years that followed. I think there is reason to believe that, in the mid-twentieth century, the experience of gay oppression provided a particular angle of vision that brought certain themes, aspirations, and civic desires to the foreground. If we dig more deeply, what might emerge from excavating this territory? Can we learn something different about the 1960s? Does it allow us more readily to imagine placing gay back into the 1960s and seeing the decade, accordingly, in new ways?

Gay as Harbinger

In questioning the persistence of a "rise-and-fall" interpretation of the 1960s, I am not offering in its place the inverse: a story of the great march forward of progressive social and economic change. Anyone who has lived through the last decades knows that we are in the middle of an era of conservative ascendancy. In the realm of party politics, the number of Republicans has grown, and the party has moved to the right; the number of Democrats has shrunk, and the party has moved to the right. The changing tax structure and the balancing of the federal budget, the direction of social policy as evidenced by the debates over welfare, the growing disparities in income and wealth, and the composition of the federal judiciary, particularly the Supreme Court, are some of the more obvious indicators of the shift. And the conservative wave has not yet crested.

Even as we acknowledge this, we also cannot escape the fact that there are living legacies of the 1960s. Without the civil rights and black power movements of those years, we would not as a society be debating today the merits of multiculturalism. Without the resurgence of feminism in the 1960s, we would not today find women just about everywhere in public life. And without the broad cultural shifts that the era induced, we would not be living today with something thoroughly new in the history of modern Western societies—a mass movement for freedom of homosexual expression.

Yet all of these legacies, and probably others we could name as well, are still being fought over. None are secure; none offer predictable futures. If we define the dynamic edge of the 1960s as those forces campaigning for a just and equitable society, it is difficult to identify what is permanent about the decade's achievements *and* how those achievements position the nation to move once again in those directions. What, in other words, can the outcome of the 1960s tell us about what is to come and how it will materialize? What of the 1960s still resides with us so that a peaceful world, a fair distribution of wealth, and a civic culture in which no social groups experience forced exclusion or subordination, come closer to realization?

Let me suggest that a productive approach to these questions, and to understanding the post-'60s United States as something other than the triumph of reaction at home and abroad, might come through a look at gay America in the last generation.

One way of seeing gay as a carrier of the era's legacy is simply by acknowledging the history of the gay and lesbian movement since the end of the 1960s. By the 1970s, the black freedom struggle was in disarray, divided and wary about the future. Feminism retained a dynamic quality for much of the 1970s, but the growth of a vigorous anti-abortion movement in the second half of the decade, and the final defeat of the Equal Rights Amendment in 1982, put the women's movement on the defensive. By contrast, the gay and lesbian movement has over the last thirty years grown in size, extended its influence, and expanded its list of achievements. This has not happened at a steady pace; there have been reversals and setbacks along the way. But, overall, it is remarkable that, in the midst of a deepening conservative impulse in U.S. political life, this movement for social justice has marched forward.

One can point to a number of concrete measures of change. Since the late 1960s, a majority of states have repealed sodomy laws that were as old as the nation and that led to the arrest and conviction of large numbers of Americans every year. In several states, and most of the nation's large cities, civil rights law has been expanded to ban discrimination on the basis of sexual orientation. The federal government, which prohibited through much of the Cold War the employment of gay men and lesbians in *any* government job, has gradually relaxed these restrictions until only military service remains inaccessible. The American Psychiatric Association has eliminated the classification of homosexuality as a disease, which for decades had not only served to stigmatize gay and lesbian relationships, but also led to the involuntary institutionalization of many people.

At the level of social life and daily experience, it is not too much to say that, for millions of gay men and lesbians, the changes of the last three decades have been nothing short of revolutionary. The constant, incessant fear of discovery and punishment has abated. The sense of carrying a dreadful stigma has lifted. Instead of being weighed down by a terrible loneliness that the enforced secrecy and invisibility a homophobic society had imposed, gays and lesbians have created vibrant communities with robust institutions. Whereas in the early 1960s one could, at best, hope to find some bars where homosexuals could meet, gay men and lesbians in the last generation have invested heavily in the construction of organizations and institutions to knit people together. There are churches and synagogues for expressions of religious faith. There are health clinics, youth organizations, family services, senior citizen groups, and twelve-step programs to care for people's physical and psychological well-being. There are community centers that house an endless array of activities and services. There are political action and advocacy organizations designed to express the collective voice of the community in public affairs. There are bowling and softball leagues, bridge tournaments, running clubs, and outdoors groups that make recreation a community-building experience. Bookstores, arts and film festivals, conferences for writers, and theater workshops foster cultural expression and intellectual life. Among gay men and lesbians the impulse toward community building, certainly one of the signature impulses of the 1960s, has been extraordinary. It may not be too much to claim that, in a generation in which jeremiads about the collapse of community in America are commonplace, many gay men and lesbians have become the repository of vital wisdom about valuing and maintaining a vigorous communal life.

As with community life, so too with citizen action and empowerment. In an era in which disgust with politics and citizen apathy are widespread, in which the only mobilizations seem to be the armies of Christian conservatives on the march, the gay and lesbian community has been an important counterpoint— even though its significance has been largely ignored by progressives in the United States. At the level of both local and national politics, the community has been in an almost constant state of political agitation over the last twenty years. Some of what it has done looks like the routine operation of "interest group" politics. Thus, there are now about three dozen state federations, none of which existed twenty-five years ago. They lobby, coordinate constituent visits to the legislature, conduct voter registration, and sometimes organize statewide mobilizations. But just as often the gay and lesbian movement has kept alive a tradition of direct action and community organizing that one associates with the best of the 1960s. In 1987 and again in 1993, national marches on Washington brought out more people than any demonstration of the 1960s. Gays and lesbians organized a mass civil disobedience outside the Supreme Court in 1987, the largest ever mounted against the venerable institution. The direct action protests of AIDS activists in the late 1980s and early 1990s built on the tactics developed by civil rights and antiwar demonstrators of the 1960s and extended by the antinuclear agitators of the late 1970s. They adapted the techniques of nonviolent civil disobedience to an MTV-, media-saturated generation, devising eye-catching and attention-grabbing forms of protest. Today, groups like Digital Queers are pioneering ways of adapting cyberspace to the requirements of political organizing.

I know that, for some Americans, the above paragraphs about the flowering of a gay community and gay politics read like a litany of what's wrong with our country. For political and religious conservatives the growth of the gay movement and the rise of visible gay communities are elements of moral decay, and they have no difficulty in saying so, as public statements by Trent Lott, the Senate majority leader, Gary Bauer, a former Reagan administration official who now leads the Family Research Council, and William Bennett, a conservative educator and best-selling author, make clear. And I suspect that many on the Left, many liberals and progressives, also experience varying levels of discomfort at the spread of sexual identity politics. While they would not object to the existence of a gay movement, the steady injection of gay issues into public debate seems to them symptomatic of the collapse of the serious politics of the

1960s. Instead of an insistent focus on matters like the U.S. global economic imperialism, justice for African Americans and immigrants of color, economic democracy and the welfare state, politics has devolved into a concern with mere lifestyle issues, into trivial inessential topics like sexual freedom.

But even the ground on which an American progressive tradition has staked itself—democratic participation, expanded notions of equality, justice for all—offers a firm footing for gay agitation. If the essence of being gay or lesbian concerns the pursuit of love, affection, intimacy and passion, if it is about the building of close human relationships, then surely it is a good thing that police across the country no longer arrest tens of thousands of people every year for something as innocent as holding hands in a bar. Surely it is a good thing that, when men and women have epithets thrown at them and baseball bats swung in their direction, they feel entitled to expect that the police will apprehend the assailants rather than add to the pain of the assault. Surely it is a good thing that a group of citizens is not formally excluded from major segments of the labor market. Surely it is a good thing when they do not have to worry that the discovery of the most loving relationships in their lives could mean the loss of their livelihood.

There is yet a second, perhaps more important way in which gay not only carries forward the legacy of the 1960s but points us toward what a new progressive political vision might embody. Increasingly since the early 1970s, political conflict and social justice struggles have developed around matters that once were defined as existing within the realm of private or personal life. Increasingly, sexuality and the family have become the fulcrum not only of public discourse but of policy debates and policy making as well. The list of issues is a long one: abortion, contraception, and reproductive rights; sex education and teenage pregnancy; censorship of the arts and the Internet; wife battering, incest, and the abuse of children; no-fault divorce laws and single-parent families; rape and sexual harassment; AIDS funding and prevention strategies; and, of course, the panoply of issues connected to the gay movement. Without too much effort, most of us can probably also generate a list of headline-making scandals, paralleling each of these issues, that mesmerized the public for long stretches of time.

Interestingly, the shift of sexual and family-based matters from the realm of the private to the center of national politics has even reshaped how issues more typically associated with the quest for economic and social justice are debated. From the presidency of Ronald Reagan through the rewriting of federal welfare law in 1996, the suggestion of sexual immorality threaded its way through the public discourse about welfare. Nativist attacks on immigrants and the renewed call to restrict the number of foreigners admitted to the United States are often rife with allusions to the procreative excess of immigrant populations: their children allegedly will overrun the schools and drain the resources of other public services.

There are good reasons why, even as the remnants of the U.S. Left rail against the North American Free Trade Agreement, the International Monetary Fund, and the depredations of global capitalism, sex and the family agitate our body politic. The connections between macro-level world economics and the micro-reality of personal life are real and substantial. As the movement of global capital and the fluctuation of world currency markets make us subject to powers beyond individual control, the need for dignity, security, and freedom at the level of intimate relationships and the uses of the body have become more important than ever. Solutions to problems in these areas, of course, cannot be divorced from changes in the rules of international economics. But a politics of economic and social justice that doesn't attend openly to the felt insecurities and aspirations of people at the level of the intimate won't bring folks to the barricades either. The extension of long-standing traditions of democratic rights to incorporate the realm of the intimate, and the reframing of long-standing battles for economic and social justice in ways that incorporate the sexual behavior of peoples, seem to be a requisite for a next cycle of progressive politics and social change.

Embedded in the rise of a people who call themselves gay are some gripping questions about how capitalist societies have evolved in the twentieth century and how they might be reorganized. What has made possible the coalescence of a group of people who choose to live outside a reproductive family unit? What can this development tell us about the changing relationship of the family and the individual to economic life in an increasingly global capitalist order? What options for personal freedom *and* for new forms of community does it offer? How might "family" come to look different and have new and expanded meanings? How might we want consciously to change the structure of economic life in order to encourage the range of options that people choose in pursuit of intimacy, family, and community? Are the present ways that capitalism orders life—the privatization of reproduction and child rearing; the demand that more and more adults be drawn into the labor market; the shrinking resources available to the nuclear family—the best way to do things?

When gay liberation and lesbian feminism emerged at the end of the 1960s, these were the kinds of questions they put on the table. As movements, they not only offered incisive critiques of the organization of the family, sexuality, and gender, but they also developed in their practice ways of living that looked beyond the "Ozzie and Harriet" version of private life. New forms of invented kinship, new ways of fostering community, even new forms of conceiving children and raising them, were bred into the bones of these young liberation movements. In the 1980s, the AIDS epidemic dramatized, for those people curious enough to notice, that gay America carried within it an ethic of family and community that was deep and broad. In death as well as in life it turned out that a people stereotyped for their isolation and loneliness were able to draw into their circle caring friends, lovers, former lovers, the friends of their former lovers—people, in other words, without the formal legalistic relation of family that normally defines the limits of our personal responsibility. The compassion-numbing conservatism of the country in the late 1990s makes all this seem distant; even within the gay community, the public battle seems to have devolved into a quest for marriage. But this should not obscure for us that out of the 1960s emerged a movement that took the decade's ideals, applied them to the realm of the intimate, and over the last generation struggled against great odds to realize new meanings for human freedom and social justice.

In September 1997, in Washington, D.C., the National Gay and Lesbian Task Force held its annual Honoring Our Allies reception. As the name implies, the event is designed to acknowledge that gays and lesbians are not fighting for their rights alone and without help. That year, the honorees included Coretta Scott King, the widow of the slain civil rights leader, and John Sweeney, who had recently been elected president of the AFL-CIO; Senator Edward Kennedy presented the award to Mrs. King. The evening brought together sixty years of the progressive tradition of the United States: the labor movement, which defined the militant social justice politics of the Depression decade; the civil rights movement, which propelled progressive politics forward in the 1960s; and the liberal wing of the Democratic Party, which has been the electoral force that has institutionalized elements of a progressive vision of economic and social life in America. And the instigator of the evening was the movement which, in this conservative era, has tried to keep alive and extend a progressive American tradition.

It will be at least a while yet before a new progressive politics asserts itself as a dynamic shaping force in American society. But when it happens, as it certainly will, this even newer Left will inevitably draw upon its sense of history and the relevance of historical traditions that preceded it. It will be stronger if it is able to look to a 1960s, so emblematic of protest and political passion, in which gay is thoroughly integral, and if it acknowledges a more recent past in which gay has carried legacies from the 1960s forward, along the way enriching our sense of what freedom and social justice might mean.

NOTES

1. See, as examples, Kirkpatrick Sale, *SDS* (New York: Random House, 1973); Milton Viorst, *Fire in the Streets: America in the 1960s* (New York: Simon and Schuster, 1979); Allen Matusow, *The Unraveling of America: A History of Liberalism in the 1960s* (New York: Harper and Row, 1984); Todd Gitlin, *The Sixties: Years of Hope, Days of Rage* (New York: Bantam, 1987); James Miller, *"Democracy Is in the Streets": From Port Huron to the Siege of Chicago* (New York: Simon and Schuster, 1987); Terry H. Anderson, *The Movement and the Sixties: Protest in America from Greensboro to Wounded Knee* (New York: Oxford University Press, 1995).

2. John D'Emilio, *Sexual Politics, Sexual Communities: The Making of a Homosexual Minority in the United States, 1940–1970* (Chicago: University of Chicago Press, 1983; 2nd edition, 1998), p. 149. The information on the pre-Stonewall gay movement in this and the following paragraphs comes from chapters 8 through 12. Citations identity the location of quotations.

3. Ibid., p. 153.

4. Ibid., pp. 153, 164.

5. Ibid., p. 143.

6. Charles Kaiser, *The Gay Metropolis, 1940–1996* (Boston: Houghton Mifflin, 1997), p. 138.

7. James Baldwin, *The Fire Next Time* (New York: Dial Press, 1963; Laurel edition), p. 15.

8. Ibid., p. 21.

9. Paul Goodman, "Being Queer," in *Crazy Hope and Finite Experience: Final Essays of Paul Goodman*, ed. Taylor Stoehr (San Francisco: Jossey-Bass, 1994), p. 109.